THE UNIVERSITY CLUB
OF WASHINGTON, DC

THE UNIVERSITY CLUB

OF WASHINGTON, DC

ONE HUNDRED YEARS
OF FELLOWSHIP

Written by CHRISS WINSTON

Edited by SENIOR JUDGE LOREN A. SMITH

ISBN 0-89526-077-8

Published in the United States by
Regnery Publishing, Inc.
An Eagle Publishing Company
One Massachusetts Avenue, NW
Washington, DC 20001

Printed on acid-free paper

Manufactured in the United States of America

10 9 8 7 6 5 4 3 2 1

Since 1947
REGNERY
PUBLISHING, INC.
An Eagle Publishing Company • Washington, DC

This book is affectionately dedicated to

JAMES D. "MIKE" MCKEVITT

who exemplified the University Club ideal of good fellowship. For Mike, every day was a celebration of life, a reason for joy and laughter, and an excuse to create an event at the Club. He served it well as both its historian and its president. Mike McKevitt loved the University Club, and so this book is for him.

Contents

 A century is a long time, and there have surely been more changes in the century during which the University Club has existed than in any other. In 1904, the city of Washington had a population of just over 300,000. The built-up part of the city ended at about Park Street on the north. The city was served by four trolley lines and there were a total of seven hundred automobiles within its limits. Washington in 1904 was a capital city in which foreign diplomats assigned to it still received extra pay for a tropical station. When the University Club was founded, Theodore Roosevelt was serving as the twenty-sixth president of the United States.

Since then, the nation has come through several armed conflicts, a major depression, and several recessions. Today, the Washington metropolitan area contains four million people, and Washington is the political center of the most powerful nation in the world.

Naturally, the University Club has changed with the times. From its first home in a rented Victorian mansion, the Club constructed its own building at 15th and I Streets in 1912. William Howard Taft, the Club's first president, and then president of the United States, officiated at the laying of the cornerstone. The impressive seven-story building now occupied by the Club was built in 1920.

From its beginning, membership in the Club has come from both the private and public sectors of the city. Today, newly enlarged athletic facilities encourage fitness. The upper four floors of the Clubhouse are devoted to overnight accommodations for both members and visiting members from the numerous private clubs across the nation and around the world with reciprocal privileges. There are a number of "clubs-within-the-club": devotees of fine wines, great books, billiards, bridge, dinner dances, and an excellent speaker's program all use the Club's facilities.

Past and present members have been responsible for the remarkable progress of the Club in its first century. Present and future members will have the task of continuing that progress in its second century.

—WILLIAM H. REHNQUIST
Chief Justice of the United States

EDITOR'S FOREWORD

As a person enters the elegant front door of the University Club, having passed between the burning gas lanterns of a different era, across the cobblestone driveway, and by the understated bushes and trees, one is met with a bronze plaque. *Enter all ye who have a degree of good fellowship and learning,* it announces to the member or visitor. The words are from the University Club's first birthday banquet program and were placed at the Club's entrance in honor of a former Club president, the late James D. "Mike" McKevitt.

Chriss Winston has written a book that gives a vivid account of what has occupied the people in these sometimes tranquil and sometimes exciting precincts over the last one hundred years. No book can portray even a small part of the chronicle of what several thousand people did over a century, but the author has made a valiant attempt. You will see that yourself as you read this book. She paints a vivid picture of one hundred years of people, activities, issues, buildings, and events, putting these into the context of the great human dramas of the last one hundred years. Six major wars, the Great Depression, scandals, the growth of a government and a city. Yet all of these dramas, tragic and ennobling, or tawdry and agonizing, have been played out by human beings on the stage of history. And many of the actors and a few of the scenes have been part of the University Club.

Club members have also played out thousands of less momentous events. Squash games, grand dinners, membership ups and downs, Club renovations, and money problems. Dances and committee meetings have gone on while poker games and political deals were made. People swam and smoked cigars while lecturers talked of Antarctic adventures or the intricacies of tax law or painting in the traditional Chinese style. The actors were all part of the Club, but what is a club? What is that intangible element that draws the actors to its stage? In the simplest of terms: a club is people coming together to do things together. But a true club is something much more than that.

Former Club president John Beck mentioned something to me that might be useful in helping the reader to understand the Club. He talked about an idea that undergirds the events Chriss so effectively portrays, something we, as University Club members, sometimes lose sight of. Or maybe, like someone walking among the trees, we find it hard to visualize the whole forest. That idea is the spirit of the Club. It is not the building, the rooms, the athletics, the dining, or the parties and programs. All of these are the stage upon which the Club takes place, but they are not the Club.

What connects these actors and events is fellowship. People were in the Club because they wanted to be. Duty drove them to the Army or Navy or public service, and many members died for the nation. But duty didn't bring them to the Club. Nor did the search for wealth, though many had extraordinary success at that venture. The University Club fostered learning because so many members are and were learned in law or medicine or science or the arts. But learning didn't bring people to the Club. Power and glory were found in numerous Club members, from presidents and justices to captains of industry and military heroes. But these human aspirations didn't draw people here. Why the great and the near great, the men and the women, the specialists and the laymen, have come here is to be with others. To enjoy their company. To share a good meal. To compete with them in sport. To chat and argue with them over sports, politics, books, or the weather. In a word, "fellowship." Fellowship is the spirit of the Club. It characterizes the Club, distinguishing it in a fundamental way from a hotel, restaurant, or gym. It animates the activities that go on at the Club, and it binds people together. It binds them not with the deep commands of faith, ideology, or economic relationships. But it binds them with a tie not unlike family. This connection may be intensely deep or quite casual, as in most families. But it is there. It is the underpinning of the events and dramas this book portrays. It is the context that allows us to understand the Club's venerable history as something in which each of us still participates.

The Club is the people who compose it: the members, their families and guests, and the long-term employees, and the tie of fellowship that brings them together. Sometimes they come together for great purposes, but mostly for the everyday events that make life worth living. As you read this book, stop for a moment and reflect on the good meals, spirited games of squash or cards, warm conversations, evenings with a glass of good whiskey or a mellow cigar. Think of the good book or magazine in the library, or the enjoyable reception, or just good times you have had at the Club. Think how these experiences of yours are part of a long line of such fellowship now extending back one hundred years. This perhaps will make each of us appreciate the Club a little more for the treasure that it is, and the fellowship that pervades its rooms. May you enjoy this Club and its spirit well into the next hundred years. See you in 2104!

—LOREN A. SMITH
Chairman of the Centennial
Committee

Congratulations to the University Club of Washington, D.C. on celebrating its Centennial year. Today, the University Club continues in the same grand tradition in which it was founded in 1904. It is a first-rate facility with a first-class staff.

Since joining the Club fifteen years ago, I have often used its wonderful facilities, including the dining rooms and health club—which I still frequently use. When I began my service in the U.S. Senate in 1997, the University Club was my home. I stayed at the University Club before my family moved here from Nebraska. Over the years, I have been proud to host many out-of-town guests at the Club.

Peace and quiet are rare commodities in Washington. As a Nebraskan, I appreciate both. The University Club has been a place where I have found peace and quiet and have always appreciated that, as well as some of the best conversation I've had in this town. It is my hope that the Club's next one hundred years are as successful as its first. Even though I may not be around for the next one hundred years, I look forward to many more years at the University Club.

—CHUCK HAGEL
United States Senator

A Second Century
for the University Club

The origins of private clubs can be traced back more than three centuries to the days when men gathered in London coffeehouses and taverns for drink and conversation. Few had clubhouses until the middle of the eighteenth century, but in those days, fellowship and common interests and causes made a club, not a building. Several centuries later, shared interests and shared values, camaraderie and the company of good friends remain at the heart and soul of a truly successful club.

Clubs form for a purpose. In 1904, the University Club of Washington was no different. It was begun by a group of university-educated men to "promote science, literature, and art, and to maintain a Club House for purposes of social intercourse amongst its members and for mutual improvement." That original mission statement spurred Proctor Dougherty, William Howard Taft, and six hundred like-minded men to form a club that has stood the test of time.

As we celebrate our Centennial, the goals that served as a foundation for the new University Club remain today an integral part of this club, its philosophy, and its membership. But this is not the same club as the one that first met in the New Willard a century ago. Our goals have expanded, and our membership has changed as times have changed.

Today, men and women of almost every age, ethnic and religious heritage, and professional background make up our membership. We are a sound and growing club because we have made diversity a goal, and we are stronger for it.

We are a center of lively debate and discussion, much as the club was in its first days and has remained over the years. Our emphasis and interest in all things international give us a distinctive character that can be traced to the first diplomats who crossed the Club's threshold in 1904. Over the past decade, the Club's focus on expanding activities and events to meet the needs of our increasingly diverse membership has energized the Club and kept us relevant to contemporary society. In doing so, we continue to be a place where friends gather.

A century after its founding, the University Club maintains its ranking as one of the top professional clubs not only in Washington, but in the United States—a place where the powerful and the prominent from all walks of life come to speak, debate, dine, exercise, and meet friends. The movers and shakers of Washington can be seen every day in the Club—in the Taft Dining Room with Miss Laurence standing watch; in the steam room or on the squash court; or in the Pershing Grille debating the issues of the day at the Club Table. Yet, the Club has also created a new and unique persona as a family-friendly place where children are welcome to a degree not seen in any other club in the city. And that adds to our liveliness.

Through the good work of the Club's Foundation and the Community Affairs Committee, the Club has become a true partner in the community, acknowledging its role as a neighbor and its responsibilities to help its neighbors in need. For decades, the Club enjoyed a reputation as center of influence and intellectual thought; now we also reach out to make our community a better place. And that is good for all of us.

Athletics were not a major part of the founders' original plan. In 1936, the merger with the Racquet Club changed the Club dramatically, and athletics were embraced as an important part of Club life. That enthusiasm continues today, and as our modern society focuses more and more on health and fitness, the Club has responded with a state-of-the-art athletic facility that is second to none.

We are definitely not the same Club that Proctor Dougherty founded so many years ago. But I'd like to think that this wise man, who left us such a wonderful legacy in the University Club, would approve.

For me personally, it is a great honor to serve as the University Club's Centennial president and as the first woman to join what has been a long and distinguished line of men stretching back one hundred years to President William Howard Taft. Their vision, their leadership, their humor, and, when needed, their diplomacy has brought this Club through difficult and contentious times, through war and economic depression, through great societal upheavals and cultural change. But it has been more than any one president or board that has made the University Club what it is today. It is the extraordinary sense of community and friendship that has always characterized this Club and its membership that has made the University Club of Washington a special place indeed.

This Centennial history tells the story of our Club, but it is more than that. It is the story of the thousands of men and women who have called themselves members of this Club over the years. It is their tale of success and failure, growth and change, camaraderie and mutual support, all in the context of the times and the great city in which they lived. So, as you turn the final page, think about the next chapter of this great Club. For that is ours to write, and I am convinced that, together, we can make the University Club's second century as proud as the first.

—SUSAN NEELY
President of the University Club

ACKNOWLEDGMENTS

Beginning to thank people, no matter how deserving, over the span of one hundred years is a daunting task and risky business. But so many people, both University Club members and staff, have played a role in the researching and writing of this book, that an attempt must be made.

First, I'd like to thank the wonderful historians who came before me and without whose work this book simply couldn't have been done. Former president Cecil Wilkinson's history of the first fifty years was invaluable and much of it is included in this book as well. Ken Reese and Bob Lowenstein gave me the next forty years in their wonderful ninetieth anniversary history, which I found myself going back to again and again.

A heartfelt thank you goes to the members of the Centennial Committee with a special nod to its chairman, Judge Loren Smith, who was my patient advisor and editor throughout the process. The University Club Foundation, its board, and its president, John Chandler, are owed a particular debt of gratitude for their vision in funding this project to preserve the University Club's history for coming generations of members. Thank you on their behalf. The Club's Board of Governors, along with the Literature and Arts Committee, deserve our thanks as well for their support of this important project.

I want to thank president Susan Neely for her time in guiding this project, particularly given all she has on her plate these days. And I also want to give special thanks to each of the Club's former presidents, who took time from their busy schedules to talk with me about their memories of the Club and their tenure. Their input was extraordinarily helpful. Along with the Club presidents, a number of members helped fill in blanks, check facts, and gave me wonderful stories that have added life to the book. So, my thanks to them, and all the members of the University Club for this opportunity.

There were also a number of staff members who went above and beyond the call of duty in helping ready this book for publication. First and foremost, General Manager Albert Armstrong was tremendously helpful. Without his guidance, his suggestions, and his amazing memory, the Centennial History might have taken another hundred years to complete. Many, many thanks go to Melissa Read for her help in everything from gathering the many photos for the book to answering endless questions from me. Miss Laurence's recollections over forty years and Ghirma Meres's over thirty were remarkably helpful as well, and Howard Day's assistance in covering the Club's athletic history and in the editing phase of the book were much appreciated.

Finally, I want to thank the authors of several books that were sources of much of the information about the history of Washington in the book: Jeanne Fogle, *Two Hundred Years: Stories of the Nation's Capital*; William Oliver Stevens, *Washington the Cinderella Town*; Marc McCutcheon, *Everyday Life from Prohibition through WWII*; and, most especially, Constance Green for her wonderful book, *Washington: A History of the Capital 1800–1950*.

—CHRISS WINSTON

UNIVERSITY CLUB, SIXTEENTH AND K STREETS

The first Clubhouse at 16th and K Streets,
occupied in 1904

Chapter One

A NEW WASHINGTON—
A NEW CLUB

As Washingtonians strolled to work down Pennsylvania Avenue one Monday morning in 1882, there it sat. A shiny B&O railroad engine stranded on a set of tracks at the foot of the Capitol, like a big boat marooned on a muddy flat at low tide. Boss Shepherd, the man (other than Pierre L'Enfant) more responsible than any other for pushing Washington into the ranks of the great cities of the world, had ordered the railroad to remove the "temporary" tracks that crisscrossed Pennsylvania Avenue.

The tracks, ugly remnants of the Civil War, spoiled Shepherd's ambitious plan to turn backwater Washington into the nation's showplace city. But not everyone was agreeable. The railroad brass had not only refused to cooperate but had defiantly left an engine out on the Pennsylvania Avenue crossing. They had underestimated the unstoppable Shepherd, however, who simply sent his workmen out in the dead of night to tear up the tracks on either side, leaving the engine stuck in the middle of the Mall and the B&O president more amused than angry at Shepherd's stubborn determination. But Shepherd understood that the nation's capital was entering a new era that called for a new city—a modern city. If Boss Shepherd had his way, Washington would no longer be a dirty swamp overrun with "the infinite, abominable nuisance of cows and horses and sheep and goats running through all the streets" as one senator complained. The Boss got his way.

Shepherd paved miles of streets and built sidewalks, laid sewer lines and put up three thousand gaslights. More than sixty thousand trees were planted in glorious new gardens along the new streets. Judson Welliver, the first presidential speechwriter, claimed that Washington had more trees than Paris.

By 1881, the beginnings of a new National Museum sat imposingly on the Mall, not far from the Washington Monument. It was finally finished in 1884—thirty-six years after it was begun. Four years later, the world's largest office building at the time, the neo-classical War and State Building, now the Old Executive Office Building next to the White House, was completed. Soon, electric trolleys were puttering down the tree-lined avenues, replacing the horse-drawn cars of earlier times. Commuter railroad lines carried many federal workers, whose numbers had exploded from 7,800 in 1880 to more than 23,000 by decade's end. Meanwhile, more than one thousand vendors sold fresh fish and meats, poultry, and vegetables hauled by oxcart to the newly rebuilt Center Market at 7th Street and Pennsylvania.

It would be many more years before Major L'Enfant's vision of a national Mall, a green expanse stretching from the Capitol to the White House, would become reality, but Boss Shepherd had given Washington a heavy-handed shove toward becoming the cosmopolitan capital city of an increasingly powerful nation.

By the turn of the century, Washington was home to more than 280,000 people. Seven hundred horseless carriages sputtered down Washington's streets and the trolley lines reached from Southeast to Georgetown and north to Park Road where "civilization" ended. The indomitable Theodore Roosevelt could be seen trekking through Rock Creek Park with gaggles of foreign diplomats in tow, trying to keep up with the energetic new president, whose fondness for the outdoors led him to explore Washington's "Central Park." Roosevelt was also known to doff his clothes after a hard walk for a quick swim in the Potomac. One story has the French ambassador J.J. Jusserand, who frequently hiked with Roosevelt, stripping down on the riverbank and plunging in, only to hear Roosevelt call from midstream, "Look at your hands." The ambassador had removed everything but his gloves.

In 1903, Roosevelt dedicated Andrew Carnegie's grand library at Mt. Vernon Square; Union Station's imposing façade was rising on Massachusetts Avenue just a mile away. The Daughters of the American Revolution had laid the cornerstone of their white-pillared building on 17th Street; and in Georgetown, a new hospital had opened. Washingtonians could see Richard Mansfield in "Old Heidelberg" at the Columbia Theater or the "Wizard of Oz" at the New National Theater. By mid-decade, "cinema palaces" would also add to Washington's entertainment scene.

Change was everywhere. Boss Shepherd's $20 million explosion of new government-financed construction had transformed Washington from a muddy cow town to a bustling city of new schools, office buildings, row houses, grand mansions, shops, and hotels. And nothing was more elegant and exclusive than Henry Augustus Willard's brand new hotel. It was the city's first commercial skyscraper, with the largest ballroom in town, just steps from the Treasury Building.

A New Club Forms

The Willard family had long had a hotel on Pennsylvania Avenue near the White House. Lincoln stayed there on the eve of his inauguration, as did Taylor, Fillmore, and Buchanan. The Swedish Nightingale, Jenny Lind, called the Willard home when performing in Washington, along with a host of congressmen and generals, poets and novelists, diplomats, and other celebrities of the time. Julia Ward Howe wrote the words to the "Battle Hymn of the Republic" in her room at the Willard, and her brother, an influence peddler extraordinaire who held court in the Willard lobby, gave modern Washington the term "lobbyist."

Nathaniel Hawthorne once wrote, "Willard's Hotel could more justly be called the center of Washington and the nation than either the Capitol, or the White House, or the State Department."

So it's no surprise that when a distinguished group of local business, military, and political leaders met on February 22, 1904, to form the bustling capital's first private club, open exclusively to university-educated gentlemen, they chose the plush Red Room of the new Willard Hotel for their inaugural gathering. The time was ripe for a new club. The Cosmos Club had formed in 1878 with a bent toward those of the scientific persuasion. With the turn of the century, the much-changed Washington was drawing a new class of men—college- and university-educated men of position and power—to the city as the federal government grew. The creation of a club to provide a haven of good food and intellectual fellowship was a logical next step in the social evolution of the growing city.

The formation of the club by such luminaries as Chief Justice Melville Fuller; the Secretary of Commerce and Labor, George Cortelyou; and the Secretary of the Smithsonian, Charles Walcott, attracted the attention of the local newshounds of the day.

In a story the next day, the *Washington Evening Star* shared the details of the Club's first meeting, which was called to order by Proctor L. Dougherty, a young engineer and later District Commissioner. Dougherty, who was to become the Club's most important member for the next five decades, had been asked by the Washington Society of the Massachusetts Institute of Technology "to investigate the question of forming a University Club and to secure all possible information on the matter." As Dougherty was to do over and over again in the ensuing years, he carried out his mission to the letter.

As the organizing meeting progressed, the only small disagreement apparently centered on the cost of the annual dues, which after some debate was finally established at $20—a bargain by today's standards. But back then, hand-tailored men's suits went for as little as $12.50. Bread was a nickel a loaf. Smokers could buy "Moguls"—ten for fifteen cents, and Magruder's sold its special whiskey for a dollar a quart.

Proctor Dougherty's membership certificate

Once the issue of the dues had been dispensed with, the Red Room group then passed its first set of bylaws, agreeing that the object of the Club was "to promote science, literature, and art, and to maintain a Clubhouse for purposes of social intercourse amongst its members." They voted to elect 603 men as charter members of Washington's newest club and created a Ruling Council of twelve members and a Board of Admissions. The University Club was official. Now all it needed was a home and a set of officers.

Taft Recruited

Five days later, on February 29, a leap year decision was made to formally invite William Howard Taft, the new Secretary of War, to become the first president of the University Club. Charles Walcott was tasked with contacting Taft. At the next meeting, on March 4, Walcott brought good news. The appropriately nicknamed "Big Bill" Taft, weighing in at 330 pounds, had accepted the Club's invitation.

The former Ohio jurist had just returned from a successful stint as governor of the Philippines to take Elihu Root's place at the War Department. Taft, known as much for his sense of humor as for his size, was a reluctant politician who loved his wife, the

First Club president William H. Taft

law, and golf. Deep down, he actually aspired to a spot on the Supreme Court, not the presidency.

In his award-winning biography of Teddy Roosevelt, *Theodore Rex*, Edmund Morris tells an enlightening story of Taft's interview with reporter Kate Carew of the *New York World*:

> Carew asked, "Which would you rather be, Chief Justice of the United States, or President of the United States?"
>
> Taft quaked with self-protective laughter. "Oh, ho, ho! Of course, I couldn't answer that question." He flushed with merriment, while she thought, *He must have been a very pink and white baby.*
>
> "Who do you suppose," Miss Carew pursued, when the heavings subsided, "will be the Republican candidate for President this year?"
>
> "President Theodore Roosevelt," Taft boomed, puffing out his cheeks.
>
> "And who in 1908?"
>
> "Oh," he said, smiling, "that is too far ahead."
>
> "But I had read somewhere that perhaps you would be."
>
> Taft began to talk about golf.

Just a few months after Taft assumed the presidency of the University Club, he and his wife, Nellie, settled into a new home the pair nicknamed "Hotel du Taft," conveniently located at 1630 K Street. As it turned out, it was just across the street from the Club's first quarters at 16th and K.

But on the night of March 12, 1904, the Club was still without a home, so its first "mass meeting" was held at one of the city's favorite eating establishments, Rauscher's. More than four hundred members attended the gathering, whose agenda focused on finding a suitable site for the Club before members headed for the buffet tables. The Glee Club entertained the membership with college songs, but the highlight of the evening was the arrival of the Club's new president, Secretary Taft, who spent much of the night shaking hands with every member in the room.

One local newspaper covering the event wrote:

> Amid the cheers of 500 University men, alumni of the East, West, North and South, classes dating back to Harvard 1835, and as recent as Columbian [now George Washington University] 1903, Secretary of War Taft assumed his new duties last night as President of the University Club...It was the largest and most enthusiastic meeting of a university club ever held in the United States, and already it is not only the largest university club in the world, but contains the greatest number of distinguished men and men of greatest prominence.

[Secretary Taft] expressed his gratitude for the honor that had been conferred upon him in being chosen the first President of the Club. He thought Washington an ideal city for such an organization and he was sure it would be a great success, judging by the number present and the enthusiasm they displayed. He pledged himself to do all he could to make it the success it ought to be and would be.

THE FIRST CLUBHOUSE

It would be another three and a half months before University Club members would hold their first meeting in the first Clubhouse. The search committee had recommended an imposing building at 930 16th Street, which rented for the princely sum of $4,000 per year, totally furnished. The Board of Governors agreed; and on July 4, 1904, the University Club held a gala official opening from 9 a.m. until 1 a.m., offering members a "no charge" buffet, not unlike today's Membership Appreciation Day. As Club members strolled through the red brick mansion, with its turreted front graced by tall shade trees, they found a cozy grill room in the basement along with a kitchen, buffet, and wine room. A liquor license had been issued to the Club two weeks earlier. The first floor had been renovated to include a writing room, a billiard room, and a card room. A large room on the third floor would be used for smokers and other "men only" events. There were also very limited sleeping accommodations and even a free telephone for members' use. Everyone else paid 3.6 cents per call.

Saturday night was soon designated as "Club Night," when a "simple collation," a light meal, was served, again without charge. A piano was rented for the evening, but despite the Club's 12:30 a.m. closing time, the treasurer soon reported, "the bar is not a source of profit but a loss of about one hundred dollars since the opening of the Club to date."

No Washington club would be complete without some politicking, and the University Club's long history of political traditions began in its inaugural year. On November 8, 1904, a private wire was installed to bring the national election returns into the Clubhouse, where members awaited the outcome as they would on many election nights over the decades to come. That year, the House Committee also notified the manager that "all tipping must be stopped under penalty of dismissal."

The Club's first annual meeting took place on February 11, 1905. The *Washington Post*, in a story called "Year of Prosperity," reported that George Washington University, Georgetown, Princeton, Harvard, Yale, and Columbia led, in that order, in the number of members of the Club, and that "there are 175 colleges represented in the membership, a larger number of colleges than any other university club in the country." Washington, D.C. had obviously arrived. On February 18, Secretary Taft was reelected to a second term as Club president.

THE FIRST BIRTHDAY BANQUET

Four days later, the Club's first birthday banquet took place, again at Rauscher's. The cost? A whopping $3 for "Blue Points on the Half Shell, Sauterne, Consommé Julienne, Turban of Bass a la Neva, Filet de Boeuf Pique Jardinière, Claret, Asparagus, Cigarettes, Punch au Kirsch, Mallard Ducks, Homini Croquets, Apollinaris, Glace, Pudding Diplomate, Cigars and Café Noir."

Club president Taft, serving as emcee of the slightly unruly event, quieted the crowd with a champagne bottle "gavel."

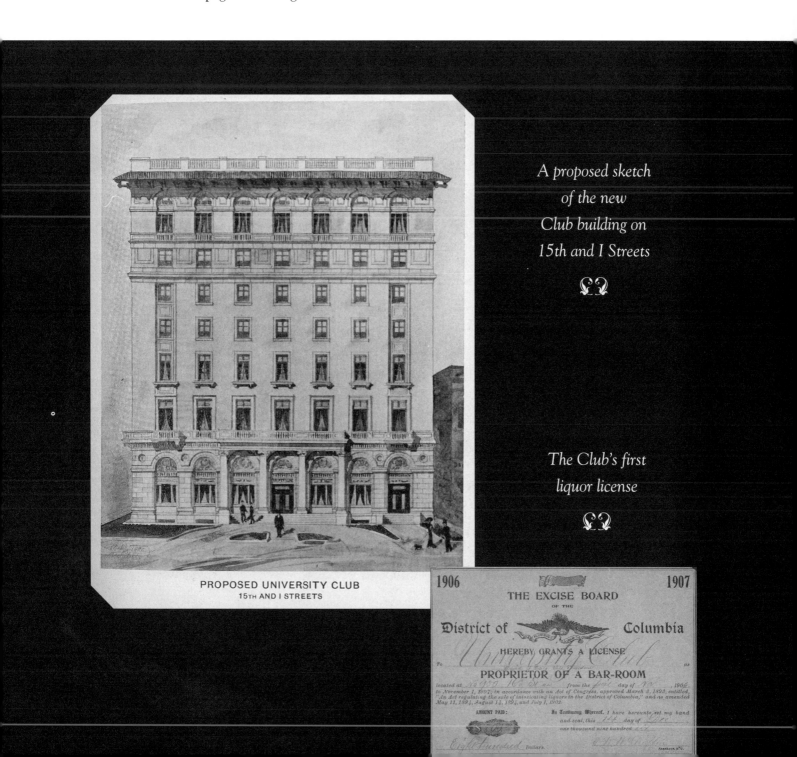

A proposed sketch of the new Club building on 15th and I Streets

The Club's first liquor license

PROPOSED UNIVERSITY CLUB
15TH AND I STREETS

1906   1907

THE EXCISE BOARD
OF THE

District of   Columbia

HEREBY GRANTS A LICENSE

PROPRIETOR OF A BAR-ROOM

"Fellow members of the University Club," he said, "you recognize in my hand the emblem of authority which has brought you to your feet and which I hope will now bring you to your seats." According to the *Star*, he was rewarded with the "wildest enthusiasm" as the crowd named him the next president of the United States and "cries of Taft! Taft! Taft! Rang through the banquet hall till the roof fairly shook. The Secretary of War sat quietly through it all with something of a twinkle in his eyes. Then [he] remarked in a mock-casual manner that he was glad the electoral vote of the District of Columbia was safe."

Not much business was done that evening, but in the months to come, members, among other things, rejected a proposal to allow billiard playing on Sundays and voted to deny membership applications from Maryland Agricultural College graduates—today's University of Maryland—as well as from all dentists. But despite the limit on Terrapins and tooth pullers, the Club managed to increase its membership to 801.

The Club's long tradition of sponsoring in-house lectures began on April 22, 1905, with a talk by Dr. Wilfred T. Grenfell of the Royal National Mission to Deep Sea Fishermen, "whose work on the coasts of Newfoundland and Labrador has so interested the civilized world."

By the time of the second annual meeting in early February 1906, Club officers were focused on the matter of finding a suitable lot and financing to build a permanent home for the Club.

Later in the month, Woodrow Wilson, then the president of Princeton, was the evening's guest of honor for another raucous dinner at Rauscher's celebrating the Club's second birthday. The *Post* reported it this way:

> Over 300 members of the University Club were assembled for the second annual banquet of that organization.... Thanks to the admirable team work of the Club and some wonderful individual plays, the pigskin of hilarity was sent flying clean and clear through the goal posts of fun. Not once did the eleven of Dullness score; not once did it race into the territory of Enjoyment's eleven.
>
> Rauscher's never presented a more brilliant picture. The variety of college colors, which were used in profusion, lent a kaleidoscopic effect to the scene. The blue of Yale, crimson of Harvard, orange and black of Princeton were in evidence, every college sitting under the shelter of the pennant that it holds dear next to the banner that soared above all in the glory of its red, white and blue....

Wilson, who would defeat Taft for the presidency six years later, spoke about George Washington in his remarks to the dinner. Taft, who was out of town, missed the event altogether. But shortly after Wilson finished, the colorful Speaker of the House, Joe Cannon, made a grand entrance into the banquet to a cheering crowd.

On February 24, Taft handed the reigns of the Club presidency to George Cortelyou, who had been Secretary of Commerce and Labor, Chairman of the Republican National Committee, and was Postmaster General at the time. Later, he would rise to become Treasury Secretary.

By now, the Club had settled into a social pattern of Saturday Club Nights and occasional lectures on a range of topics from "The Recent San Francisco Earthquake"

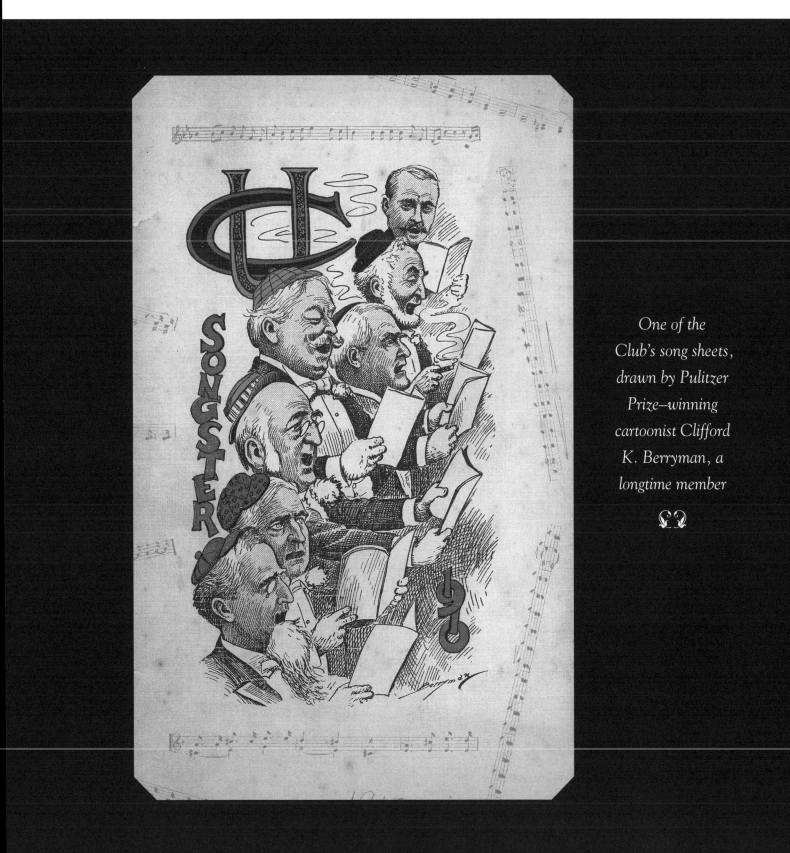

One of the Club's song sheets, drawn by Pulitzer Prize–winning cartoonist Clifford K. Berryman, a longtime member

to "The Poet, John Greenleaf Whittier"—a tradition that continues to this day. But it wasn't all seriousness. The members also voted to purchase a player piano to bring a little music to the house. Song sheets from the time can still be found at the Club—titles like "Landlord, Fill the Flowing Bowl," "Bill Bailey," and "There is a Tavern in the Town."

1907 dawned with the Club having rung out the old year with a deficit, and an increase in the membership dues came under consideration. The third annual banquet was moved from Rauscher's to the Raleigh Hotel. Members were serenaded by Irish tenor George O'Connor, who would be a Club favorite for more than forty years. Graduates from 144 colleges and universities attended the dinner, which was highlighted by the appearance of Vice President Charles Warren Fairbanks.

Although Fairbanks wasn't on the "toast list," he was called upon to speak and observed wryly, "I know you are men of a liberal education, for I see that nobody has refrained from either drinking or smoking. Some who have done so much of both must,

I think, like myself, have been graduated from a denominational institution." J.J. Jusserand, the French ambassador who had once doffed everything but his gloves when swimming with T.R., also spoke that night.

Meanwhile, Cortelyou informed the members he could not serve a second year as president, and on February 28, 1907, Dr. Charles D. Walcott, Secretary of the Smithsonian, became the third president of the Club. The Special Building Committee continued its search for land on which to build a permanent Clubhouse, coming close to purchasing several properties. In the end, however, they decided to continue the search. By November, with a deficit still hanging over the Club, the first increase in resident dues was approved at a special membership meeting.

The Club's third birthday dinner, held at the Raleigh Hotel

Just months before he won the Republican presidential nomination, Secretary Taft once again assumed the emcee duties at the Club's fourth banquet in 1908. That year, one of the speakers was the new Japanese ambassador, Harvard graduate Baron Takahira, who said, "The sentiment manifested in receiving me makes me feel how friendly you are to my country."

Secretary Taft graciously responded, "The suggestion of war between the United States and Japan is the suggestion of a crime against humanity." Prophetic words.

The banquet was attended by more than 350 members and a host of luminaries—from the dean of the diplomatic corps to the chief of staff of the Army, from the president of the University of Virginia to a Supreme Court justice—and many others who spent much of the evening making lengthy toasts on a variety of subjects. Finally, toastmaster Taft "concluded the speechmaking [according to the *Herald*] by thundering, 'I hereby declare this legislature adjourned.'"

TAFT GETS THE NOD

Four months after the Club banquet, on June 18, fireworks and band music filled the night at 16th and K when word came to the Club that William Howard Taft had, indeed, won the Republican presidential nomination earlier that day. University Club members lined up behind a band rented for the occasion and marched across the street to "Hotel du Taft," where the new nominee had just finished dinner. Soon, the street was filled with the sounds of the song first heard at the Club's 1906 banquet, "Taft for me, Taft for me...U-ni-u-ni-u-ni-ver-sity..."

Taft, clearly deeply touched by the outpouring, spoke to his fellow Club members:

You don't expect me to make a speech tonight—much less a political speech. A great honor has fallen upon me today—to lead a great political party in the contest that is to come. This expression of good fellowship I value greatly, as I deem it an expression of good-will from my fellow Club members.

We are neighbors. I don't regard it as a political demonstration at all, but merely as the good wishes of my neighbors. It is one of your number upon whom a great honor has been conferred and to whom you are here to extend congratulations...I thank you, gentlemen, for your good fellowship. I thank you in behalf of the real ruler of the family, the lady who is, I hope, near by looking on and listening. For those who conduct themselves properly in their family life, no greater need of approval could be desired. I am most deeply indebted to you all.

Although Taft was overdue at the White House that evening, the Club members formed a double line from the gate of the Taft home to "escort" Taft to the Club's front door. One newspaper reported that the oversized presidential candidate had actually been carried along by the crowd, but given the jovial Taft's size, many think the story is more legend than fact. Taft did sign the Club register that night, however, and then at the suggestion of one of the Club members, hopped on board the Army wagon that had brought the band and rode to the White House "in style."

On November 3, 1908, William Howard Taft became the twenty-seventh president of the United States. Proud University Club members heard the news of Taft's 321–162 electoral vote victory over William Jennings Bryan on a private wire brought to the Club especially for the evening. Though no historical record of that night exists, the sounds of singing and celebration could no doubt be heard by anyone passing by the corner of 16th and K that election night.

A New Home Is Found

The Club celebrated its fifth birthday with big news. Members at the 1909 banquet learned that the Building Committee, at long last, had optioned four lots at the northwest corner of 15th and I Streets, McPherson Square, for the grand sum of $72,500—less than $10 per square foot. To fund the costs of constructing the eagerly awaited Clubhouse, the officers, with Club president Charles Walcott in charge, announced the formation of an independent building company capitalized at $200,000 in open stock. At year's end, the *Star,* in its morning editions, reprinted the architect's drawing of the proposed new Clubhouse after a lively membership meeting held the night before gave the project an enthusiastic thumbs-up.

While members waited for the new building to be completed, Club activities continued as usual. Perhaps the most unsettling lecture topic in the Club's long speaker series was 1910's "The Hook Worm, Its Cause and Its Cure." The sixth annual banquet will go down as one of the University Club's most historic, with the new president of the United States holding court as the night's most honored guest. According to the *Herald,* Taft "broke his custom, formed when he started making dinner addresses as the Chief Executive, and stayed until the end of the long programme."

But Taft wasn't the only celebrity in the crowd that night. Members of the Cabinet and the Congress dressed the dais, along with Admiral Robert E. Peary, the discoverer of the North Pole. Some believe that it was at this University Club banquet that Senator Chauncey Depew, who was serving as emcee, was thought to have joked to the portly Taft, "I observe that you are enceinte. What are you going to call the offspring?"

Laughing, Taft supposedly responded, "If it's a girl, I'll call her Charity. If it's a boy, I'll call him Courage; but if, as I suspect, it is nothing but wind, I'll call it Chauncey Depew."

At the annual meeting in 1910, Senator Stephen B. Elkins of West Virginia was elected to serve as the Club's fourth president, but sadly, Elkins would die in office ten months later. In February 1911, Gardner Williams, who had returned from gold mining in Rhodesia, found himself the Club's next president.

Despite the heavy responsibilities of the Oval Office, President Taft headlined the seventh and eighth banquets, which were both held at the Willard. On February 27,

1912, a wistful and perhaps even melancholy Taft told his fellow Club members as they celebrated the Club's eighth birthday:

"A university club is an outgrowth of university life that has a peculiar fitness. It provides for an association of men who have been used to association under the conditions likely to make the sweetest memories, and that lead to the continuance of those associations as far as may be under the auspices of such a club. It is the institution where public opinion of the best character ought to be formed, and I doubt not that it is."

Acknowledging Taft's tough reelection battle, Senator Joseph W. Bailey, a Texas Democrat, made a little news that evening when he denounced Theodore Roosevelt's third-term ambitions, saying "if the present President is not a good enough Republican to succeed himself, he must be a good enough Democrat to do so." Two months later Club members would put politics aside and celebrate the long-awaited laying of the new building's cornerstone. The festivities began late on the afternoon of April 10, 1912, as Masons from the local temple marched to the new site at 15th and I Streets and then, with the Marine Corps band and mounted police leading the way, continued on to the Club's old quarters on 16th Street. There, the parade circled around, and after several hundred Club members joined in, marched down Vermont Avenue back to the building site.

President Taft, a Master Mason himself, led the officers of the Grand Lodge of the District in the traditional ceremony. After applying the square, level, and plumb line to the cornerstone, the president spread the mortar with a silver trowel, still a part of the Club's historical memorabilia collection today, and the cornerstone was, at last, put in place. Construction was officially underway and a new era for the University Club had begun!

The Club's second home, built in 1912,
on 15th and I Streets

Chapter Two

THE UNIVERSITY CLUB
BUILDS A HOME

oss Shepherd would have been proud of the University Club's new home. It was a grand building, everyone agreed. The Club stood six floors high, on a spot not too many blocks from where the Boss had built his own mansion twenty years before. But then, it was a time of grand undertakings in Washington and the world. Just a few years before, Washingtonians had hopped the trolley across the river to Fort Meyer to watch demonstrations of the Wright brothers' astonishing new airplane. They strolled through the National Museum of Art for the first time, where Whistler's dreamy portraits and newly donated old masters adorned the walls of the central hall.

A little more than a year after the Club's official opening, the SS *Ancon* would become the first ship to pass through the "eighth wonder of the world," the Panama Canal. Women were marching in the streets of Washington and New York and in towns and cities across the country, demanding the right to vote. Change was everywhere.

In the nation's capital, the population tipped 330,000 in the 1910 Census and kept climbing. Trolleys clanged across the Aqueduct Bridge into Rosslyn as the suburbs were expanding, and development spread, spurred by the city's powerful national banks. Riggs National Bank's influence reached into the Treasury Department itself—literally. For years, Charles Glover, the bank's president, had his own desk in the main Treasury Department, where he was the first to hear about the department's monetary actions. It took a new president and comptroller of the currency, John Skelton Williams, to try to rein in the practices of the Riggs and the other banks. But that didn't stop Glover from clobbering Williams with his walking stick in Lafayette Park. A man, he believed, had unfairly maligned him and his bank. In the end, the courts ruled in Glover's favor.

15

Over the decades, Washington's banks would become one of the mainstays of the University Club, often paying the initiation fees and dues of their senior members until tax law changes and industry consolidation, for all practical purposes, ended the role they played in the Club's history.

With Washingtonians swept up in baseball fever that spring of 1912, President Taft set a precedent that continues today by throwing out the first ball of the season, thus beginning the tradition of "opening day." That year, the Club also hired its first manager, William Gaines, for the princely sum of $2,000 a year. In November, University club members were mourning President Taft's election loss to Woodrow Wilson in a hard-fought, three-way battle that saw Theodore Roosevelt emerge from retirement to head the Bull Moose Party ticket.

A Gala Opening

In those days, Washington was nicknamed the "city of conversation" and on New Year's Day, 1913, there was plenty to talk about. The University Club had opened the doors of its new building the night before, to much public acclaim.

The *Star* reported in its January 1, 1913, edition:

Today is a good deal more than New Year's Day for members of the University Club—more than the beginning of another year.... Early last evening the members of the Club began the use of the new Clubhouse. Billiard and pool balls clicked on the tables in the spacious basement room, the handsome 'grandfather's' clock chimed the hours in the reception hallway and polished ash trays received the first tarnish from cigar ashes.

Throughout the evening the bellboy, in new red-coated uniform, kept busy opening the front door for members who desired to...admire the beauty and enjoy the comforts of the new home. They strolled through the many rooms from basement to sixth floor finding much to admire in decorations, fixtures, mantelpieces, furniture—in fact, equipment and architecture generally.

The main entrance is on Fifteenth Street, opposite McPherson Park, and there is a rise of only three steps to the reception hall with its tiled flooring. As one enters, the first sight is a flight of marble stairs that leads to the floors above. On the left of the reception hall is what is known as the college room, furnished with many big easy chairs and leather couches.... On the right of the entrance hall are a guest room, where visitors will find comfort while waiting for members, a grill room of cozy sort and the office with its telephone switchboard.

There is a ladies' entrance from the I Street side of the building, with a small hallway and a daintily furnished reception room. An elevator to the ladies' dining room two floors above is close to it.

It was an impressive building, with English tile floors, chestnut-paneled rooms, massive fireplaces, and French rugs and draperies, along with a state-of-the-art kitchen and thirty bedrooms on the fourth and fifth floors.

The Italian Renaissance–style building was designed by George Oakley Totten, Jr., a charter member of the Club. In the end, the construction bill came in at $176,000, and when other charges, furniture, and equipment were added, the total topped out at $243,000. Now all the Club members had to do was pay for it.

UNIVERSITY CLUB OF WASHINGTON

Ninth Annual Banquet

THE Annual Banquet will be held at the NEW WILLARD on Saturday evening, February 8, 1913. Save that date. President Taft will attend.

THE BANQUET COMMITTEE

A ticket to the Club's ninth birthday

A special meeting of the membership was called and two hundred members met on January 6, 1913, just days after the gala opening, and voted unanimously to increase dues from $30 to $50 a year, along with a $50 initiation fee. The Ruling Council, which had been in place since the Club's beginning, was also replaced by a fifteen-member Board of Governors.

A month later, the Club held its ninth birthday banquet at the New Willard Hotel, although the event's name was changed that year to "annual dinner." The bittersweet evening served as a farewell to President Taft, who had attended and spoken at each of the Club's dinners during his presidential term.

That evening, Colonel George Harvey, editor of *Harper's Weekly*, called Taft "the worst-licked, the least-sore and the best-liked of all our Presidents." Charter member

Oliver Metzerott presented the much-beloved president with a gold key to the Club-house and told him, "Nine years ago when the University Club was new-born and homeless, you did us the honor to become its first President... Now that we have entered our new home, we are anxious for you to know how much we appreciate that friendship and how great is our admiration for you. So we take this opportunity to present to you this, the only key to the Clubhouse, and to assure you that it represents what you, sir, have won—the key to all our hearts."

President Taft, who would soon join the faculty of the Yale Law School, responded, "And so my friends, I came here to say good-by, to testify to you my appreciation of your good will, and to say to you that I carry away with me, as one of the delights of my Washington life, the good fellowship of the University Club.... I count it a happy part of my life that it was thrown in Washington when the University Club was begun, and when it has sprung into such a degree of prosperity and such full spirit of that club fellowship that insure its constituted life and usefulness. And now, good-by. I will be with you every once in awhile."

That year, there was an attempt to allow a limited number of members who "have attended approved universities or college but have not received their degrees therefrom." It was rejected; but a year later, members had a change of heart and voted to allow one hundred associate members. In its promotional brochure, designed to showcase the new Clubhouse, prospective members were told that the University Club "is intended to be national headquarters for university and college men... where character and culture are standards and congeniality and good fellowship reign." According to the booklet, 219 American and foreign universities and colleges were represented by members in professional, artistic, scientific, literary, business, and public service life and "yet retain their fraternal college spirit, which it is the special aim of the Club to foster."

A New Era

On March 4, 1913, Woodrow Wilson became the twenty-eighth president of the United States. The Taft era was over for Washington and for the University Club. That February, Myron Parker, prominent civic leader and former District Commissioner, was named the Club's sixth president. In the summer of 1913, the newest Club manager, Lewis Cochran and the House Committee butted heads after the Committee directed Cochran to put on luncheons at thirty cents and forty cents, against the manager's better judgment. When the Board ruled against them, the Committee lost their battle for the "nearly" free lunch.

That fall, the Club hosted one of its most memorable events of the time—a reception honoring the Prince of Monaco—spending $25 for extra music for the evening.

Once again, the *Star* carried the details:

His serene highness, Albert, Prince of Monaco, Duc de Valentois (and a dozen other titles) is prouder of being able to write after his name 'member of the Institute of France' than of all these titles. This was stated at the University Club last night, where the Prince of Monaco was a guest at a reception a short time after his arrival in Washington from the West. The prince is the first reigning sovereign to visit Washington in many years. The prince, in whose domain is Monte Carlo, was accorded the reception by the University Club in recognition of his achievements as a scientist, which include researches in oceanography, meteorology and anthropology.

Six hundred members celebrated the Club's tenth anniversary in white tie and tails at the New Willard on February 18, 1914. Although President Taft's absence left a big hole to fill, literally and figuratively, it was a star-studded evening nonetheless. Vice President Thomas Riley Marshall was the main speaker, who concluded his mostly humorous remarks with this advice: "Don't take yourselves too seriously. The trouble with Americans is they want to settle everything and settle it now. Leave something for the boys to do."

The new dean of the Yale Law School, William Howard Taft, sent a letter to his University Club friends with his congratulations on the Club's tenth birthday, while Secretary of State William Jennings Bryan, sipping grape juice, regaled the crowd with tales of his early campaigning.

CHANGE TAKES OVER

With suffragettes marching in city streets, the Board of Governors voted in the fall of 1914 to let the Executive Committee "use its discretion" in the matter of permitting ladies' nights, and in raising the price of alcoholic drinks if need be. In those pre-Prohibition days, a member could get a good whiskey highball for twenty cents.

By mid-decade, more change was in the air. Henry Ford was turning out almost a quarter of a million Tin Lizzies a year—and pricing them at just $360. More than fifty movie companies were pumping out silent films headlined by stars like Mary Pickford and Charlie Chaplin. Americans were reading the *Saturday Evening Post, Ladies' Home Journal,* and Booth Tarkington, and complaining about the federal income tax, which was about to be ruled constitutional by the Supreme Court. Some things don't change.

On Lincoln's birthday, 1915, the cornerstone for an imposing new monument to the fallen president, designed by architect Henry Bacon, was laid on the banks of the Potomac. At the University Club, members had comfortably settled in their new Clubhouse. With the decade-long effort to build a home for the Club finally completed, the focus turned to increasing membership, expanding Club activities, and turning up the pressure on members slow to pay their bills. Club membership in that year's secretary's report clocked in at just over 1,200. The board authorized the Club's new manager, Kieran Lowry, to hire a man "to keep the Club free from insects and mice at $90 a year." Club historian Cecil Wilkinson, in his fifty-year Club history, couldn't resist commenting that, "this was no reflection on the Committee on Admissions."

The eleventh annual dinner, held on February 25, 1915, was highlighted by a mock trial on the capabilities or incompetence of the university-educated man, which the *Star* trumpeted as: "Banqueters Acquit the College Man: Hold Him Not Guilty of Charge He is Improperly Trained for World's Work." Myron Parker was elected to another term—the third of what would be eight that he would serve.

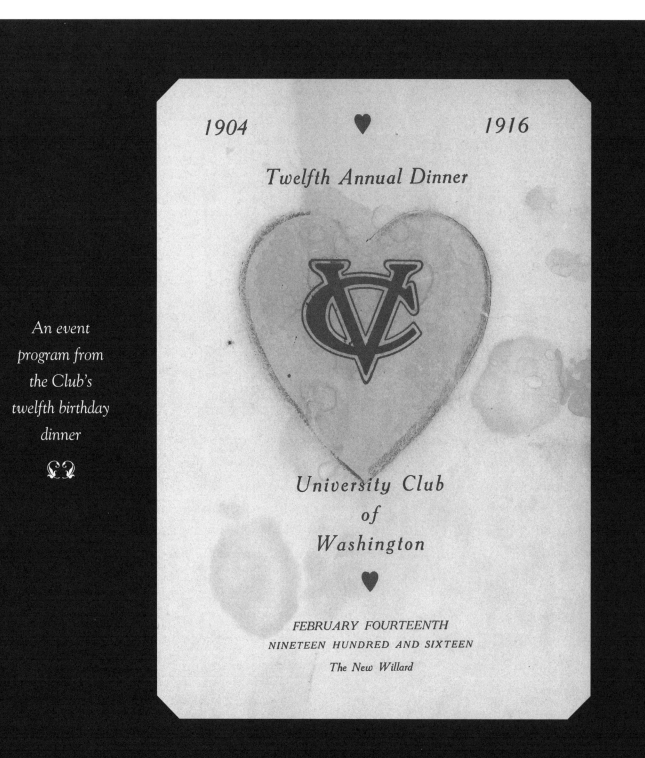

An event program from the Club's twelfth birthday dinner

1904 ♥ 1916

Twelfth Annual Dinner

University Club
of
Washington

♥

FEBRUARY FOURTEENTH
NINETEEN HUNDRED AND SIXTEEN
The New Willard

WAR ON THE HORIZON

In the year that followed, however, the winds of war sweeping Europe threatened to draw America into the fray. In May, the *Lusitania* was sunk without warning by a German submarine, killing nearly 1,200 people, including more than one hundred Americans. So, it wasn't surprising that the Club's annual dinner that Valentine's Day, 1916, was a little more serious than the good-humored evening members had come to expect.

The *Star* described it this way:

> Patriotism, with "preparedness" as a necessary adjunct, was the keynote of the speeches at the annual banquet of the University Club at the New Willard Hotel last night. The members and their guests were roused to high enthusiasm as the speakers, Democrats and Republicans alike—casting politics aside—urged the need today of Americans for America first, last, and all the time. The sentiment of those who sing "I Didn't Raise My Boy to be a Soldier" was vigorously criticized by the Rev. Dr. James Shera Montgomery of the Metropolitan Methodist Church, who in a ringing speech, declared that he knew of no holier altar upon which to offer his own son than that of the country's service, if necessary, in time of war.

As the months went by, war fever raged in Washington, and the University Club was not immune. In June, the Congress passed the National Defense Act, which increased the size of the country's standing army to 175,000. That same month, 116 University Club members, dressed in white flannel trousers, dark coats, and straw hats, proudly marched in a Preparedness Parade on Flag Day, June 14, while the Board of Governors' minutes began to show the remitting of dues by members who had been mustered into the armed forces. Along with its dances and lectures that November, the Club also invited members of the Plattsburg Military Training Camp to the Club for an evening event.

War might have been on the horizon; but this was Washington, after all, and in Washington, politics must go on. And it did. Woodrow Wilson was reelected that fall, and at the University Club a "post-mortem" discussion of the 1916 election was held. Senators, congressmen, and other campaign politicians hotly debated the implications of Wilson's reelection, but the Club, always bipartisan, gave each side equal time.

While the war sometimes dampened spirits, Washingtonians, like most Americans, also found themselves caught up in a dance craze that had started with the turkey trot and the bunny hug, but peaked when Vernon and Irene Castle wowed Broadway with their Castle Walk and fox trot. So, bowing to popular demand, the Club, in 1916, also loosened up a little and began what has become a long tradition of dinner dances. Then, the price of admission was just $1.50.

The new year, 1917, began amid the ominous signs of an American entry into the war. This year was the end of the "age of innocence" as one social commentator called the war era, and was also the end of one of the Club's traditions—its annual dinner.

The New Willard was once again the site for what was to be the thirteenth and final annual banquet. The days when William Howard Taft could draw more than six hundred members to cheer on their president were over. Fewer than 175 attended the Valentine's Day dinner, which featured stirring remarks, nonetheless, from Colonel George Harvey, editor of *Harper's Weekly*, who called for the United States to enter the war immediately. The colonel's speech was apparently so inspiring that members, wearing multi-colored hats, leapt spontaneously from their seats numerous times to break into one rousing rendition of the "Star Spangled Banner" after another.

Just two months after Harvey's call to action, Germany's torpedoing of three American merchantmen assured war. President Woodrow Wilson asked Congress on April 2, 1917, for an official declaration of war against Germany, and Washington turned into a war capital overnight. The New Willard bellhops drilled on the hotel's roof, and young men raced to enlist. Washington, then a city of 350,000, exploded to 526,000 in the first twelve months of war, straining city services, housing chief among them.

As the war went on, University Club minutes show that the influx of tens of thousands of government workers flooding Washington impacted the Club's ability to provide accommodations for non-resident members. One solution was a proposal to rent a building nearby to help house these short-term residents. Instead, the Club offered temporary memberships at $7.50 for military men and civilians engaged in the war effort.

That spring, the Club's entertainment program had a decidedly military flavor to it. Members watched official British war films and listened to an address titled, "The Navy—Our First Line of Defense."

The Board of Governors also authorized the purchase of a service flag to honor members who had answered the country's call to duty. Eventually, eighty-seven stars would grace this proud flag honoring those serving in the first World War. Although soliciting for charitable causes was not allowed in the Clubhouse, an exception was made that fall for the YMCA's fund-raising drive for the war effort.

November also saw the local D.C. prohibition law, passed earlier that year, go into effect. The District was two years ahead of the rest of the country in outlawing liquor. Meanwhile, prices, pressured by the military's needs for food and other goods, pushed costs higher and higher. By the end of the year, the Club was forced to increase its room rates for permanent guests by twenty percent, doing the same for temporary guests.

In April 1918, the board declared that "we conform absolutely and gladly with the wishes of the local food administrator." The government had asked restaurants to voluntarily stop serving dishes using wheat products until after the fall harvest. Most complied, but a few ignored the request, and the University Club board wanted its support for the food administrator's rationing policies made clear.

On November 11, 1918, the war ended with the signing of the Armistice and members once again flocked to the newly reconstituted dinner dances. The Meyer Davis Orchestra provided the music for the popular buffet affairs, which saw the price increase to a whopping $2. When the board met in December, reports show that University Club members had purchased nearly $425,000 in Fourth Liberty Loan bonds, and an army captain, attending the meeting, thanked the Club for "the wonderful way in which strangers who were here in war services had been treated."

An aerial view of the Federal Triangle,
completed in the mid-1930s

Chapter Three

1920s–1930s:
BETWEEN THE WARS

With the "war to end all wars" officially over, Congress turned to other pressing domestic issues and, in 1919, took historic action by passing not one but two new amendments to the Constitution that would radically change the country and its culture. First, on June 4, 1919, Congress approved the Nineteenth Amendment to the Constitution, giving women the right to vote. But Speaker of the House and University Club member Joe Cannon had his doubts.

He wrote, "I have had five generations of feminine influence in my own family to advise me, appeal to me and command me. My mother...was my first counselor....then my wife took her place when I first came to Congress; then my daughters insisted on telling me what their father ought to do; later my granddaughters entered the family council and now in the first year of woman suffrage, my great-granddaughter in language not strictly parliamentary but understood by her great-grandfather, gives advice and consent."

Six years earlier, a number of Club members had protested to the board concerning allowing ladies in the Clubhouse. The minutes reported that the House Committee "had the situation in hand." It wasn't the last they would hear from the ladies.

On October 18, 1919, the Eighteenth Amendment—Prohibition—also passed in Congress, setting the stage for one of the most controversial and eventually colossal failures of social policy in the country's history.

POSTWAR WASHINGTON

In the 1920 presidential election, voters rejected Democrat James Cox and his support for the League of Nations and against Prohibition, opting instead for Republican

Warren G. Harding. The heir to the Washington Post fortune, Edward Beale McLean, a University Club member and owner of the ill-fated Hope Diamond, chaired the Inaugural Committee. The new administration would bring big changes to Washington—some sorely needed—with "tempos," temporary office buildings and barracks built during the war, still cluttering the once beautiful Mall.

As the Roaring Twenties kicked into high gear, the Charleston raged and classics like "Ain't We Got Fun" and "Second Hand Rose" were popular favorites. Sinclair Lewis's *Main Street* could be found in the drawing rooms of America and the University Club library and writers like F. Scott Fitzgerald, Edith Wharton, and Zane Grey were rapidly becoming popular favorites.

After the war, normalcy had quickly returned to the University Club, although the Club did lose a number of its members to resignations—going from 825 resident members to 747—including a little-known Assistant Secretary of the Navy by the name of Franklin D. Roosevelt, who returned home to New York.

By 1920, Tuesday evening dinner dances were once again drawing large crowds, where they spun to songs like "Mah Lindy Lou" and "A Pretty Girl is like a Melody," while the lecture series returned to more mundane topics. Daniel Roper, a University Club member, was commissioner of the Internal Revenue Service, which had become all the more important with the passage of the Sixteenth Amendment—the income tax. Commissioner Roper commandeered ten of his assistants for a seminar at the Club to discuss "vital problems of tax administration, including methods of rounding up tax dodgers, traffic in 'dope' and 'moonshine' whisky, operation of the child Labor Law, income and excess profits, the new luxury tax and other subjects of popular interest."

Washington Stays "Wet"

Although Prohibition was now the law of the land, enforcement in Washington, as in most of America, was a spotty proposition at best. One bootlegger even had his own office in one of the House office buildings to keep the Hill supplied.

The *Washington Herald* described the city's drinking "problem" this way:

> Cocktails continued to be served as usual. In fact, it became a point of honor to serve cocktails. Folks seemed to imagine that if they didn't serve cocktails other folks would think they were obeying the law, and such a thought, to a liberty-loving people, was unbearable.

A *Charlotte News* reporter wrote, "Washington is wet. I mean it is wringing, dripping wet. Intoxicants are sold in cafes, drug stores, hotels, and almost everywhere."

One Prohibition agent toured the country testing how long it took to buy illegal alcohol. New Orleans held the record at thirty-five seconds. Washington clocked in at two hours and eight minutes.

While Club records discreetly ignore the entire issue of Prohibition, it's hard to imagine that the Club, unlike the rest of Washington, went totally dry—laws or no laws. Godfrey Munter, a Club member for more than seventy years, once confirmed what most members have always believed. According to Munter, a noted local attorney and former head of the D.C. Chamber of Commerce, a drink could be had at the University Club just as in most of the capital's eating establishments. Whatever was going on behind the scenes, resignations still plagued the Club in 1920. So when the Officers' Club, located on Dupont Circle, gave up its building, the University Club was happy to welcome forty-two of its members. Club members also voted to increase the dues from $50 to $60 a year.

The Club Carries On

With hundreds of women marching in the city streets for voting rights, one might have thought that women's suffrage was the only voting issue in Washington in those days. Not true. District residents were also continuing their efforts to gain voting representa-

tion. But when the National Press Committee for District of Columbia Suffrage asked to send a speaker to the University Club to argue its cause, the board voted to "ignore" the request. It was an interesting decision, considering that three prominent members of the Club would serve as commissioners of the District of Columbia—Myron Parker, the longest serving president; Proctor Dougherty, the Club's preeminent founder; and J. Thilman Hendrick, a local stockbroker.

In the spring of 1921, Harding moved into the White House, a new president for the nation, while the University Club reelected its long-term president, Myron Parker, as its chief executive for the eighth and final time. The Club kept a full social calendar that year. There was a chess exhibition, dinner dances, motion pictures for the children, and a stimulating round of lectures. Some forty-nine members, however, enjoyed none of the festivities after being shown the door, figuratively speaking, for non-payment of Club dues and debts. As the Club continued to face financial problems, it was forced to

President Myron Parker's letter to members about the Club's financial problems

MYRON M. PARKER
1913-1921

In a circular letter, dated May 19, 1921, President Parker poured out his soul:

It is a source of deep regret that some of our members indulge in constant criticism respecting their Club and its management and this in the presence of strangers and new members. It seems to me that it would be much better were they to speak of the comforts and privileges they are permitted to enjoy here. One of this number was recently invited by the Executive Committee to appear before them that he might make plain his grievances. Nothing from his standpoint seemed to be right; everything was wrong from top to bottom. In all his statements there was nothing concrete. Over two hours were wasted in listening to this member without any definite benefit having been derived. His desire seemed to be to get more and better things for less money. . . .

In a word, the issue is clear. We must have more members or more money — both preferred.

toughen its payment policies, which caused some controversy and consternation, as shown in President Parker's letter to members:

> It is a source of deep regret that some of our members indulge in constant criti-cism respecting their Club and its management and this in the presence of strangers and new members. It seems to me that it would be much better were they to speak of the comforts and privileges they are permitted to enjoy here.

Parker then complained about one individual who had appeared before the Executive Committee to express his unhappiness with the Club, saying:

> His desire seemed to be to get more and better things for less money... In a word, the issue is clear. We must have more members or more money—both preferred.

James Wesley Fowler

Wesley Fowler, who was a fixture at the Club for fifty-five years

Six months later, Colonel Parker, credited as the driving force behind the building of the Clubhouse, resigned and was replaced by Martin Knapp, a judge of the Commerce Court. Ladies became an issue again that year as one member proposed banning smoking in the ladies' dining room. Apparently, liberation had reached the women's floor of the University Club, where some members' wives had taken up the cigarette craze. The board declined to act on the suggestion.

On September 21, 1921, a man who was to become a fixture at the University Club's front door for the next fifty-five years—Wesley Fowler—began his record-setting service. That year also saw Frank L. Carter, who had been associated with the Club since 1907, take over the general manager duties from Kiernan Lowry.

TECHNOLOGY CHANGES THE WORLD

In 1922, despite the popularity of that newfangled invention, the radio, the board tabled a proposal to install a "wireless telephone so as to receive broadcasting from the Westinghouse and Naval Air Stations." Apparently, the technology wasn't up to snuff, according to the governors, who announced, "This system has not been sufficiently developed."

The Club's lecture series reflected the country's fascination with manned flight when Brigadier General William "Billy" Mitchell addressed members on "The New Era of Aviation." It wasn't the first time the Club had shown an interest in "flying machines." Eleven years before, the nation's capital had been treated to a grand aerial exhibition, and the exciting show had officially kicked off at the University Club. Well-known aviator J.A.D. McCurdy delivered an address to the Club on the history of aeronautics, taking listeners back to Leonardo da Vinci's fascination with flight and returned them to the present and McCurdy's own experiences, including his failed attempt to fly from Key West to Havana. The aeronautical action then moved to the Hill. Taking off from a field in Anacostia, McCurdy and a number of other celebrity aviators entertained members of Congress, military officials, and federal staff with their daredevil flying skills, even going so far as to buzz the Capitol dome.

As the new aviation industry began to make the world "smaller," the Club's interest in all things international was evident in its "World Correspondents Nights"—a series of talks by reporters covering France, Russia, and China, among others.

On August 8, 1922, the Club held its first field day at the Columbia Country Club, where members ponied up $1 for greens fees. It was the first in what was to become a long history of Club athletic competitions.

Another tradition began that fall, when a group of some ninety physicians and surgeons—all Club members—formed an internal "club within a club" called Wapiya, a

Sioux Indian name for medicine men. It wasn't long before the Club had gained a well-deserved reputation as a meeting place of prominent Washington doctors.

The Club received a number of gifts that year, including one of the engraved invitations to the 1845 Inaugural Ball and two finely mounted specimens of speckled trout. The artist Walter Cox also offered to donate an oil painting of William Howard Taft, which hangs in the Taft Dining Room today.

The following year, on February 10, 1923, the annual board meeting adjourned on a somber note when word came that Club president Martin Knapp had died earlier that day. Six months later, in an odd coincidence, the nation would lose its president when Warren Harding died of an embolism while on a visit to California. "Silent Cal" Coolidge would step up to the plate and become the thirtieth occupant of the Oval Office.

When the University Club Board reconvened a few days after Knapp's death, it selected Dr. Daniel W. Shea, professor of physics at Catholic University, as the Club's eighth president. Despite a booming economy, Club finances were also on the agenda as the board voted to levy a $20 assessment against all resident members. Other "important" matters included providing "adjustment" for Godfrey Munter, who complained that his coat and hat had been damaged while left in the Clubhouse, although the board wanted it understood that they were setting no precedent.

Entertainment in the Club that year was a reflection of the culture and society swirling about Washington in those heady days between the wars. Ladies were invited to attend many Club activities, so it's not surprising that Club records show a packed social calendar of dinner dances, musical nights, Oriental interpretative dance recitals, and lectures.

MORE MONEY PROBLEMS

The following year, 1924, saw the annual board meeting focused once again on familiar goals: "(1) a substantial curtailment of the accounts payable and the bills payable; and (2) the collection of as many as possible of the accounts receivable that were delinquent more than one year."

But the board added two new objectives that year—building three more stories to the Clubhouse, which had been long planned, and attaining full title to the property through the purchase of all remaining bonds and stocks. It also voted another members' assessment of $20. Later that month, Dr. Shea was reelected to a second one-year term. During the year, smokers prevailed when the board voted to allow smoking on the second floor of the Clubhouse, although the dining room, with its expensive and easily ruined linen tablecloths, remained off limits.

Despite the board's refusal to purchase a radio two years before, members were clearly fascinated with the new technologies that seemed to appear almost daily, even if their leadership was less enthusiastic. In October, members took matters in hand and passed a hat to buy the Club's first radio.

One "Club Night" announcement asked: "The mysteries of radio transmission of pictures through the air. . . . Telegraph, telephone, radiograph, radiophone, are we coming to television? Let's all come and have a peek at this new wonderland of science." Although it seems anachronistic now in the era of ten-digit direct dialing, the Club's telephone number in those days, dialed by operators, was Franklin 6327.

Dinner dances to popular songs like "Tea for Two" and "California Here I Come," continued to be the favorite Club entertainment, but musical evenings and dance recitals also remained popular, along with the lecture series highlighted that year by "The Resurrection of King Tutankhamen" given by Dr. Mitchell Carroll, editor of *Art and Archaeology* magazine.

THE CLUB TURNS TWENTY

1924 had special importance for members, who celebrated the twentieth anniversary of the Club's founding with a rousing dinner held in the Clubhouse on February 27. Honoring the Club with his presence was the venerable William Howard Taft, now Chief Justice of the United States—the office to which he had aspired all along.

Speaking to the audience of 150, Taft said that he was now a member of a "cloister club where speechmaking was taboo" and "members of that club with oratorical ability have to suffer." The toastmaster on that special birthday was William Mather Lewis, president of George Washington University. The *Washington Post* wrote that "George O'Connor regaled with his vocal antics, assisted by Matt Horne at the piano," which was carried live by radio station WCAP. Not long after, the Club received many messages from non-resident members who had listened to the festivities on the "wireless."

President Shea wrote to thank the Radio Division of the Chesapeake and Potomac Telephone Company for arranging the broadcast, saying that it had been heard, "at such distant points as Youngstown, Ohio, Asheville, North Carolina, and Elkhorn, West Virginia."

In the years to come, Washington's growing power and influence would draw more and more people to this once sleepy Southern city. No one could say that about the nation's capital anymore. The sounds of clopping hooves had been replaced by the roar of engines and honking horns. William Howard Taft himself had been the first president to have an automobile in the White House. By 1925, automobile traffic in Washington had become a stop-and-go affair as the suburbs grew, and more people drove to work. Even with a twenty-two-mile-per-hour speed limit, there were nearly 9,400 accidents in Washington in 1925 alone. Air travel was also beginning to come into vogue, and the price was right—only $30 to fly from Washington to New York. Moreover, Washington was becoming one of the country's favorite vacation spots.

More and more people were arriving in the capital every day, and many needed a place to hang their hats or find a little friendly conversation. The University Club certainly filled the bill, but financial troubles continued to plague the Club in 1925, despite a number of actions taken by the board, beginning in 1923, to remedy the situation. The board had tried to accommodate delinquent members whom they hoped would return themselves to good standing if "kept on the rolls until they could adjust their affairs which had been very much disturbed by the War." But, finally, the governors had no choice but to pull the memberships of a substantial number of those far past due in their bills, writing off $2,691 in the process. A year later, they were forced to write off another $4,000 owed by men in the armed forces who had enjoyed Club privileges during the war. During 1924, membership slipped further to only 548 members. On Valentine's Day, 1925, Dr. Lewis H. Taylor, a well-known surgeon, assumed the Club presidency with the Club facing serious financial problems. One of these was increasing food prices, which had risen more than seven percent over the past year. Yet another assessment of $20 was levied to keep the Club afloat.

THE PERSHING TRADITION BEGINS

Still, Club activities continued unabated. With the Army band providing the music, one of the most colorful events in the Club's history was held in 1925—a gala reception honoring General John J. Pershing, the great hero of World War I. Little did members know that General Pershing would play a bigger role in the life of the Club years later. The Dance Committee reported that "our lounge offers a ballroom setting unexcelled anywhere in Washington" and that the Club had instituted the "Club Table" in the center of the dining room where single stags could dine with others. The Club Table can still be found in the Grille today, named after Black Jack Pershing himself. While members hashed over the issues of the day in the Grille, the radio bugs that year were entertained with a lecture on "The Secrets of Radio Transmission."

1926 saw ladies finally allowed to eat in the main dining room, at least on Sunday evenings. Membership had remained relatively constant during the previous year, but once again members were assessed $20 to cover operating deficits, which were aggravated by the continuing rise in food prices: almost ten percent that year. Proctor Dougherty, the founding father of the Club and one of its stalwarts over the years, was honored by being named a commissioner of the District of Columbia that year.

BEFORE THE FALL

The years leading up to what was to be the nation's worst financial disaster—the Great Depression—were relatively quiet ones for the University Club, other than its seemingly never-ending economic woes. Charter member Oliver Metzerott, a former Maryland state senator, was elected Club president on February 17, 1927. After four years of assessments, members threw in the towel that year, voting to increase annual dues to $80. The Club also increased meal prices five percent, but the minutes show an average loss of 8.3 cents per member meal.

In 1928, Herbert Hoover won a landslide election over Al Smith, but the change of administrations impacted the Club very little. Despite food costs, the price of a plate luncheon was reduced to sixty-five cents in an effort to attract new members, but the Club's rolls continued to dwindle. In his annual report to the board on February 9, 1929, Metzerott announced a loss of more than $4,500 during the previous year, along with the loss of another 103 members. In response, the governors created a special recruiting commission to reverse the trend that was playing havoc with the Club's finances.

Later that month, George F. Snyder, solicitor for the Canadian Pacific Railway and one of the Club's most active and ardent supporters, became the eleventh president of the Club. Mid-year, the board set a series of new goals for the Club, which included:

1. An effort to acquire all of the stock of the Building Company, by gift or otherwise
2. The building of a three-story annex on the property north of the Clubhouse for storage and Club facilities
3. The remodeling of the present bedroom floors
4. The addition of athletic facilities on the roof
5. The providing of additional space for ladies on the first floor
6. The refurnishing of the House

All of this was to be done on a budget of $85,000. Little of this ambitious agenda was ever completed. In November, the board voted to allow women into the main dining room on nights other than Sunday, when "co-educational programs were on the social calendar."

THE CRASH AND THE CLUB

October 29—Black Tuesday—the stock market crashed as panicked buyers wildly sold a record 16,410,030 shares. The *New York Times* called it "the most disastrous trading day in stock market history." A month later, the New York Stock Exchange had dropped $26,000,000,000 in value.

The day after the crash, the president tried to calm the nation, saying, "The fundamental business of the country…is on a sound and prosperous basis."

In reality, the nation was in terrible shape and so was the University Club. Its credit was badly extended, and it faced the harsh reality of trying to meet an unsecured bank loan. To pay its obligations, the Club needed $25,000, but the bank refused financing without personal guarantees. Five members of the board—Henry Blair, Oliver Metzerott, Harry Rust, Sr., George Snyder, and Stanley Smith—volunteered to underwrite the loan, which took more than seven years to repay, when the Clubhouse was sold in 1937. Each of the generous underwriters paid $100 every quarter on the principle—no small amount of money in those days.

For the next two years, however, the Club would buck the national tide, like Washington itself, which, as the nation's capital, was somewhat insulated from the economic tidal wave overwhelming the rest of the country. Surprisingly, the membership increased from a low point of 451 in 1929 to more than 700 by 1932. During that time, initiation fees were allowed to be paid at $5 a month, but a better explanation for the membership increase may be the election of Lewis Lofton Moneyway as head of the Committee on Entertainment. His efforts as an impresario turned the Club into a "cultural center," bringing well-known musicians into the drawing room for recitals covered by the local papers. He also arranged lectures and plays that kept the Club filled with members and their spouses. In 1929, Fred DeWitt Shelton began the Club Bulletin, which is still a Club mainstay today, and Adele Lovelace began what was to be an extraordinary forty-eight-year career with the Club.

At the 1930 annual meeting, president Snyder was reelected to a second term, and William Howard Taft was made an honorary life member "as of the day of his resignation from the Supreme Court of the United States." Unfortunately, the Club's much beloved first president would die in March of that year. Looking to save the Club a little money when money was tight, Snyder took on what some might consider a quixotic quest. He argued to the IRS that the Club should be exempt from taxes, as the Cosmos Club was, because it was not a "social, athletic or sporting" club, which were required to pay taxes. Although the court case stretched on for four years, in the end, the Club lost its battle with Uncle Sam.

By 1931, not only had membership increased substantially, the Club had reduced its financial liabilities to $16,000. Still, in the annual meeting that year, members were told that "general financial conditions"—more than one thousand banks closed their doors in 1930—made negotiating a loan to enlarge the Club impossible. At that meeting, the man responsible for the creation of the University Club, who had refused to allow himself to be nominated at that historic founders' meeting, Proctor Dougherty, at long last, was elected to serve as the Club's twelfth president.

Though the vast majority of members supported the Club's proposed $250,000 expansion, one disgruntled owner of a few shares of stock in the Building Company, which actually owned the Clubhouse, went to court to stop the effort. Long and bitter litigation ensued that would finally be dismissed in 1935. Despite detailed building plans and a substantial increase in membership, men who had joined on the promise of a larger facility and major structural improvements began to resign, and the Club saw membership drop from 717 to 582 in just one year. It appeared that the Depression had finally crossed the Potomac.

At 15th and I, members saw the first signs that the economic storms beginning to blow in Washington would sweep through the University Club as well. To meet coming obligations, the board, headed by newly reelected president Dougherty, cut the size of the Club staff and approved a five percent reduction in pay.

And if the times weren't bad enough, in April, the Bulletin reported, "Heads bloody but unbowed as a result of two defeats at the hands of the Racquet Club, the University Club ping pong team is still seeking fields of combat." Still, Maestro Moneyway continued to work his magic that year, with a round of first-rate entertainment including musicals, lectures, and dances.

Massive public works funding and government employment had largely protected Washington from the economic catastrophe hitting most of America. But by the end of 1932, tens of thousands were out of work in this city of 486,000. As times grew tougher, more than a few in Washington welcomed the election of New York governor Franklin Delano Roosevelt, a former University Club member.

The White House may have changed hands, but at the Club, like so many other institutions in Washington, finances remained the same—dangerously thin. In May, the board directed the Executive Committee to "handle all questions relating to open accounts of the Club with certain of its larger creditors and to negotiate settlements which.... would be to the Club's best advantage." Before the next meeting, the treasurer had delivered promissory notes to a baking company and a dairy company to cover unpaid Club bills. In January, the Club defaulted on interest payments due on its stock, although half of the interest owed was paid later.

At the 1933 annual meeting, president Dougherty told members, "The year just past has been one of difficulties which have been largely met." But the difficulties were far from over. The previous year had seen yet another decline in membership, which had dropped to 435 members. It was understandable why Charles A. Douglas, a brilliant international lawyer famed for his trial work, was reluctant to serve as the Club's next president—the thirteenth. Although he acquiesced, his term was one of the Club's shortest when he fell on the Club's marble grand stairway and broke his leg. A committee formed to find a successor to the unlucky thirteenth, and T. Howard Duckett, a distinguished attorney and banker, was chosen to lead the Club in the difficult year of 1933.

The board adopted a resolution to extend an invitation to President-elect Roosevelt and his Cabinet to become honorary members of the Club. There was one exception, of course. Should any Cabinet officers be female, they would be offered the guest privileges provided to the wives of members. Frances Perkins, the Secretary of Labor, became the first woman to serve as a Cabinet officer.

Happy Days Are Here Again—Almost

Just a couple of weeks before the 1934 annual meeting, the "noble experiment"—Prohibition—officially ended across the country and at the University Club, thanks to the passage of the Twenty-first Amendment. It took the governors exactly two days to vote to "officially" begin serving alcoholic beverages in the Club. But restocking the lounge was an expensive venture and the financially strapped Club again suffered from a case of insufficient funds. Proving that necessity truly is the mother of invention, Club members were asked to trade cash for IOU's to fund the restocking effort, and it didn't take long for good whisky and good fellowship to flow once again in the rooms of the University Club.

But the end of Prohibition wasn't the end of Washington's economic problems. Federal salaries had been cut, and while banks were beginning to reopen, many still remained in receivership. When the Club gathered to celebrate its thirtieth birthday in 1934, Duckett delivered the unpleasant news that membership had dropped precipitously to 388—the lowest in Club history. That translated into a loss of more than $11,000 in dues income. The Club found itself in debt: $51,000 due to creditors, $27,000 owed on notes, and more than $10,000 in bills payable. Despite this bleak situation, Howard Duckett agreed to serve another term on what some thought was a sinking ship. But he was about to get a top-notch first mate.

Frank Davies was a highly experienced hotelman who took on the difficult job of general manager for the Club. His first crisis was meeting the payroll, which was overdue. Davies went to Duckett and a new member, Claude Houchins, with his problem. The pair each loaned the Club $1,500, and the barmen, waiters, and housemen got their badly needed paychecks.

But paying the staff was only the first problem Davies would have to solve. Money was so short that as soon as members' bills were out, he would make the rounds downtown, asking them to pay immediately. Most complied. Other innovative solutions were found to help put the Club on a better financial footing and fund some needed repairs. One member of the board, J. Raymond Hoover, came upon the idea of selling $50 notes to members, which would mature in eighteen months and pay three percent interest. The plan raised $4,500 to repaint the faded interior and help put the Club back on a cash basis.

While the board struggled with finances, members were still enjoying Club activities. Musical performances—vocal and instrumental—continued, as well as poetry readings, plays, and even a little vaudeville. But nothing could top one of the Club's most unusual lectures of all time. M.W. Sterling, chief of the Bureau of Ethnology, gave a "graphic talk with illustrations, on his journey among the Head-Hunters of the Amazon." As the annual report of the Entertainment Committee put it, he "taught us how to cure and reduce the heads of our enemies, and we went home feeling that we could do a good job if the Lord would only deliver them into our hands." Member and later Pulitzer Prize–winning cartoonist Clifford K. Berryman gave a "crayon talk" on "Presidential Candidates as Portrayed by Partisan Caricaturists."

Although Club rules prohibited a third presidential term, members overrode their rules and elected Duckett a third time. By 1935, the two thousand cherry trees that Mrs. William H. Taft had gratefully accepted from the mayor of Tokyo in 1911 had become one of Washington's wonders. That year, the city held its first Cherry Blossom Festival, a sure sign that both spring and a better economy were returning to Washington. Another sign was the rise of federal employment, which went from 63,000 in 1933 to 93,000 by 1935 as the New Deal took hold. In 1940, that number would hit 166,000.

Adding to the economic upturn was a public works program that saw the completion of the Federal Triangle, the Supreme Court, a second House office building, and other government buildings along the Mall, bringing jobs and increasing prosperity to the capital.

A year later, though, the Club still wasn't out of the economic woods. Large tax bills were still to be paid, among others, but the membership drain had stopped. At the annual meeting in February 1936, Duckett proudly reported an increase of fifty-six new members. After three terms as president during difficult times, he was no doubt relieved to at last be succeeded by Stanley Smith, an international lawyer, who became the fifteenth president of the Club.

On May 22, 1936, the board heard disturbing news from a specially appointed committee charged with assessing the Club's financial situation and making recommendations for its future. The Club's total obligations, they were told, had reached nearly $175,000—not exactly small change in those times. Two hundred new members would be needed to balance the books, and that was not a realistic possibility. Neither was a bank loan or individual arrangements with the Club's various creditors.

A RADICAL SOLUTION

That left a radical option—to sell the Club's building and merge with the Racquet Club, which had suffered similar problems during the Depression. It had actually been forced to reorganize under bankruptcy laws at one point, and like the University Club, continued to struggle financially. The board, seeing no other realistic option, voted to sell the building and set a $300,000 price tag.

While it may have been a marriage made in "Hooverville" rather than heaven, it seemed to the board to be the Club's only way out of its financial hole.

On August, 21, 1936, more than one hundred members turned out for a meeting to consider the proposed consolidation. The resolution, adopted that day, authorized the president and secretary of the Club to move forward on the consolidation effort. Three blocks over at the Racquet Club, the merger was a little more controversial, where some members objected to the two boards' agreement, especially the decision to retain the University Club moniker. One opponent of the consolidation complained at the Racquet Club's September 23, 1936, meeting:

> Aside from the library of the University Club, we have no need of anything they have in the line of furnishings and I sincerely doubt if the library would be of any benefit to us, although, of course, it would be necessary to the educated gentlemen who are destined to inherit us. We are selling our birthright, our name and our all for a mess of pottage in the form of whatever members of the University Club is able to bring to the new coalition . . . and there is no assurance that they will be able to bring a sufficient number to assure the future of the Club.

The historic trowel used by General John J. Pershing to lay the cornerstone of the Racquet Club on February 12, 1921

The naysayers lost the day, however, and the merger of the two clubs was assured. If that good news wasn't enough to buoy the spirits of the members of both clubs, a month later the University Club board received an offer from John L. Lewis, head of the United Mine Workers of America, to purchase the University Club's building at 15th and I for $275,000 in cash.

And so it was agreed. On December 1, 1936, the University Club's new address would be 1135 16th Street—the avenue of the presidents—where the Racquet Club-house had stood regally since General John J. Pershing himself laid the cornerstone in 1920. Black Jack Pershing's trowel has now joined William Taft's as one of the Club's historic treasures, along with Charles Lindbergh's letter to the Racquet Club accepting honorary membership in 1928. The letter hangs today in the Pershing Grille.

The University Club welcomed the sixty resident members of the Racquet Club to its ranks, along with their more than eight hundred associate, non-resident, and other members. One of those was John Brabner-Smith, an emissary of the attorney general of Illinois, who became Special Assistant to the U.S. Attorney General in 1932. Brabner-Smith had come to Washington seeking help from the "Feds" to rein in Scarface Al Capone and his gang, who were terrorizing Chicago. Working with a colleague in

Congress, Brabner-Smith was successful in passing legislation that gave the FBI the authority to move against Capone. The gangster was subsequently convicted of income tax evasion and imprisoned, effectively ending his reign of terror in the Windy City. While at the Department of Justice, Brabner-Smith was also involved in the historic Lindbergh kidnapping case.

Another new member was William H. G. FitzGerald, who would later become the ambassador to Ireland and the driving force behind the Club's position as the premier squash facility in Washington.

Adele Lovelace remembers that officials of both the University and Racquet Clubs "knocked themselves out trying to make the merger of the two diverse groups a happy fraternity... The Grille became a very lively and noisy place, but for a time the UC group's good fellowship did not invade the RC regulars—many had rough edges."

The University Club not only inherited a spirited, athletics-oriented membership, but also one of Washington's architectural treasures in their new Clubhouse. The seven-story building was designed by architect Jules de Sibour, a native of France and graduate of Yale, and built by the "man who built Washington," premier developer Harry Wardman, who also constructed the Wardman Park Hotel, the British Embassy, and the Hay-Adams Hotel, among many other Washington landmarks. Harry Wardman's great nephew, Michael, is a Club member today.

The building, opened in 1921, has a raised terra cotta base in a modified Georgian style. When the University Club moved into its luxurious new headquarters, the building housed a spacious first floor lounge that could seat 160; an air-conditioned dining room with 140 places; and the front desk and offices. On the second floor, members found a men's grille room along with a reading room, the co-educational "Cockatoo Lounge," billiards and cards areas, the beautifully paneled boardroom, and one small private dining room.

The third floor was home to the ladies' powder room, Club offices, and fourteen bedrooms, while the top four floors were dedicated to more bedrooms, for a total of 105.

The new building also offered members athletic facilities for the first time, including four squash courts, four bowling alleys, a swimming pool, a small gymnasium, steam room, rubbing tables, boxing, fencing, and a barber shop.

The first post-merger Club president won election in a coin toss that decided whether the first president was to be an "old University-ite or an old Racqueteer." Spencer Gordon, who had headed the Racquet Club, won the toss over Stanley Smith and became the sixteenth chief executive of the substantially larger, better financed, and better housed University Club. In April 1937, Club treasurer Claude Houchins reported a profit by the Club of nearly $9,000 for the first quarter. By the end of June, the Club boasted a total of 1,795 members. Happy days were back.

The following year, 1938, Stanley Smith returned as president of the Club—able now to claim service as both the fifteenth and seventeenth president. In June, Frank

Davies, who had served ably as manager in the former Clubhouse, was appointed manager of the newly combined Club.

THE WINDS OF WAR

As much of America was finally coming out of the Depression, cheering on Seabiscuit, and dancing to Benny Goodman, the Club was also climbing back onto steady financial ground just in time to see the world come apart once again. British Prime Minister Neville Chamberlain returned from Munich, telling his people as he stepped from the plane, "My good friends, for the second time in our history, a British Prime Minister has returned from Germany bringing peace with honour. I believe it is peace for our time . . . Go home and get a nice quiet sleep."

Eleven months later, on September 1, 1939, Hitler's Nazi blitzkrieg struck Poland and Chamberlain's "peace" was shattered. Britain declared war as Hitler stormed across Europe. Yet, at the University Club, as in most of Washington, life went on with an eerie normalcy, though with an underlying sense of uneasee. Tea dances, a Halloween dance, and the New Year's Ball highlighted the year as swing was quickly becoming the rage and songs like "Deep Purple," "Over the Rainbow," and "You Must Have Been a Beautiful Baby" poured from the radio. A stag Monte Carlo Night and even a demonstration of hypnotism kept members' minds off the brewing controversy overseas. The biggest excitement that season in Washington was the visit of King George VI and

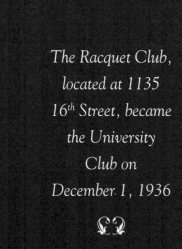

The Racquet Club, located at 1135 16th Street, became the University Club on December 1, 1936

Club's longest standing members and is seen most nights having dinner in the Taft Dining Room.

While members were reading *Grapes of Wrath* and tapping their toes to the music of Tommy Dorsey, once again, the winds of war were blowing "over the pond." But it was a war that the majority of Americans wanted nothing to do with. A Roper poll taken that year found that sixty-seven percent of the country thought America should remain neutral. The nation's isolationism wouldn't last, as Roosevelt revved up his mighty oratorical skills and legendary arm-twisting abilities to gain support for his belief that America should go to the aid of the hard-pressed British.

In February 1940, lawyer George Ward succeeded Stanley Smith as Club president. Three months later, in May, Winston Churchill became prime minister and Roosevelt was well on his way to an overwhelming victory over Republican Wendell Wilkie and an unprecedented third term. By September, the capital was moving toward a war footing, and the University Club's board voted, as it had during WWI, to remit the dues of all members called into military service. During the year, the Clubhouse was refurnished and redecorated, but the Club still managed to eke out a $4,600 profit. By October, the influx into Washington of men anticipating war pushed Club membership to a then all-time record high of 1,761.

King George VI and Queen Elizabeth of England

The University Club celebrates its forty-fifth anniversary—1949

Chapter Four

1940s: Washington at War

On December 7, 1941, "a day that would live in infamy," imperial Japanese forces rained a deadly shower of bombs on Pearl Harbor, and America's "neutrality" ended with one of the most despicable acts of diplomatic and military treachery in history.

The following day, President Roosevelt traveled up Pennsylvania Avenue to formally ask Congress for a declaration of war. Sixty million Americans listened to his five-minute speech—the largest radio audience in history.

That same day, Baron Ulrich von Gienanth, attaché and head of the Gestapo's espionage operation in the United States, strolled down 16th Street to the Club from the German embassy, located farther up Massachusetts Avenue. When Club general manager Frank Davies saw von Gienanth approach the building, he grabbed for the phone to alert the FBI. (The University Club had an established relationship with the FBI both before and during the war.) The call wasn't needed, however. Not surprisingly, the baron was already under surveillance.

Davies greeted von Gienanth at the door but, uncharacteristically, did not offer the German his hand. The baron handed him a joint resignation letter from himself and three other German diplomats who had been University Club members, calling the situation merely a difference in politics, nothing personal. He then asked for a statement of their accounts and offered to write a check. When told the Club no longer would accept his check, the baron produced a big roll of bills and paid in cash.

The two Japanese diplomats who were members never appeared, and the Executive Committee abruptly ended their memberships. Somehow, they did manage to pay their bill.

Despite his country's declaration of war against the United States, von Gienanth continued his espionage activities over the next weeks. In response, the American government took action on December 29 to isolate all foreign enemy diplomats. The Germans and Italians went to the Greenbrier, while the Japanese went to the Homestead.

Before war broke out, the Club had opened its bowling alleys to ladies for the first time, for mixed doubles on Friday evenings—a move that would not only impact the social structure of the Club but prove to be the single most important source of Club leadership for years to come. Informal afternoon and cocktail dances were also gaining popularity over the more traditional evening affairs. On Christmas morning, 1941, with Washington now at war, the Club began a tradition that lasted for many years—providing a hearty Yuletide breakfast for all members who lived in the Clubhouse. It was the calm before the storm.

Not long into the New Year, members found themselves preparing for air raids and the Club insuring itself against war damage for $370,000. Happily, no claim was ever filed. Frederick Gibbs, meanwhile, became its nineteenth president in February 1942. As war consumed the nation, the city's pulse raced while "dollar-a-year" men poured into Washington. At the Club, the "no vacancy sign" was always out in those days, with nearly one hundred percent occupancy. The Club's bedrooms were full with visitors from Oxford to Melbourne, along with a growing list of new members; at the annual meeting, members were warned that any of their friends considering applying for membership should do so immediately, as the days of a waiting list weren't far away. While the Club showed a profit, reports show that food costs, pushed by war shortages, rose more than seventeen percent over the previous year.

National Airport, opened in 1941

But a full house at the Club shouldn't have been a surprise. All of Washington was filling to the brim with war workers and foreign visitors. Seventy thousand people had moved to Washington in the first year after Pearl Harbor alone. The city was overwhelmed. Traffic, never good, now slowed to a snail's pace even as streets were widened to accommodate the increasing congestion. The summer before, National Airport had opened, bringing even more people into the already crowded city. Restaurants were overbooked, and housing was tight and getting tighter as five thousand new government workers a month poured into Washington.

For the Club, business had never been better. In fact, it was packed. At the 1943 annual meeting, the Club treasurer announced that receipts for 1942 had been thirty-three percent higher than any other year in Club history. Mr. Gibbs was reelected and later that spring the membership topped 2,100. But circumstances were far from easy. The Club faced the difficult problem of a growing demand for services while rationing and a lack of suitable help complicated general manager Davies's already difficult job. Sunday dinners were sacrificed to the war effort, and it was "first come, first served" on the nights the dining room was open.

On February 20, 1944—just three and a half months before D-Day—the Club celebrated its fortieth birthday, though not in its usual fashion of a grand black-tie dinner and plenty of speechifying.

The *Star* reported:

> The University Club, whose pattern has been woven brightly into the fabric of social life in Washington, on Tuesday, will round out its fortieth year. Food ration points being the rare items they are, the Club has muted the trumpet which would ordinarily flourish the fanfare upon such an auspicious occasion.

Instead, the Club put its memorabilia collection on display. The article did note, however, that more than six hundred stars now made up the Club's service flag, including eight members who had died for their country.

The twentieth president of the Club—Dean Hill Stanley, a prominent lawyer, came into office on Valentine's Day, 1944, to find a waiting list for membership for the first time in the Club's history. Over the summer, the Allies landed on European beaches and rolled north toward Germany. Spirits were rising, even if some spirits were hard to come by. Because the war made the importation of Scotch difficult, if not downright dangerous, the Executive Committee voted to limit the sale to eight bottles a day.

Scotch wasn't the only essential in short supply. In the 1944 Club elections, one candidate for Club president, who owned an antifreeze company, gave members of the Board of Governors free "samples" to help alleviate their winter rationing problems.

Filled with optimism in September, the committee made the Club's first plans for a victory celebration, deciding to close the bar to all but members and "persons holding unexpired guest cards" on that joyous day. It would come less than a year later, on May 8, 1945, just three weeks after the death of Franklin Delano Roosevelt. His loss left the nation grieving for the president who had brought them through war and served longer than any man before or since.

PEACE RETURNS

The University Club could now claim another of its own in the Oval Office. Then–Vice President Harry S. Truman had accepted honorary membership in the Club just three months before he found himself "imprisoned in his white jail." Keeping to tradition, the

Club kicked off 1945 with its New Year's Day Governors' Reception and continued to hold its popular stag nights, inviting wounded soldiers and sailors from the service hospitals for one such event. Another highlight of the social season was a twelve-piece all-women's band from Mary Washington College, which rattled the walls in the lounge where members and their wives danced the night away. But the event of the year was, no doubt, a demonstration by Tarbell, the "world-famous magician and mental scientist." So many members and their wives wanted to attend the magic show that the Club was forced to rent the ballroom of the Mayflower Hotel to accommodate the crowds.

On August 14, VJ-Day was declared, and soon rationing would become nothing more than a quaint story for members to tell their grandchildren. With the war's end, the Club returned to normal life, and members were happy to hear they could once again host private luncheons and dinners. 1945 was a year of major financial restructuring for the Club and saw the Racquet Club officially deed over its remaining interest in the Clubhouse.

1946 was gloriously uneventful, as were most of the late '40s, with the Club records showing the election of Sterling Ely, a chemist and attorney for Union Carbide, as the twenty-first president of the Club. President Ely supervised a major renovation and redecorating program, and at the next annual meeting dues were raised to $100. In April 1947, the Board of Governors' proposal to install Muzak in the Clubhouse met with a determined opposition. The anti-Muzak members held the canned music "hostage," demanding that free cheese, which had been a fixture in the grill room, be reinstated before they would agree to the expenditure. The "cheese-heads" won the day. So did the technology buffs, who proposed and passed a motion to buy the Club's first television set.

In the fall of 1948, feisty Harry Truman defied the pundits to win the presidency in one of the great surprise elections in history. Earlier in the year, Cecil J. Wilkinson, the author of the Club's fiftieth anniversary history, was not so surprisingly elected the twenty-second president of the Club in February 1948. Happily, Wilkinson and the board faced few burning issues, and over the next year, applications for membership continued to soar. The Club also began a major air conditioning project—a welcome move in steamy Washington. Ladies could now bowl on both Thursday and Friday evenings. Cocktail dances were back, and more formal dinner dances were on the horizon. As the library continued to grow, members played tournament bridge along with the usual cards, and the Club's annual field day of golf and good fellowship was also held. One member was called on the carpet by the Executive Committee for "parking his dog overnight in the check room," and the use of dice in the Club was "permanently prohibited," following a small altercation.

There were big doings on the sports front, as well. With the 1936 merger, athletics had become a major part of Club life. The new Clubhouse, with its swimming pool, ping-pong tables, bowling alleys, and squash courts, gave the University Club facilities

The University Club of Washington

IMPORTANT—Please read carefully.

May 1, 1944.

Dear Member:

For the first time in its history your Club has reached the total of resident members permitted under the By-Laws and there are now pending a large number of applications which has necessarily created a waiting list. We are also nearing the point when the limit on associate members will be reached. The members will realize, therefore, that any delays which occur in the election of their nominees will primarily be occasioned by this fact.

In order to insure that the Club may be able to offer its benefits to all resident and associate nominees as early as practicable, the attention of the members is directed to the following rules affecting the membership:

1. A resident member who enters the Armed Forces and receives a commission and who is ordered away from the Washington area * is eligible to be placed upon the absent membership list and change of dues to $5.00 per year, plus tax, but only so long as he is absent from the Washington area.

2. A resident member entering the Armed Forces in any capacity below a commission is entitled to remission of all his dues during such service and the full use of the Club, but only so long as such status continues. If he later receives a commission, he should immediately notify the Secretary of the date and place of assignment.

3. A non-resident member moving to or establishing an office or place of business in the Washington Area is required by the By-Laws immediately to notify the Secretary as to his change of status.

4. A resident member who moves his residence or place of business so that neither is within the Washington area is required by the By-Laws immediately to notify the Secretary of his change of status.

5. A non-resident member is not entitled to absent membership when he enters the Armed Forces unless he has previously been a resident member and has paid the resident initiation fee.

Failure of a member to notify the Club of his change in status will result in his receiving a bill at some later date covering past dues which may be embarrassing to such member as well as the Executive Committee whose duty it is properly to bill members.

The attention of the Executive Committee has been directed to the fact that some members of the Club who have been accorded the privilege of being placed on the absent membership list because they have been assigned to military duty outside of the District area have returned to the District, thus becoming resident members again and subject to the payment of resident dues, but have been using the benefits of the Club without notifying the Secretary of their return. This is most unfair to the other members and will not be countenanced by the Executive Committee.

The cooperation of all the members is earnestly solicited in the observance of the above rules.

By Direction of the Executive Committee,

ROBERT R. FAULKNER, Secretary.

————

* i.e., to a point more than thirty miles from the zero milestone located in the ellipse south of the White House.

A wait list letter from 1944

45th ANNIVERSARY
FEBRUARY 26 1949
—
SUPPER

The forty-fifth anniversary celebration was a gala affair highlighted by talks from the Club's remaining founding members

University Club Marks 40th Milestone

By Cecil J. Wilkinson.

The University Club, whose pattern has been woven brightly into the fabric of social life in Washington, on Tuesday will round out its 40th year.

Food ration points being the rare items they are, the club has muted the trumpet which would ordinarily flourish the fanfare upon such an auspicious occasion. Instead of a dinner commemorating the completion of four decades of uninterrupted existence, the club will note its birthday quietly, with only a collection of memorabilia on display in the clubhouse on Sixteenth street reminding members of the anniversary.

The red room of the old Willard Hotel was the scene of the genesis meeting of the University Club on February 23, 1904. Proctor L. Dougherty, who was later to become a District Commissioner, presided; Ralph P. Barnard served as secretary.

Club's Incorporators.

The club had been incorporated seven days earlier, the incorporators being Ellis Spear, Proctor L. Dougherty, Edwin H. Fowler, Wallace Donald McLean, Isaac R. Hitt, jr.; George O. Totten, jr.; Ralph Barnard, Colin H. Livingstone and James R. Wood.

The certificate of incorporation recites that "the particular business and objects of this corporation are educational, literary, musical, scientific, for the promotion of the arts and for mutual improvement."

Some 600 college and university men were the charter members of the club, Of these, 20 are still affiliated with the organization: Ralph P. Barnard, Henry P. Blair, Arthur H. Brown, Reed Paige Clark, Angelo Conti, Proctor L. Dougherty, Henry R. Gower, Robert S. Hume, Tracy L. Jeffords, Harry M. Kaufman, George W. Koonce, Dr. James G. McKay, Wallace D. McLean, Stuart McNamara, Ernest W. Marlow, Oliver Metzerott, Harlan Moore, Dr. Luther H. Reichelderfer, George W. Stone and Norman E. Webster.

Taft Was First Club President.

The first president of the club was Secretary of War William Howard Taft. He was elected at a meeting of the club's council on March 4, 1904. The following have since served as president of the club: George L. Cortelyou, Charles D. Walcott, Stephen B. Elkins, Gardener F. Williams, Myron M. Parker, Martin A. Knapp, Daniel W. Shea, Lewis H. Taylor, Oliver Metzerott, George F. Snyder, Proctor L. Dougherty, Charles A. Douglass, T. Howard Duckett, Stanley P. Smith, Spencer Gordon, George S. Ward, Frederick R. Gibbs and Dean Hill Stanley.

The 1944 officers of the club are Dean Hill Stanley, president; Andrew D. Sharpe, first vice president; Cecil J. Wilkinson, second vice president; Robert R. Faulkner, secretary; H. Stewart McDonald, assistant secretary; Henry H. Elliott, treasurer; Allen G. Gartner,

The governors of the University Club in its 40th year. Top row, left to right: H. Clifford Bangs, Allen G. Gartner, Percy W. Phillips, H. Stewart McDonald, Edward Stafford. Middle row: Cecil J. Wilkinson, Godfrey L. Munter, Andrew D. Sharpe, Sterling Ely, Capt. Francis G. Ulen, U. S. N. Bottom row: Dale D. Drain, Oliver Metzerott, Frederick R. Gibbs, Dean Hill Stanley, president; George S. Ward and Henry H. Elliott. Absent from the picture are J. Thilman Hendrick, T. Howard Duckett, Claude M. Houchins and Robert S. Faulkner.
—Louft & Wolf Photo.

assistant treasurer. These officers and the following are governors of the club: Dale D. Drain, Sterling Ely, Frederick R. Gibbs, Godfrey L. Munter, J. Thilman Hendrick, Claude M. Houchins, Oliver Metzerott, Percy W. Phillips, Edward Stafford, George S. Ward, H. Clifford Bangs, Capt. Francis G. Ulen, U. S. N., and T. Howard Duckett.

First Quarters.

The first quarters occupied by the University Club were at the southwest corner of Sixteenth and K streets. This house was leased by the club on June 15, 1904.

Across K street was the residence of William Howard Taft, former president of the club, and on the evening of the day in 1908 when he was nominated for the presidency of the United States the club members jubilantly serenaded him, singing "For Taft's a Jolly Good Fellow." Later the nominee went to the clubhouse and from there was escorted to a horse-drawn Army wagon and transported to the White House to confer with Theodore Roosevelt. Meantime, the Taft boys—Robert and Charles—were shooting fireworks on the club lawn.

During those early years the annual dinners of the club, held at local hotels, were noteworthy occasions, attended by hundreds of men prominent in national political life and in the affairs of the District.

Contemporary newspaper accounts record that at the 1905 banquet, at Rauscher's, Club President Taft "used an empty champagne bottle as a gavel" and that Baron von dem Bussche of the German Embassy, one of the speakers, was greeted with cries of "Hoch der Kaiser" and toasts to Emperor William and to the German universities.

Service Flag Has 600 Stars.

Today there are more than 600 stars in the club's service flag; eight members have died in the service of their country.

In 1905 the club minutes reveal, a proposal to permit the playing of pool and billiards on Sundays was rejected.

President Woodrow Wilson of Princeton University was one of the speakers at the 1906 dinner. At that affair, a cigar, three feet long, was presented to Uncle Joe Cannon, Speaker of the House of Representatives, and the following song, to the tune of "Everybody Works But Father," was chanted to him:

"Everybody knows Joe Cannon—
*   He'll be here after while,*
With a big cigar for a headlight,
*   Surrounded by a smile.*
He cheers for dear old Wabash,
*   Where the moonlight used to shine;*
Now he's left his fireside
*   For a good old college time."*

At the 1908 dinner one of the speakers was the Japanese Ambassador, Baron Takahira, who "received a thunderous welcome" and who said, "The sentiment manifested in receiving me makes me feel how friendly you are to my country." At this dinner William Howard Taft was quoted as saying that "the suggestion of war between Japan and the United States is a suggestion of a crime against humanity."

The Evening Star's column-long accounts of those salad-day dinners were liberally illustrated with cartoons by Clifford Berryman, long a member of the club.

The librarian of the club at that time was Gifford Pinchot, head of the Bureau of Forestry.

New Clubhouse.

In 1912 the club moved to its own clubhouse, located at the northwest corner of Fifteenth and I streets. This building was designed by Architect George O. Totten, jr., a member of the club. One of its features was a series of carved stone heraldry of leading colleges and universities on the Fifteenth street facade and on the I street side.

In 1936 the University Club sold this building to the United Mine Workers of America which has since occupied it as a national headquarters. At that time the University Club and the Racquet Club merged and the lares and penates of the former group were moved to the Racquet Club's 105-bedroom building at 1135 Sixteenth street, opposite the National Geographic Society. The club building, designed by Architect Henri de Sibour, had been erected in 1921.

The University Club today has the largest membership in its history—2,301, including both resident and nonresident.

an unmatched athletic edge in the city. In 1949, the Club reaffirmed its reputation as one of the nation's premier squash facilities when it established two major squash competitions, the national Woodruff-Nee Invitational and the William H. FitzGerald Cup, both of which continue today. Ambassador William FitzGerald, a member since the merger with the Racquet Club, began playing squash almost seventy years ago, and it has been his love of the game, along with tennis, that has earned him innumerable honors over the years, including his selection as 2003 Naval Academy Alumnus of the Year. A graduate of the Harvard Law School as well, he founded the FitzGerald Cup to pit Washington squash players against Baltimore's best—a competition which, today, has become one of the most prestigious in American squash. As the Centennial year approaches, Ambassador FitzGerald can also claim the title as longest-serving member of the University Club.

Whatever the Club's fortieth anniversary had lacked, its forty-fifth anniversary more than made up for it, in both song and celebration. Ohio Senator Robert A. Taft, the son of the Club's first president who, as a boy, had once set off fireworks on the Club steps, gave a memorable speech full of personal anecdotes about his father. The Club's remaining charter members each spoke to the gathering as well. President Wilkinson showed a slide presentation of the Club's history as a musical quartet sang songs from "Sweet Adeline" to "Happy Days Are Here Again." Finally, the lights dimmed and the staff brought out a huge cake with forty-five candles gleaming in the darkness. As members broke out into song, it was evident that a decade of world war and personal sacrifice had ended on a happy note.

Rationing takes a toll on Club dining during the war

> ## The University Club of Washington
>
> March 31, 1943
>
> ### IMPORTANT PLEASE READ ! ! !
>
> Dear Member:
>
> The reduction in food, both processed and meat, has made necessary an explanation in detail and an appeal to each member for his whole-hearted cooperation in the present war emergency.
>
> The Rationing Authorities have limited the Club to approximately 60% of the processed foods (that is, canned, frozen and similar products) used by it in December 1942. Beginning March 29, 1943, the Club will be able to obtain under rationing regulations approximately 40% of the total quantity of meats, butter, cheese, shortening and oils consumed in December, 1942. In other words, assuming that the meats, butter, cheese, shortening and oils altogether used in December weighed 7,000 pounds, the Club will be able to obtain under the rationing approximately 3,000 pounds of these products. The 3,000 pounds may be divided amongst these products as the Club sees fit, but it is apparent that the Club having used in the basic light month of December, 1942, 5,900 pounds of meat, to say nothing of butter and other fats, very little meat or butter will be obtainable. The months of April and May normally are months of very heavy consumption.
>
> It requires no argument or striking emphasis to appreciate the difficulties facing the Club in serving meals to its members which require any of the foregoing articles of food.
>
> As an initial step in meeting the necessities of this situation, the Board of Governors has directed the discontinuance of all group meals, whether served in the private dining rooms or in the other dining rooms of the Club.
>
> Meatless days must be established in view of the limited amount of meat allocated to the Club. We are in no position to designate any particular meatless days during the week, since this depends on local distribution by our suppliers. Because many of us are accustomed to eating fish on Friday, it is probable that this day will be one of our meatless days. However, this will be dependent upon circumstances as they arise.
>
> The members can very materially assist in this situation if they will conscientiously avoid as far as practicable, inviting guests to dine at the Club. With rationing as it is, every guest served consumes food that well may have to be denied a member. We are not insisting at this time, and we hope it will not be necessary to insist, that members entirely forego entertaining guests at meals. The Board of Governors still feels that if the guest privileges are moderately used, members may continue to invite their casual business and social guests to the Club to dine, as well as the members of their immediate family or house guests, without impairing the ability of the Club to continue to serve adequate meals. It is essential, however, that members desist from bringing groups of guests to the Club to dine and they should urge the members of their families to desist from inviting such groups.
>
> No action is, therefore, being taken to limit guest privileges. We hope that this appeal will be earnestly considered by all the members, communicated to their families, and a sincere effort made by all Club families to help the Club in this emergency. If this is done, we feel confident that drastic restrictions on guest privileges will not become necessary in the immediate future.
>
> Sincerely,
>
> BOARD OF GOVERNORS.

The Club's fiftieth birthday—1954

Chapter Five

1950s: A Quieter Time

A world weary of war once again faced the prospect of international conflict when North Korea crossed the 38th parallel on June 25, 1950, and invaded its South Korean neighbor. The United Nations stepped in, but it was the United States that stepped up to the plate, sending thousands of troops to fight what would be an inconclusive war. Twenty-five thousand Americans would lose their lives before an armistice was signed in July 1953.

At home, as the Cold War heated up, the nation was embroiled in what came to be called the "Red Scare." A little-known senator from Wisconsin, Joseph McCarthy, turned the Capitol upside down with anti-Communist hearings on Soviet espionage. This led to McCarthy's censure by the Senate and a controversy that continued into the 1990s.

Still, much of the decade was a quiet time for America. It was the '50s—when everybody liked Ike and loved Lucy. Elvis and Marilyn became the new stars in the heavens, along with a Russian "tin can" called Sputnik that spurred a space race. You could send a letter for a two-cent stamp, and a family of four could live on $60 a week.

In 1954, the Supreme Court, under the leadership of Chief Justice Earl Warren, one of the University Club's most prestigious members, handed down its historic *Brown v. Board of Education* ruling. The great jurist once said, "Everything I did in my life that was worthwhile I caught hell for." This ruling would be no exception—the controversial decision changed America forever.

In the early years of the decade, H. Stewart McDonald took the reins from the dedicated and droll Cecil Wilkinson and oversaw an increase in both the Club's initiation fee and yearly dues—$150 and $125 respectively—to cover significantly rising costs. A new Westinghouse twenty-inch television was installed in the Men's Grille, while dances and bowling were still in vogue. A group that had been meeting regularly each week for twenty-five years—the "Little Pealers"—continued their "quiet" luncheons with cards afterwards, where there was always somebody buzzing about something. A mystery of sorts puzzled Club members when an old bookplate was discovered by the Club librarian in a collection in Philadelphia. The "University Club" plate had a book in the center, atop Ionic columns, with the year 1891 on its cover. Since the University Club wasn't formed until 1904, it took a charter member to solve the mystery.

Cover of the November 1955 newsletter

The University Club of Washington

Nov.   **1955**

"*The object of the Club shall be to promote science, literature, and art, and to maintain a Club House for purposes of social intercourse amongst its members and for mutual improvement.*"
—ART. II, BY-LAWS

CALENDAR OF ACTIVITIES AND NEWS EVENTS

Saturday, November 5—Cocktail Dance.......................5:30 to 8:30 p.m.
Wednesday, November 9—Lecture night .... 8:15 p.m.
Saturday, November 19—Cocktail Dance.................. 5:30 to 8:30 p.m.
Mixed Bowling League:
    Thursday, November 3..................Buffet, 6 p.m.; Bowling, 8 p.m.
    Friday, November 4 ....Buffet, 6 p.m.; Bowling 8 p.m.
Men's Bowling League: Monday and Tuesday nights...................8 p.m.
Monday, November 7 and 21:
    Inter-Club Duplicate Bridge Matches......................8 p.m.

Proctor Dougherty informed the Club that there actually had been a University Club back then, but it had been absorbed into the Potomac Club.

Along with real mysteries, the Club was also enjoying the donation of a collection of mystery books, as well as the newly published *Caine Mutiny* and a member's new book, *Of Men and Mountains,* by Supreme Court Justice William O. Douglas.

During the early '50s, as today, social and athletic activities abounded at the Club. Athletic Director Billy Whipp taught members' sons how to box, and Sande Williams's Orchestra furnished the music for many of the Club's Saturday cocktail dances.

One evening, the wife of a member, nicknamed "Pulani," brought in a troupe of local Hawaiian musicians and dancers. Pulani herself taught ancient and modern interpretative hulas, and sang and danced. In June 1951, the Board of Governors voted to let women use the swimming pool two nights a week, but four months later pulled the plug on ladies' swimming when the Sports Committee objected, arguing that the change would have required hiring an extra attendant and installing a sterilizer for the swimsuits. Some wags, no doubt, wondered, "What swimsuits?"

Members watched films at the Club like "East Africa and the Belgian Congo"—areas of interest then just as they are today. Non-resident member J. Forbes Amory, a fellow of the Royal Geographic Society who led the first American safari to the Belgian Congo, gave an accompanying lecture. By 1952, the Club had hit a new membership record—2,508. Charles Pledger, Jr., a well-known trial lawyer and the first local attorney to be elected to the American College of Trial Lawyers, became the Club's twenty-fourth president while the great military hero of World War II, General Dwight D. Eisenhower, was elected the thirty-fourth president of the United States. Election night at the Club was a gala affair, complete with ticker tape and a tabulation board. Ladies were permitted on both the first and second floors that evening, which ended with a midnight buffet for the politikers. Christmas dinner that year was $3.25 for roast turkey and add-ons, from blue points and caviar canapés to vegetables, salads, and desserts. The New Year's Eve dance was a little more expensive—$7.25 per person—but members got noisemakers, a "dunce" cap, and a hot midnight buffet for the price.

Club bulletins were filled with the comings and goings of members heading off to exotic locales like Mexico City and Athens to take up new positions in the world of business and diplomacy and returning from places like Baghdad and Moscow. Over the years, the careers of Club members in the international arena have kept many a moving van busy in Washington.

Frank Carter, who had served as general manager at one time, retired in 1952 after forty-five years of loyal service to the Club. In 1953, as part of the lecture series, members heard from Dr. Julius Amberson of the U.S. Navy's Department of Tropical and Arctic Medicine, who discussed his adventures in Greenland and Alaska.

On February 19, 1954, with former president Cecil Wilkinson chairing the festivities, it was back to the Willard (no longer new) for the Club's Fiftieth Golden Jubilee Celebration, held, as always, in grand style.

That year, James M. "Jim" Johnston, the founding partner of one of Washington's leading investment firms, Johnston Lemon & Co., succeeded Charlie Pledger as president of the Club. In the '60s, Johnston was also one of the owners of a new Washington Senators expansion team, organized after owner Calvin Griffith moved the original Senators to Minnesota.

Club records show that fifty-two years after he had written the letter that led to the formation of the University Club, Proctor Dougherty was still serving his fellow members as the chairman of the Committee on Literature and the Arts. A new manager, Mendell Rice, also took over the "back of the house" for Frank Davies that year, but at the Club's front door, Wesley Fowler was still greeting members as he had for more than thirty years. Most of that time, a large oak pegboard listing every member's name stood at the entrance to the lobby, overseen by the infallible doorman. Fowler, whose amazing memory never failed him, put a peg next to each member's name as he crossed the threshold, and in those days, many of those members headed directly to the Grille.

THE MEN'S GRILLE—WHERE THE ACTION WAS

In the '50s and '60s, the Men's Grille was a lively place, full of lobbyists and lawyers, politicians and Hill staff, bankers and businessmen, where "everybody knew your name." One member everyone knew was a shrewd Irishman often called the "Artful Dodger of the New Deal." Tommy Corcoran, who was known to buy drinks at the bar for the gathered crowd on many an occasion, had been a member of FDR's "brain trust." "Tommy the Cork," as FDR nicknamed him, is credited with shaping some of the most important and controversial legislation of the New Deal. But he was only one of many colorful characters who stopped in the Grille for a drink or two several nights a week. One of those was a young congressman from Massachusetts by the name of John F. Kennedy. Kennedy occasionally stayed at the Club, but he was a familiar figure in the Grille in the early '50s, when he dropped by for drinks and, rumor has it, often a quick snooze on the library sofa. Some members swear the young, up-and-coming Massachusetts politician was finally banned from the library when his snoring disturbed the reading of the Club's more studious members. Others say it was his habit of tearing out articles from the Club's newspapers that he found interesting that finally earned him the door. Whatever the truth, then–Senator Kennedy married in late 1953 and, though never an actual member, his days at the Club were officially over. John wasn't the only Kennedy to stay at the Club. Ted, Bobby, and Sargent Shriver have all used the Club's privileges at one time or another.

The politician-fathers of two later senators were also Club members in those days—Connecticut Senator Thomas J. Dodd, father of current Senator Christopher Dodd, and Congressman Howard Baker, Sr. of Tennessee, father of former Senate Majority Leader Howard Baker, Jr. of Watergate fame. Senator Norris Cotton of New Hampshire was another Club regular, along with many House members.

The Grille was a great place for political action, but the third-floor card room, now the site of the Club's executive offices, was another. A dedicated group of card "sharks" played bridge, poker, gin rummy, whist, and dominoes there over lunch and after work. The leaders of the pack were George Hughes and another Massachusetts Congressman, Tip O'Neill, who would go on to be one of the most powerful Speakers of the House in history. O'Neill was a great fan of horse racing, but for him, there was nothing like a good game of cards. From the late '50s into the early '90s, he was a University Club regular, where he would play with friends and "enemies" alike. His regular crowd included lawyers, businessmen, and other politicians, such as then–Vice President Richard Nixon, Republican Senator Karl Mundt, and Congressmen Jamie Whitten and John Bell Williams, to name just a few. Many members recall seeing O'Neill and Nixon square off for high-spirited games of gin rummy lasting long into the night.

Another Club regular was "Honest Mike" Kirwan of Ohio, who came to Congress during the Depression. He won his election to Congress when, nearly broke, he told voters he wanted to go to Washington because he needed a job. His honesty earned him a seat in Congress for the next thirty-four years. It was at the University Club that Kirwan and O'Neill became friends, which led to Kirwan's decision to put O'Neill on the leadership track by appointing him to the Democratic Congressional Campaign Committee. Leo Diehl, Tip O'Neill's chief of staff and closest confidant, was also often seen in the Grille.

Senator Thomas J. Dodd

Tip O'Neill wrote in his autobiography, *Man of the House*, that he was one of a "group that played poker every Wednesday night at the University Club. Those card games were a great way to meet some of my colleagues and to learn what was going on in their districts all over the country." In his biography of O'Neill, called *Tip*, John Farrell quotes the speaker's description of his nocturnal visits to the Club this way: "You would get there about 6 p.m. You would eat and sit around until 8 p.m. You would talk about legislation, you would talk about sports, you would talk about your district. At 8 p.m., you drew and had a couple of poker games."

If he didn't get a winning hand, however, O'Neill often played all night and "walked home through Washington's deserted streets in the early morning hours or saw the Capitol dome at dawn." Mrs. O'Neill was known to call, looking for the big Irishman, but Tip supposedly had the Club operators well trained to cover his tracks.

Speaker of the House of Representatives Tip O'Neill

It usually went something like this. Millie would start calling the Club around 11:30. "When are you coming home?" she'd ask. "I'll leave about 12:30," Tip would tell her. His chauffeur, Joe, knowing the routine, would curl up on the billiard table in the card room that Speaker Sam Rayburn supposedly slept on once, too.

At 1:00 a.m., Millie would call again. "I'm behind," Tip would plead. Usually, according to onlookers, to the tune of a "bankrupting" sum like twelve cents.

Another hour would go by, and the phone would ring again. "I've got to wake up Joe," Tip would explain to Millie, and the pair would usually leave forty minutes later. O'Neill continued to play cards at the Club after his retirement from Congress until his death in 1994.

Of course, in those days and into the '60s, politicians, businessmen, and other professionals worked at a slightly different pace than the hard-charging crowd of today. Most Club members arrived at their offices very early in the morning—many by 7 a.m. They worked until 12 or 1 p.m., then headed to the Club for a carafe of martinis, followed by a heavy midday meal (not infrequently with a bottle of wine.) Cards were often "dessert," bridge the Club favorite. Some would take a steam or a swim, then head back to the office for a few hours. By 5:30 or 6, they'd be back in the Grille for a drink or two before calling it a day or dining at the Club Table or with their wives in the Taft Dining Room.

Others might hit the squash court, as the University Club was considered one of the city's premier squash facilities. By 1955, the annual squash players' dinner had become a fixture, and that year a senior official from the State Department spoke on "the importance of squash in developing qualities of sportsmanship." The Club made the pages of *Sports Illustrated* a few months later, when the magazine devoted three full-color pages to four sporting prints owned by the Club. They had originally been purchased by a Racquet Club member, who had been given the task of acquiring titles "relating to manly sports."

THE LIVE-INS

Many of the regulars in the Men's Grille in '50s and '60s were "live-ins." Over the decades, the Club has been home to innumerable people, from journalists to judges, military men to politicians. After the 1992 election, Vice President Dan Quayle and his wife, Marilyn, were residents for a short time at the Club. Of course, not all residents were permanent. As one member put it, "In those days, when there was a problem in a marriage or a divorce, you could always find someone hanging around here until the smoke blew over."

Today, only five members call the Club their permanent home, but at periods in the Club's history, especially during and after wars, the Club's residential floors often bulged at the seams. In the early '50s, when Washington was hit by yet another housing shortage (especially near the Capitol, where several apartment buildings had been torn down to make room for a new House Office Building), a number of congressmen made the Club their home address. Unlike today, many congressmen back then went solo to Washington, leaving their families at home. With housing hard to come by, a group lived at the Club off and on during the '50s and '60s. One of those was Congressman James Delaney of New York, chairman of the powerful Rules Committee, who led the fight to limit the use of chemicals and pesticides in food products. Another was one of the Club's most popular live-in politicians—Senator Theodore Green of Rhode Island, who served in the Senate from 1936 to 1954. When he retired at the age of ninety-three, he was, at that time, the oldest man to serve in the Senate—a record just recently broken by the late Strom Thurmond, who retired from the Senate in 2000 at one hundred.

Congressman James Delaney

Member Ray Brophy remembers that Senator Green was famous for being tight with a dollar, following Yankee tradition. "He would go to a reception in the Club and stuff his pockets with whatever was served on the tables. He'd get one drink and have a wonderful time."

John Wigger, then a lawyer with the Department of Justice's antitrust division, first moved into the Club in 1948 because of its lively, congenial atmosphere and its convenient location. Back then, there were one hundred bedrooms and about fifty permanent residents; congressmen and senators, Hill staff, and a judge or two all called the Club home, but the living was hardly luxurious. Granted, a barber was available on site, along with a valet who cleaned residents' clothes and did minor tailoring. But spartan rooms, shared bathrooms, and no central air conditioning were the order of the day, although when Washington's summers kicked into high gear, electric fans were available. In fact, one of the first acknowledgments that the Club was in need of some updating was the decision in the 1950s to begin installing air conditioning and generally upgrading the accommodations. All the guest rooms were closed in the mid-1960s for renovation.

One of the "resident" judges at the Club was Chief Judge Marvin Jones of the Court of Claims. It was thanks to his residency in the Club that the Court moved from its quarters in what is today the Renwick Gallery to its current location on Lafayette Park. During the '60s, it seems Mrs. Kennedy wanted to renovate the Renwick and the Judge wanted to keep his court within walking distance of the Club. Being a buddy of Lyndon Johnson, he cut a deal. The court would move to accommodate the former First Lady but would be given space in one of the planned Executive Office Buildings on the square.

Bryce Rea took up residence at the Club in 1972. A renovation in the late '80s caused Rea and Wigger real heartburn when then–general manager Jack B. Quick decided to close down the Club on Friday and Saturday nights. Permanent residents had to pack up for the weekend and find other quarters, although Rea did sneak back in one weekend—only to get a tongue-lashing from the unhappy Quick. Clarence Pechacek, who joined the University Club in 1938 after riding a caboose from his hometown of Sioux City, Iowa, to attend Georgetown Law School, was also a longtime resident member. A dancer and bowler, the popular Pechacek remains another of the Club's longest standing members—more than sixty-five years.

Another permanent resident still at the Club is Dick Peterson, who has lived in the Club for the better part of twenty-five years. A long-time member of the House Banking Committee staff, Peterson remembers being well taken care of by Mrs. Harrison, the Club's former housekeeper, whom he described as much like a "super house mother in a frat. She picked up our laundry, made sure our rooms were clean and even sewed on our missing buttons," he fondly recalls. Peterson says that Club security wasn't as tough as it is today, though. Once a hobo wandered in the Club's back door and went down to the gym, where he showered, shaved, helped himself to a suit of clothes left by an unsuspecting member, and headed back out the door. What the ill-fated member wore that day remains lost in the annals of Club history.

THE BOWLERS TAKE CHARGE

The Club bowling alleys were a major center of energy and activity in the 1950s and '60s. Members bowled in leagues on Mondays and Tuesdays, and the alleys became a social scene on Thursdays and Fridays when mixed teams took to the lanes. Couples like the Becks, the Engels, the McCoys, the Ellises, the Donovans, the Jernbergs, the Baldwins, the Whytes, the Chandlers, the Harrises, the Phillippses, the Carmans, and the

Donalds were some of the mainstays of the bowling leagues for more than three decades. There was always a bartender on duty—often LeRoy Harper, who began his service with the Club in 1963 setting pins and serving food and drinks in the bowling alley. Today, LeRoy is the most familiar fixture in the Pershing Grille, where he has bartended for more than twenty years, becoming one of the members' favorites in the process.

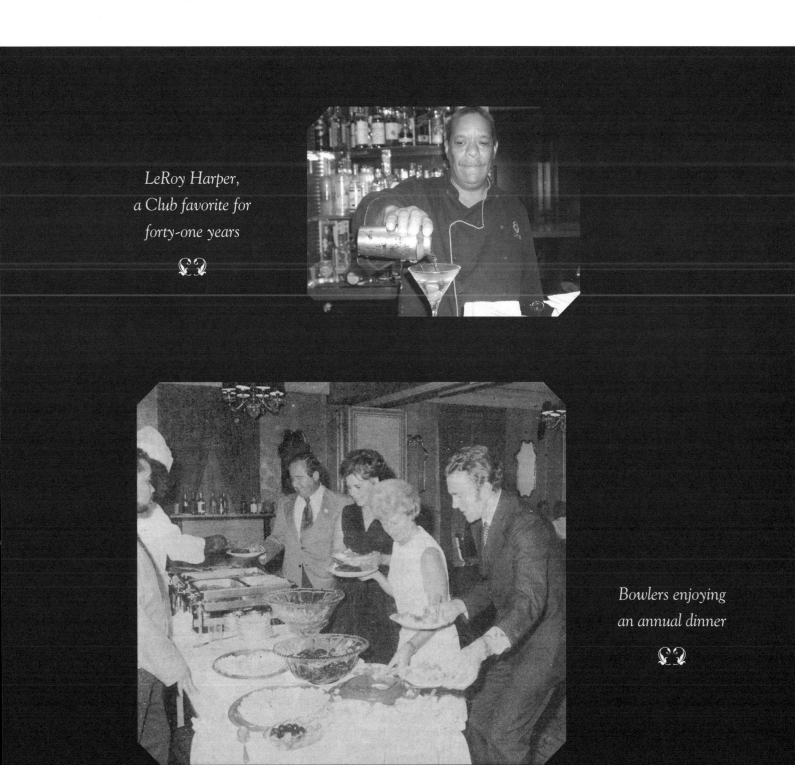

*LeRoy Harper,
a Club favorite for
forty-one years*

*Bowlers enjoying
an annual dinner*

Back in the '50s and '60s, however, couples would typically enjoy a few friendly games and then mosey up to the Peacock Lounge. There pianist Art Carchedi would hand out song sheets, and the good times would begin, with Gene McCoy usually leading the way. But the bowlers were more than just a group of fun-loving friends. Over the years, they became the Club's social and leadership nucleus, the people behind so much of what happened in the Club over the span of nearly three decades. Many served on the Club's various boards and committees, planning some of the most entertaining evenings the Club has seen before or since. For years, nearly every Club president was a bowler. Former president Keith Engel says, "It started with John Beck, Lee Ellis, myself, Dale Jernberg, Gene McCoy...about eight or nine or ten presidents in a row were bowlers."

THAT'S ENTERTAINMENT

When it came to activities, bowling wasn't the only entertainment—far from it. In the 1950s and into the '60s, members kicked up their heels at evening tea dances held in the library. Many members still fondly remember those dances as the highlight of Club life in those days. With their wives dressed to the nines, members rolled back the carpet in the library, moved the tables, and danced the evenings away. One of the best and most prominent dance couples was Arthur and Leona Keefer, who would later endow the Club's library, making one wonder if the tea dances had left the Keefers with a soft spot for the normally quiet and sedate room.

In 1956, there was a changing of the guard as Arthur Winn, managing partner of LaRoe, Winn and Moerman, assumed the Club presidency. Winn, who joined the Club in 1940, was a distinguished attorney with a quotable sense of humor. His description of a hog, in the eyes of a meatpacker, as "not a pet but an articulated group of pork cuts" was once humorously quoted by Justice Felix Frankfurter in a landmark decision involving government compensation for wartime meat purchases. Winn's tenure saw more improvements in the Clubhouse, including the installation of new automatic elevators. The next year, members were asked to specify their favorite dishes for potential inclusion on a new Dining Room menu. Broiled pheasant and roast mallard duck came in first and second in the game category. Blue and Camembert won the cheese competition. Later that year, the Board of Governors began considering proposals to amend the bylaws to admit members' widows at a charge of $50 a year. In 1958, dentist Marc Burton took the reins from President Winn, and in April, Mrs. Catherine O'Connor Roberts, widow of John O'Connor Roberts, was elected the first widow member.

Athletic trainer Billy Whipp, a former professional boxer who had been at the Club when it was still the Racquet Club, got a raise that year to $80 a month for nine months of the year, and expanded his repertoire to include jujitsu and fencing. One longtime member recalled many years later that, "an amazing number of our younger members were instructed by Bill Whipp in one form of mayhem or another when they were boys." Whipp was also a friend of the great Jack Dempsey, and rumors persist that Dempsey once spent a day at the Club training with his buddy Whipp.

The inflation that had come and gone over the years hit once again in 1958, and resident dues rose from $150 to $240 per year, while the price of a haircut went up to $1.15. More importantly, scotch and bourbon highballs shot up to 80 cents. Martinis with vodka, however, were slashed from 72 cents to 65 cents.

But leave it to the University Club members to find a real bargain. On April 30, 1959, the first of what would become annual international odysseys got underway when fifty-five members and wives climbed aboard a chartered DC-7 prop jet at National Airport and flew off on a Club-sponsored thirty-three-day visit to thirteen European countries. All this for a grand total of $668 per person, including transportation, lodging and meals. Remembering the wonderful time that was had by all, John Beck, one of the original travelers, refers to it today as the "If it's Tuesday, it must be Belgium" trip.

The friendships that grew out of that first trip lasted a lifetime and helped form the social nucleus of the Club for many years. Many members of this prestigious group of "Globetrotters" would later become the Club's presidents and board members over the next three decades.

The first trip was so successful that another trip to Europe followed the next year, and in 1962, most of the members of the mixed bowling league took off on a round-the-world jaunt that included Japan, Hong Kong, Thailand, India, and Egypt. In 1964, the next Club trip was even more unusual, when members ventured to Eastern Europe and Russia, staying in a hotel right on Red Square at a time when the Cold War was red hot. The trip was arranged by Adele Lovelace, one of the Club's longest serving staff members, and also included stops in Scandinavia.

President John Fitzgerald Kennedy

Chapter Six

1960s: Progress
and Discontent

The decade that would witness both the grief of war and the pride of great achievement began with the hope and promise of a young new president. John Fitzgerald Kennedy, who had ruffled a few feathers at the University Club in his younger days, defeated Richard Nixon in the narrowest election victory in the nation's history until the election of 2000.

In 1963, Dr. Martin Luther King, Jr. gave his "I Have a Dream" speech to tens of thousands gathered at the Lincoln Memorial. Americans were fascinated with new push-button phones and Polaroid color film. Magazine writer Betty Friedan published *The Feminine Mystique,* and the women's movement began its drive for full equality.

In the mid-1960s, the British invaded America, infecting the teen population with Beatlemania, and America invaded Vietnam. LBJ pushed the Civil Rights Act of 1964 through a reluctant Congress. In 1968, killers gunned down Dr. Martin Luther King, Jr. and Robert F. Kennedy and brought riots and destruction to Washington. By decade's end, the anti-war movement was rocking the country, and Richard Nixon sat in the Oval Office.

But the world stood still on July 20, 1969, and watched in wonder as Apollo astronaut Neil Armstrong bounced down a shiny ladder and planted Old Glory on the face of the moon. All America was euphoric.

It was hard to believe that only ten years had passed since the seven Mercury astronauts were first introduced to the American public, quickly becoming international celebrities and the heroes of the decade. With a following much like that of today's rock stars, the amiable astronauts were mobbed for photos and autographs wherever they went. One Saturday in 1962, not long after John Glenn's ride into the history books as the first American to orbit the earth, a few lucky University Club members were surprised to see the astronaut and his six Mercury colleagues at a large table having lunch with NASA administrator and Club member James Webb. It didn't take long for members and staff to begin clamoring for autographs. Webb later said that he had been seeking privacy for the seven astronauts—a nearly impossible task since Glenn had grabbed the world's imagination with his three orbits in Friendship 7. Years later, as a United States senator, John Glenn would be a University Club visitor on many occasions.

Two years before the "spacemen's" visit delighted Club members, Harvey Gram, Jr., a top executive with former president Jim Johnston's investment firm, became the Club's twenty-eighth president in 1960. That same year, one of the Club's longest-serving staff members would begin her tenure as well.

Laurence Belanger, "Miss Laurence," greeting members in the Taft Dining Room since 1960

MISS LAURENCE ARRIVES

On May 3, 1960, a young French-Canadian woman began what has become a four-decade reign as queen of the Taft Dining Room. For forty-four years, Miss Laurence Belanger has graced the University Club with a special charm that has made the Taft one of members' favorite spots. Miss Laurence has presided over dinners of statesmen and spacemen (she was there for the Mercury 7 visit), judges and diplomats, lawyers and lobbyists, with a warmth and grace that has endeared her to the members over the years. The feeling is mutual. Miss Laurence says of the Club, "This is my family."

THE SQUASH COURT REBELLION

Under the supervision of Miss Laurence, the Dining Room became a place of quiet elegance, but the Club has had its noisy moments, too. In 1962, the squash courts became the "controversy coming out of the basement," according to one member, and rocked the boat and the board. The squash fraternity argued that the four squash courts, which dated back to 1921, were in dire need of renovation. The plaster walls were deteriorating and didn't meet regulation squash standards of the day. A number of renovations, including that of the Dining Room, were already on the schedule, but when the squash players discovered plans to build a bakery over the courts, effectively preventing their renovation, a small rebellion erupted. The players nominated their own slate for the Board of Governors, and luck was on their side when a snowstorm on voting day kept many members home. A little bad weather wasn't about to keep the squash enthusiasts away from the Club. They were there en masse, soliciting votes, and in the end, "the basement" triumphed. Carl Phillips was elected Club president, and with a little diplomacy, the differences of opinion on the renovations were reconciled. Five of the happy squash players that year won the National Team Singles squash title for the first and only time as members of the Washington, D.C. team. They included John Davis, Grenville Emmet, George Rogers, Jack Sloat, and Bill Wilson.

In 1964, a new president, Frank Carman, officially opened the new Dining Room, celebrated for the rich elegance of its formal wood paneling. Carman, a scientist, had been a "dollar-a-year" man during World War II heading the War Production Board's plastics division, a crucial part of the war effort due to the scarcity of rubber. He was also a member of the Club's "Globetrotters" and bowling league. It was on his watch that the Club voted to increase the initiation fee to $600 to keep pace with rising costs.

Although relations between the United States and the Soviet Union were still frosty after the Cuban missile crisis three years before, the Soviet ambassador attended a cocktail reception and buffet dinner to send off the Club's "in-house tourists" on their trip to Russia and Scandinavia that year.

As Americans pushed the frontiers of new technology throughout the decade, the Club took the plunge in 1966 and began computerizing members' accounts—giving each member his own number. This also solved the perennial problem of deciphering members' signatures, which the board had concluded was a lost art. That year also saw the loss of the Club's founding father, Proctor Dougherty, who had done more than any other member to get the Club off to a sound start and keep it on a solid footing for more than sixty years.

Another changing of the guard took place in 1966, as Howard A. Donald became Club president. In April of the following year, Paul Burley began what would be an eighteen-year career as general manager.

THE HOUSE NEXT DOOR

On a cold March morning in 1968, longtime resident John Wigger awoke at 4 a.m. to the sounds of a loud explosion and shattering glass. He was soon to learn that a bomb had been detonated at the Russian embassy next door, blowing out 240 windows on the south side of the University Clubhouse and rousting the thirty resident members out of a sound sleep. Luckily, no one was hurt. Pipe bombs had become a fairly regular occurrence in the neighborhood; the Aeroflot office, which was then just a block a way, was a frequent bombing target.

Once the damaged rooms had been repaired, the residents were welcomed back to the Club by new president Joseph Whyte. All told, thirty-four additional bedrooms, newly redone, were retained for transient members and guests.

The Russian embassy bombing was only one more chapter in a long, fascinating history between the University Club and the House Next Door, which have stood side by side for more than eighty years. Ironically, one of the captains of capitalism indirectly provided the diplomatic headquarters for the country in which Communism took root when railroad tycoon George Pullman built the mansion in 1911. Originally, the imposing building was a wedding gift for his daughter, who was marrying a young congressman. Two years later, the mansion was sold to the Russian Czarist government. After the Russian Revolution in 1917, the great house became the property of the new Soviet Communist regime until the disintegration of the Soviet Union in 1988. Today, it belongs to the Russian government. Judge Loren Smith remembers a day before the Soviet government fell when members came out to find their cars, parked in the Club's driveway, covered in ashes. As the turmoil in Russia worsened, the embassy staff was busy burning sensitive documents—so many, in fact, that eventually every car next door got a "top secret" dusting. But the official changing of the guard came later. On December 24, 1992, University Club members saw that the Soviet flag was still flying, but on Christmas Day, it was the old Russian tricolor waving atop the Pullman mansion.

For many years, the embassy was a place of intrigue and espionage, where some of the Cold War's most famous spies made contact. The American intelligence services—especially the FBI—had more than a passing interest in the comings and goings at the embassy. The not-so-secret relationship between the University Club and the FBI goes back a long time—some say at least forty years. During most of that time, the law enforcement agency rented eight rooms in the Club on four different floors, which were used for surveillance of the embassy. After the fall of the Soviet Union, the FBI scaled back to only two rooms on the top floor, and today, the FBI no longer has guest "lodgers" in the Club at all. When FBI agents were in residence, however, their rooms were always locked, and no one on the Club staff was allowed access. Whenever there was a need for maintenance, agents would cover their equipment while the work was underway. Contrary to the Club's most notorious rumor, there never was a tunnel between the two buildings—not even from a bowling lane, as many members believe to this day. Monty Spindler, Club president from 1985–1987, tried to convince members that the tunnel's existence was pure myth in an article in the Club's 1985 fall Bulletin. When the United States recognized the Soviet Union in 1933, the Bulletin reported, the Soviets began to remodel the embassy and obtained a permit from the District government to build a tunnel to the then Racquet Club, which the Soviets hoped to buy. When the Club declined their offer, the Soviets abandoned their idea for a tunnel connecting the two buildings and so, contrary to popular belief, the tunnel was never built.

Rumors, though, die hard. In April 2001, Russian ambassador Urily Ushakov held a reception and dinner celebrating the wit and wisdom of former Ambassador to Russia Robert Strauss at the ambassador's residence. Ambassador Ushakov, referring to the tunnel, said the best way to bridge the gap between the United States and the Russian Federation was with wit, not by digging tunnels.

During the Cold War, the University Club and the Russian embassy learned to live and let live as neighbors—most of the time. University Club member John Walker, a national security and intelligence expert, once told the story of a Soviet intelligence official whom the FBI had under daily surveillance from its post at the University Club. The agents became so used to his habits while waiting for him to make contacts that they had come to believe the man was under "complete control." But on the day the spy was to make contact with his key "source," he walked in the front door of the Club and right out the back. After two years of surveillance waiting for that moment, they lost him completely.

Sometimes, however, the FBI got its man. One CIA official met Walker for lunch in the Grille every couple of weeks. Walker's friend was, apparently, in a particularly jovial mood one afternoon when, over lunch, he neatly folded a handful of paper airplanes. He then proceeded to sail every one of them off the Club's second-floor terrace into the courtyard of the Russian embassy, just to see who would come out and pick them up. What he didn't count on, and neither did Walker, was getting nabbed by FBI agents as the pair left the Club. It seems the government wanted to know why someone at the University Club was sending secret messages to the Russians. The idea wasn't as farfetched as it might have seemed then, since we now know several master spies, including Robert Hanssen, made contact at the embassy. Walker and his friend had to convince the FBI that the airplanes were nothing more than a practical joke. "The FBI," Walker said, "doesn't have much of a sense of humor."

In 1988, as excitement was building over the extraordinary political situation in Eastern Europe and the Soviet Union, Premier Mikhail Gorbachev took Washington by storm with a two-day visit to meet with President Reagan and President-elect Bush. Wowing usually hard-to-impress Washingtonians, who lined up five-deep to catch a glimpse of the charismatic leader, the Soviet premier leaped out of his motorcade not far from the University Club to shake hands with the crowds like a seasoned American politician. The Gorbachevs were staying, of course, at the House Next Door, and members tell of being met at the corner and escorted into the Club by security personnel during the big visit.

GATEWAY FOR THE POWERFUL

The University Club has seen many of Washington's most powerful cross its threshold. In December 1963, just a month after assuming the presidency, President Lyndon Johnson visited the Club for a dinner honoring Senator Thomas Dodd, held in the Governors' Room. Always the politician, the president shook every hand in the room. It wasn't Johnson's first trip to the University Club, however. He had been a guest for a testimonial dinner thrown in the library for Senator Theodore Green when the Texan was the powerful Senate majority leader.

In the '60s, much as it is today, seeing members of the Supreme Court at the University Club wasn't unusual. Justices William Brennen, Jr., Hugo Black, Byron White, and Warren Burger were regular users of the Club's dining rooms and athletic facilities. One evening, Warren and Burger both dined at the same time in the Taft —one the current Chief Justice and the other the former. Meanwhile, one floor down, members were just as likely to see Justice Byron "Whizzer" White smashing a squash ball—his favorite pastime at the Club.

Chief Justice Earl Warren was a great frequenter of the Club in the '60s and a big fan of the Washington Senators. Members remember that he loved to talk baseball in the showers—especially when Ted Williams became the manager. In some ways, Justice Warren was just "one of the guys." One member walking into the shower got the shock of his life when he realized, "I was suddenly looking at the first Chief Justice I've ever seen with his clothes off." Another member, Gordon Silcox, had the same experience.

"I tell people I once had a conversation with the Chief Justice and neither one of us had any clothes on. Just what do you say to Mr. Chief Justice under those circumstances?"

Another member says he walked into the steam room one day and there sat the chief justice, along with half a dozen other men reading their newspapers. "You don't see that nowadays. When I walked in, the only guy who looked up was Warren and said, 'Hi,' and he looked back down. A friendly guy."

Justice Warren was a great fan of the swimming pool and could regularly be seen tearing up the lanes. He and his wife, Honey Bear, and their children dined most Fridays in the Taft Dining Room, always at the same table—in the corner by the flag, Miss Laurence remembers.

Justice William O. Douglas, who lived at the Club occasionally over the years, was also a fan of the Taft Dining Room and would often eat dinner with his wife, Cathy. When Cathy graduated from law school, the Douglases celebrated at the Taft.

Chief Justice Earl Warren

In the 1950s, Douglas was not only a justice of the Supreme Court and an author of several books; he was also a well-known environmental activist who led the effort to preserve and protect the C&O Canal. At one point in 1954, when there was talk about turning the historic waterway into a highway, Douglas hiked the towpath from start to finish—a 184-mile trek—attracting other supporters to his cause as he walked. Douglas won his fight to save the canal when it was named a national monument in 1961 and a national historic park in 1971.

Some of the canal ended up at the University Club, however. After Douglas's many hikes up and down the banks, he would often return to the Club, where he was living at the time, violating the rules by tracking up the floors with his muddy boots.

During the '60s and '70s, the bowling alleys and the Peacock Lounge continued to be centers of activity, where members kicked back and kicked up their heels. As it had for decades, the "5:30 Club" continued to hold court in the Grille, where a rotating group would gather for drinks and conversation every evening.

The '60s ended at the Club on a particularly high note, when members and their wives danced the night away at the Gold and Silver Ball in November 1969. The Club Bulletin's review of the evening described the sold out event:

> From the gold-togaed Caesar on the stairway to the sparkling tables and chandeliers, the Gold and Silver Ball on November 22 was a glittering success. The ethereal strains of the harp played by Miriam Millies greeted you as you entered. The sound snapped to a frisky foxtrot in University Hall, where Ted

In November 1969, the Gold and Silver Ball, featuring not one but two bands for dancing, was one of the Club's most memorable evenings in its long history

MIDAS TOUCH—Faye Webster and husband George help golden harpist Miriam Millies tune up before Gold and Silver Ball.

Alexander and his orchestra played to an ever-crowded dance floor. In the Men's Grille, Sammy Ferro and his group picked up the beat to a quick-stepping cha-cha and enthusiastic "hip" swingers.

Partygoers had such a good time that manager Paul Burley had to hold Ted Alexander over until 1:00 a.m. for the dancers who didn't want the evening to end.

The Club celebrated its seventy-fifth birthday

with a gala in 1979

Chapter Seven

1970s: RESIGNATION AND REINVIGORATION

On March 20, 1973, Judge John Sirica strolled out of his office to find convicted Watergate burglar James McCord standing in his reception area. In his hand, McCord held a letter for the judge, who had yet to sentence him. After bringing in some of his staff, Sirica read the contents of the letter. As history knows, McCord broke his silence and blew the whistle on Nixon administration higher-ups, who had pressured the seven burglars to keep quiet about the burglary and even commit perjury. Three days later, "Maximum" John Sirica, as he was known, walked into his crowded courtroom and read McCord's headline-making letter. That decision would change the course of a nation and bring down a presidency.

John Sirica, who became known as the "Watergate judge," was a boxer and a great friend of Jack Dempsey, as well as a former prosecutor. He was also a prominent member of the University Club, as so many extraordinary jurists have been over the years. For Sirica and for the nation, McCord's letter marked a historic moment. And like so many times before and since, a University Club member was in the thick of it. Twenty-five years later, another Club member, Kenneth Starr, would find himself in the eye of a similar political storm. University Club members and guests have often been at the center of national politics, one way or another. Some have been politicians themselves: Tommy Corcoran, Tip O'Neill, Richard Nixon, George H. W. Bush, Tom Foley, Jack Kemp, Pat Buchanan, and Dan Quayle. Others have covered them: Marvin Kalb, Bernard Kalb, Eric Severeid, John Daly, Jane Pauley, and Chris Bury. Some have even earned a living making fun of them, such as Mark Russell.

1973 was a year of scandal and turmoil that reflected what would be a difficult decade for America. The U.S. signed a peace agreement that January, although the

Vietnam War would not actually end for another two years. Unlike previous wars, however, it had had little effect on the Club. By the spring of 1973, the Nixon administration was reeling under the weight of the Watergate scandal, and Lyndon Baines Johnson was dead at sixty-four—some say of a broken heart.

The previous year, University Club member Myles Ambrose, Nixon's Commissioner of Customs, was appointed to head the White House Office of Drug Abuse Law Enforcement to help coordinate federal and local efforts to fight drugs and crime. Ambrose, still an active member today, is credited with the establishment of the Drug Enforcement Administration, created in 1973.

Nixon, however, was about to face his own legal troubles as Congress moved toward impeachment. On August 9, 1974, President Nixon resigned his office, and Gerald Ford was sworn in as the thirty-eighth president. In November 1976, the defeat of Gerald Ford brought Georgia Governor Jimmy Carter to the White House and saw the death of University Club member William O. Douglas after thirty-six years of service on the Supreme Court. Minorities and women were demanding inclusion in every part of society, and institutions across America were adapting to the realities of a changing culture. By decade's end, the country found itself embroiled in the Iranian hostage crisis.

For many Americans, much of the '70s was spent sitting in long gas lines or watching the seemingly endless rise in prices due to skyrocketing inflation. The University Club was not immune to inflation's effects. Despite heroic efforts to keep costs down, initiation fees and dues nearly doubled during the decade. In an acknowledgment of the ever-expanding Washington's suburbs, the distance requirement for non-resident membership was set at fifty miles, to either home or office, from the zero milestone on the Ellipse south of the White House.

Australian Ambassador Sir James Plimsoll, center right, with Mr. and Mrs. Frank Carman, Mr. and Mrs. John Beck, and Lecture Committee chairman Roy Sexton

John Beck, whose service would earn him the title "Member of the Millennium" three decades later, became the first Club president elected in the '70s. Beck, a highly respected attorney, had originally joined the Club in 1956 after being recruited by long-time members Clarence Pechacek and Jim Johnston. One of the mainstays of the bowling league over the years, Beck and his wife, Helen, and a group of members reinvigorated the "Globetrotters" in 1971. The group had been dormant for several years, but president Beck brought wanderlust back to the Club with a trip to Nepal, Kashmir, and several other exotic locales.

GOING INTERNATIONAL

University Club members' fascination with the international community and foreign affairs was the impetus behind what became one of the Club's all-time favorites programs, the Small World Series, begun during Beck's term. Over the years, the popular program brought decades of dinners and diplomats, lectures, slide shows, and live per-

formances to the Club, giving members new insights into the history, culture, politics, and economies of countries around the world. In 1973, the gracious Korean ambassador, Mr. Kim, and his wife gave an "artful presentation" of Korean culture and food.

In January 1975, the Small World Series sponsored a particularly memorable evening called "Joie de Wien." The Club put on a champagne reception to welcome the Austrian ambassador, Arno Halusa, and his wife, along with embassy staff. Following a dinner featuring Austrian specialties, the ambassador spoke to the crowd and then showed two films on Austrian composers and the famous Spanish Riding School in Vienna.

KANGAROO COURT—(L to R) Board Member Robert Willey, Mrs. Hershel Hurst and Mrs. Willey appear ready to adjudge Mr. Hurst (right) cultural Attache of the Australian Embassy, guilty of a stellar performance as emcee of the Australian presentation inaugurating the Small World Series October 29th.

With the merger in 1936, athletics became central to the Club's mission and purpose, but it took until 1972 for the Club to elect its first former professional athlete, Washington Redskins back Cliff Battles, as its president. Battles, whom the Pro Football Hall of Fame calls "one of the most brilliant running backs pro football has known," voluntarily left the NFL after his sixth season in 1938, despite his record-setting performance in the season's final game, when Washington defeated Green Bay for the divisional crown. He and Redskins owner George Preston Marshall had a parting of the ways when Marshall refused to raise Battles's $3,000 a year salary. So Battles took a job coaching at Columbia University for $4,000.

*Harness racing
at Rosecroft
Raceway on
June 4, 1971*

PARI-MUTUAL FEELINGS—Four distinguished bookies from the Club (l. to r.) Board Member Arthur F. M. Harris, Frank Kley, John W. Chandler and Leonard A. Tousignant congratulate each other and owner-driver Robert Poore who copped the $3000 purse aboard Neusha in the University Club Handicap at the Club's visit to Rosecroft Raceway for a night of harness racing on June 4.

FABULOUS FORECAST—Jeanne Dixon's '72 predictions for this quartet must have been on the rosy side as Mr. and Mrs. Galen C. Winter (l & r) and their guests (c) ring in the New Year at the Governors' Reception and Dance.

*The 1972
Governors'
Reception*

"When People Liked to Dance"

Events and activities of every kind were the hallmark of the '70s in the Club. In 1971, members could do the "bump" at the fall formal, "Roman Holiday," where the waiters dressed in appropriate "Roman" attire. Fred Peratine and his orchestra provided the music, and the Club chef crowned the evening with "magnificent omelet delights and crepe Suzettes." The following spring formal, the "Greatest Show on 16th," had a circus theme complete with palm readers, "he and she dancing tigers," animal cages, clowns, and three orchestras.

The Club's sports fans could wolf down a sumptuous brunch and then board a bus to Redskin games or catch a "London" double-decker bus for an evening of racing fun at Rosecroft Raceway. There were co-ed wine tastings, and bridge and dominoes tournaments. The William Howard Taft Lecture Series featured illustrious speakers such as Dr. Lev Dobriansky, who lectured on Russia, and Mort Caplin, IRS commissioner under President Kennedy, who explained the intricacies of the dreaded agency in his 1975 speech "You and the IRS."

The Club's "Theater Party" goers saw first-rate comedy and drama at many of Washington's finest theaters, ranging from Neil Simon's "The Prisoner of Second Avenue," starring Peter Falk, to "The Time of Your Life," with Henry Fonda in the lead at the Kennedy Center. Others saw "Conflict of Interest" at Arena Stage with Dane Clark. Still others enjoyed a performance of Eugene O'Neill's "A Long Day's Journey into Night" at Catholic University's Hartke Theater, starring the first lady of the American theater, Helen Hayes. But the Club itself was often the scene of comedy revues like the Hexagon Players and the British Embassy Players, the perennial Club favorites for many years.

Members were kept entertained at the 1972 "Greatest Show on 16th"

A group of ex-congressmen called the Jack Rabbits Club met regularly on Mondays to talk over the great issues of the day. There were many regulars at the Club who were or had been Hill staffers. One, the staff director for the House Agriculture Committee, had the same lunch every day at the Club for years—two stem martinis, a grilled cheese sandwich, and a hefty number of cigarettes. Don Baldwin once asked him why he had the same exact lunch every day. Because, he told Don, he'd sat down once and calculated just how much time he saved every year by not looking at the menu.

SAYING GOODBYE

Cliff Battles handed off the Club presidency to Geoffrey Creyke, Jr. in the Watergate year of 1974, and the Club lost one of its "own" when Wesley Fowler, who had stood guard at the Club's door for more than half a century, left to enjoy a richly deserved retirement. No one could ever match Wes Fowler's ability to remember the name of every member and even former members gone for many years.

One UC member, who worked in the international arena, told the story of a secret meeting he arranged once with the Shah of Iran. "We needed a place where we could talk quietly and privately." So he took the monarch to the University Club. And it worked. No reporters. No Secret Service. But as the pair strolled through the front door, Fowler announced in his best welcoming voice, "Good evening, Your Majesty. I haven't seen you since 1954."

The Club's longtime masseur, Lars Korsstrom, whose "magical" hands and $6 massages had become near legendary, was the victim of a mugging in 1974, and died from his injuries. At the time, the eighty-one-year-old was still handling a full schedule of "treatments," a combination of vigorous exercise and a relaxing massage.

Some changes in the Club's athletics took place in the '70s when Bill Whipp retired after fifty-two years teaching boxing and fencing at the Club. Bill preached that he never smoked, drank, or gambled. He died on his one hundredth birthday.

Club president Geoffrey Creyke, Jr. headed the receiving line at the annual Governors' Reception on New Years Day, 1975, greeting members in the lounge. After the reception, members were treated to a dinner of oyster bisque, black-eyed peas and "enough sea and turf food to delight everyone and restore their energy for the dancing hours of 6:30–9:30."

Arthur Harris's term as Club president, which began in 1976, was cut short by his untimely death, and Ed Melton was elected to fill the vacancy in 1977. That was also the year the Club lost another of its longest-serving staff members—Adele Lovelace, who was honored at a farewell dinner as she headed off to retirement. Ms. Lovelace lives in Florida today. After the loss of so many of the University Club's favorites, 1978 was a much happier year and a milestone in Club history.

HAPPY BIRTHDAY, AGAIN

Keith Engel, a senior partner with a national accounting firm, became the Jubilee Year president upon his election in 1978. Members celebrated the Club's seventy-fifth birthday in style with a series of memorable activities held throughout the Diamond Jubilee Year. On February 16, 1978, the Club kicked off the yearlong celebration with a stag luncheon in the tradition of the Club's 1904 dinner. In May, the ladies were included as the Club held a spring formal, complete with big band music. As the leaves turned

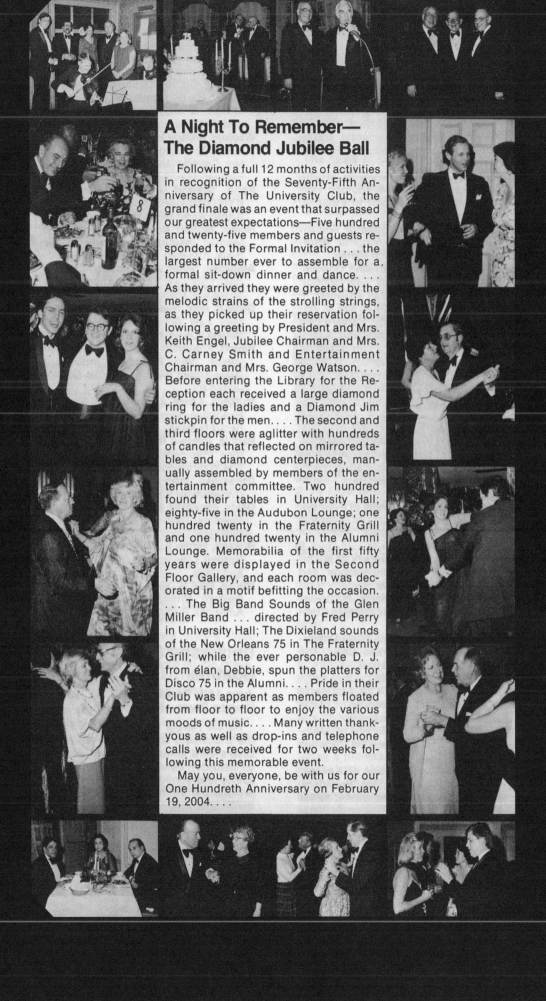

A Night To Remember—
The Diamond Jubilee Ball

Following a full 12 months of activities in recognition of the Seventy-Fifth Anniversary of The University Club, the grand finale was an event that surpassed our greatest expectations—Five hundred and twenty-five members and guests responded to the Formal Invitation . . . the largest number ever to assemble for a formal sit-down dinner and dance. . . . As they arrived they were greeted by the melodic strains of the strolling strings, as they picked up their reservation following a greeting by President and Mrs. Keith Engel, Jubilee Chairman and Mrs. C. Carney Smith and Entertainment Chairman and Mrs. George Watson. . . . Before entering the Library for the Reception each received a large diamond ring for the ladies and a Diamond Jim stickpin for the men. . . . The second and third floors were aglitter with hundreds of candles that reflected on mirrored tables and diamond centerpieces, manually assembled by members of the entertainment committee. Two hundred found their tables in University Hall; eighty-five in the Audubon Lounge; one hundred twenty in the Fraternity Grill and one hundred twenty in the Alumni Lounge. Memorabilia of the first fifty years were displayed in the Second Floor Gallery, and each room was decorated in a motif befitting the occasion. . . . The Big Band Sounds of the Glen Miller Band . . . directed by Fred Perry in University Hall; The Dixieland sounds of the New Orleans 75 in The Fraternity Grill; while the ever personable D. J. from élan, Debbie, spun the platters for Disco 75 in the Alumni. . . . Pride in their Club was apparent as members floated from floor to floor to enjoy the various moods of music. . . . Many written thank-yous as well as drop-ins and telephone calls were received for two weeks following this memorable event.

May you, everyone, be with us for our One Hundreth Anniversary on February 19, 2004. . . .

The Club's seventy-fifth birthday celebration— 1979

that fall, members were treated to ten-cent beer in the second floor Grille starting at noon. Their spouses could join them that evening for dining and dancing.

On February 17, 1979, a glittering Diamond Jubilee Ball capped off the anniversary festivities. More than 525 members and guests packed the club, which had three bands in three different rooms. Club manager Paul Burley and his staff had certainly outdone themselves.

THE SPORTS BANQUETS—A NEW TRADITION BEGINS

In December 1979, the Club began one of its most popular traditions with the first annual Sports Banquet. The speaker for that first banquet was the Washington Redskins' punter from 1968 to 1979, Mike Bragg, who holds the record for most punts in Redskin history—896. He once said, "Punting a football was probably the easiest thing I ever did, looking back at it. But, I had passion. If you don't get turned on [by your passion], you won't fulfill it."

Bragg was introduced at the banquet by Club member Pete Larson, another former Redskin. Pete carried the pigskin for D.C.'s favorite football team in the 1967–1968 season. Ten years later, Larson would become Club president, following in the footsteps of Cliff Battles. The Club's Sports Committee chooses the speaker for the Sports Banquet, who is given the Thomas Gardiner Corcoran Award at the dinner. The winner must be a scholar, an athlete, and involved in public service. Speakers in the past have included House Majority Leader Tom Foley, Solicitor General Ken Starr, Senate Majority Leader George Mitchell, Senators Al Simpson and Howell Heflin, Chief Justice William Rehnquist, and Congressman Jim Ryun. Basketball coaches Michael Jarvis of George Washington University and Gary Williams of the University of Maryland have also been Corcoran Award recipients.

Today, the banquet has become one of the Club's best-attended events.

WHEELING AND DEALING AT THE CLUB

The Club was the setting for a little international wheeling and dealing as the tumultuous decade of the '70s ended. The Carter administration had shifted American diplomatic recognition from the Republic of China (Taiwan) to the People's Republic of China, which was to become official on January 1, 1979. It didn't take long for the ownership of the last Chinese ambassador's residence, owned by the Taiwanese government, to become an issue. Under normal circumstances, the imposing frame mansion, on ten acres near the National Cathedral, would pass to the People's Republic. But there was nothing normal about this transfer of diplomatic recognition. One of those who opposed President Carter's decision was a fellow Democrat from another era—Tommy Corcoran,

Roosevelt's "get-it-done guy," who remained a powerful lobbyist in Washington and a member of the Club. Tommy's son, Tim, also a Washington attorney, is a member of the Club today.

The University Club provided the setting as a deal was cut to keep the residence out of Communist hands just days before the transfer was to take place. As member Jack E. Buttram describes it, "one evening in late December 1978, in the dining room of Washington's prestigious University Club.... I handed over a check for ten dollars to Thomas Corcoran as consideration, and took possession, in the name of the Friends of Free China, of a ten-million-dollar parcel of property. I had to get my son to write his personal check since we had rushed to Washington so fast in a private plane that I had left my money and checkbook at home."

By decade's end, the relationship between the United States and the People's Republic wasn't the only change afoot. The Shah of Iran, whom Wesley Fowler had greeted so warmly, was out of power, as Jimmy Carter was soon to be. And there was change at the Club, too.

A former Racquet Club member by the name of King, a lawyer and part owner of the Redskins, had become the Club's first Jewish member when the two clubs merged in 1936. Several other Jewish members joined the Club in the '60s, breaking down once and for all any religious barriers that still existed.

In 1977, the Club took another step toward modernizing its membership policies by voting in its first African-American member, Wesley Williams, a prominent lawyer with the powerhouse firm of Covington and Burling. Williams, a graduate of Harvard Law, was recruited and sponsored by Ambassador Richard Fairbanks, former ambassador-at-large for the Reagan administration and former Middle East Peace negotiator.

With change in the air, women members couldn't be far behind...or could they?

Today, women are seen in every facet of the Club;
they were admitted in 1984

Chapter Eight

1980s: CONTROVERSY
AND CHANGE

In her book, *Unlimited Partners*, Elizabeth Dole likes to tell the story of the time she had a business meeting with an important lawyer at the Metropolitan Club when she was a White House staffer. As she approached the entrance, a very officious doorman barred her way.

"You can't go in there," he said.

"I beg your pardon," the then Miss Hanford replied.

"Women are not permitted in the Club."

"I'm sorry. I don't think you understand. My name is Elizabeth Hanford, and I'm here to meet with some attorneys from Cleveland. We have an appointment."

"I'm sorry, ma'am. If you were the Queen Elizabeth, I couldn't let you into the Metropolitan Club."

Those were the early 1970s. By the mid-1980s, institutional barriers to women and minorities were disappearing all over Washington. But the University Club, like so many other professional clubs, remained an all-male bastion.

Justice William Douglas's wife, Cathy, ran into the same kind of roadblock as Elizabeth Dole when she wandered into the Men's Grille one evening looking for a bite to eat after using University Hall for a meeting. The maitre d' politely informed her that women were not allowed. She couldn't believe it, in that day and age, and complained to her husband. The pair headed down to the Taft Dining Room, where Miss Laurence heard Douglas tell his liberated young wife, "Give it a few years, and you will come to the Grille." He was right, but it wasn't an easy transition.

The decade of the '80s was a time of great social and political change in the country. In 1980, California Governor Ronald Reagan was elected the fortieth president of the United States after beating out a large field for the Republican nomination and the incumbent, Jimmy Carter. It was during the Wisconsin Republican primary that one of the University Club's favorite masseurs, Luis Manrique, spent a week with another Republican presidential contender and later Reagan's vice president, George H.W. Bush, helping the candidate deal with the stress of the campaign trail.

Gene McCoy, an active member of both the Bowling League and the card-playing crowd, became the thirty-ninth president of the Club in 1980. Over the years, McCoy, one of Washington's premier lighting specialists and, as one member put it, an expert in "back of the house" matters, provided invaluable contributions to the Club through several major renovations in the late '70s and again in the '80s, volunteering his expertise to work with the contractors.

In September, Howard Day succeeded Tommy Lane as the Club's athletic director and began the programs that would push the Club into the leagues of the finest private athletics centers in Washington.

But it was the ongoing controversy of admitting female members that marked the greatest change in the Club since its merger with the Racquet Club five decades earlier. In the *Washington Star* on February 16, 1980, the paper's popular gossip columnist, The Ear, wrote, "Sound mind, sound body, sound off... Roars of outrage are echoing round the super-stuffy University Club here, Earwigs. A proposal is being bandied about to admit the Fair Sex to Full Membership." It would take four more years before the Ear would be proven right.

Athletic Director Howard Day and squash pro Ghirma Meres give a squash lesson

OPENING THE DOOR TO WOMEN

Traditionally, women had been allowed only in the Taft Dining Room, the bowling alleys, and the women's lounge for cocktails, card playing and the sing-alongs with Art Carchedi. Julia M. Walsh, the first female member of the American Stock Exchange and the first female president of the Greater Washington Board of Trade, was the wife of member Thomas Walsh, then vice chairman of National Permanent Federal Savings and Loan. Despite her position in the Washington business community, she couldn't become a member, and her husband left the Club because of it.

Former president Keith Engel remembers the first time a woman officially sought membership in the Club. It was in the late '70s. "Strangely enough, in all of the years of the club, no woman had ever been put up for a membership," says Engel. When the woman's nomination came before the Board of Admissions, she was "black-balled," but Engel says, "There was a lot of feeling that we should have women members."

President Engel sent out a questionnaire to all members asking their reaction to a proposal to allow a limited female membership with reduced dues—reduced because there wouldn't be any facilities for them in the gym or swimming pool. Sixty-two percent of the members returned the questionnaire and favored the change. But a few of the swimmers, who liked things the way they were, raised some objections.

But times did change. The first woman member, Jo Anne Murray, was a young architect and a graduate of the University of Maryland, the daughter and granddaughter of members. In March 1984, her father, Francis A. Murray, Jr., a real estate executive, proposed her for membership along with James Van Story, a Maryland insurance executive. Ms. Murray told the *Washington Post* at the time, "I have a lot of clients downtown and needed a meeting place to entertain in quiet surroundings. My father is on the board of directors of many clubs and institutions in town, and we considered several... But all of the key clubs are all-male."

The move to admit women came at a time when the Club's membership included House Minority Leader Robert Michel, Archbishop James A. Hickey, and several Supreme Court Justices. Just two months later, the Supreme Court would rule, in a job discrimination suit, that law firms could not discriminate on the basis of sex, race, religion, or national origin in promoting associates to partnerships. At the time, the Club had 2,350 members, an initiation fee of $2,500, and dues set at $900 a year.

Presiding over the controversy at the time was Dale Jernberg, a highly respected banker, who had been elected to the Club presidency in 1982. Jernberg became a member of the Club in 1965, when the president of his bank at that time suggested he join. Dale and Mary Jernberg were very active Club members, especially in the mixed bowling league, where they bowled for many years.

Jernberg was in the final weeks of his term when the issue of a woman member surfaced for the second time in the Club's history. He told the *Post*, "The bylaws don't specifically prohibit women. It's just never been done."

Attorney Lee Ellis, the head of the admissions board, said, "I'm not surprised that we have a well-qualified woman applicant. It's not life or death or the end of an era. It's just a reflection of the way Washington is in 1984.... I think she will be judged just like anyone else."

But both Ellis and Jernberg were to be disappointed. The board rejected Ms. Murray's application, much to the dismay of her father and a number of other members, and the Club lost some business over the decision. The D.C. Bar Association's young lawyers section, which had held its annual dinner at the Club for a number of years, decided to move the event. It was in the midst of the continuing controversy over admitting women that John Chandler, vice president of York International, was elected the Club's forty-first president. Facing objections from both sides, he received letters from a few members who felt they would be unable to belong to a club that discriminated against women.

As the debate raged on inside the Club, outside, the Supreme Court rulings on discrimination issues, EEOC rulings, and a general change in people's attitudes toward the opening up of institutions and organizations to women was remaking the societal landscape. Moreover, women were moving into every area of business and politics, so it was clear the matter was far from settled. On June 14, 1984, a special meeting was held for all members to reconsider a recommendation, first proposed on Jernberg's watch, to amend the bylaws and allow women members in every category. More than two hundred members showed up and two-thirds voted for the proposal.

Right after the meeting, John Chandler and Frank Murray had a drink in the Pershing Grille, where Chandler asked Murray if his daughter was still interested in membership. She was, and when her application was taken up again a month later, this time she won approval. Five years of fractious debate had ended, and a new era for the University Club had begun.

In March 1992, Linda Woolley, director of public affairs for ITT, became the first woman elected to the University Club Board of Governors. She has been followed by a parade of talented and capable women moving through the ranks of Club leadership. President Maurice "Mo" Whalen, who took office in 1995 and is the father of five daughters, put special emphasis during his tenure on appointing women to committees and as committee chairs, giving them the opportunity to gain leadership experience. One of those was Susan Neely, Special Assistant to the President and Director of Communications for the Department of Homeland Security, who has been a very active member on a number of committees since joining the Club in 1991. Ms. Neely now serves during the Club's Centennial year as the first woman president of the Club.

New IRS Rules Impact Club

As tradition-shattering as the decision to admit women was, it wasn't the only change in the '80s to impact the Club in a significant way. On the downside, the IRS eliminated the deductibility of initiation fees and dues as business expenses. Meals bought for business purposes were still deductible, but at only fifty percent instead of the full cost. These changes had a profound and negative impact on Washington restaurants and clubs, which depended on a steady stream of lawyers and lobbyists for whom the business lunch had become a way of life.

On the other hand, an IRS decision in May 1984 allowed members' gifts to a club foundation for charitable purposes to be considered tax-deductible contributions. To take advantage of the change, Dale Jernberg, Tom Donahue, and Keith Engel put together legal documents to create a new Club trust—the University Club Foundation. With no regular source of funding, however, the new entity did little in its first years, but the Foundation would become a major force behind the Club's many philanthropic activities in the '90s.

A QUIET COUPLE OF YEARS

In 1985, Montgomery "Monty" Spindler, former head of UniRoyal's government relations office, was elected president of the Club—the man who had tried in vain to put the rumor of the tunnel to the House Next Door to rest. The "women's issue" had finally been decided and the Club's new data processing system had gone online in 1984, under the supervision of Jack B. Quick, who would become general manager two years later. So, happily for Spindler, his term was relatively free of controversy.

His vice president, C. Carney Smith, the well-known head of a life insurance association, had been very involved in the Club's management for many years and was pegged to move up to the presidency next. His unexpected death, however, elevated then–treasurer Lee Ellis, a partner in the prestigious law firm of Baker and Hostetler, to vice president, while retaining the treasurer's job. When Spindler's term ended in March 1987, Ellis, at only forty-two, became one of the Club's youngest presidents. Like so many Club leaders, Ellis had joined at John Beck's suggestion in 1973, and he and his wife, Paula, were part of the bowling crowd.

RENOVATIONS AND MAJOR CHANGES

As Ellis took over, yet another controversy was beginning to brew. The Club was overdue for another round of renovations and changes. Women had been members for nearly three years but, for all practical purposes, had no facilities. Some male members were still unhappy that women were there at all. Financial problems had plagued the Club for several years, and the bylaws prohibited the raising of dues and fees easily. Ellis's solution was to appoint a special planning committee in April 1987, and the board hired a club management consultant, Bill McMahon, to work with the committee to address the many problems facing the Club. The committee produced a $2.5 million improvement plan for the Clubhouse—the Red Book—the first major renovation in twenty-five years. The plan was approved after a close and contentious vote at a special meeting in January 1988. Most controversial was the plan's recommendation to replace the beloved bowling alleys with a physical fitness center. In the end, the bowlers, who had led the Club over the years, unselfishly put their own wishes second, and sacrificed the bowling alleys for the good of the whole Club.

The next step was to find the financing to underwrite the improvement plan. In the mid-1980s, the Club had met an important milestone by paying off its mortgage, but it was still without the capital to proceed on the improvement plan. Dues were increased as a first step, but the bulk of the money came in December 1988 when Riggs Bank provided a $2.5 million renovation financing loan.

The major renovations got underway in 1989 as Pete Larson, the head of a successful real estate company, was elected Club president. Larson, a great running back at Cornell, had played pro ball as both a Redskin and as a New York Giant. Larson, an active and popular member who had been instrumental with Ellis and others in putting together the renovation plan, had the dubious honor of serving while dust was flying and hammers were disturbing the usually quiet atmosphere of the Club. As East Germans were tearing down the Berlin Wall half a world away, the Club was knocking down a few walls of its own to make way for a new athletic facility, and some members weren't happy about it. A nod of thanks is owed to Bill Schofield and Joe Connor, who volunteered untold hours to move the renovations forward.

At the end of the decade, Paul Burley, the Club's longtime manager, admired for his ability to produce lavish events, retired after eighteen years of good food and good fun at the Club. Many were sorry to see him go. Jack B. Quick, the Club's chief financial officer, who surely had the most memorable of names, took over as Club manager and oversaw the construction, which proved to be quite a challenge. At the end of what was admittedly a difficult year for everyone involved, Larson opted not to seek a second year as president, and Bernie Casey, another of John Beck's law partners and both a swimmer and a squash player, became the Club's forty-fifth president. After the rough going of the previous year's renovations and with the Club facing fifty-four straight months of losses, Casey and the board, which had several new members, decided a change in management was needed. The board turned to long-time member Ray Brophy to lead the effort, and the search to find a new manager was on.

ACTIVITIES ABOUND

With all the controversy and renovations that characterized much of the '80s, one might wonder how anything else went on, but events and activities from sports to special dinners to lectures series highlighted every year. The Board of Governors' New Year's Day Brunches, long a Club tradition, continued through the '80s, as did the annual Candlelight Ball. In 1986, the Club kitchen outdid itself with a special Christmas Eve dinner, modeled after the first Christmas dinner at the White House hosted by John and Abigail Adams in 1800. Called "A Most Sinful Feast," by Mrs. Adams, it included crab claws with dill mustard sauce, winter squash soup, baked ham from the smokehouse, and beef bouilli with horseradish sauce.

In October and December, a two-part lecture series on World War II was held with both films and lectures. In between, the Club heard former Defense Secretary Clark Clifford speak on the historical significance of World War II.

The popular Small World Series continued to provide members with lively international programs such as one from the "Republic of China on Taiwan," which included a fashion show and dancing. The Noon Forum Lecture Series heard from a long list of distinguished leaders, including former Agriculture Secretary John Block, who spoke on American farm policy. CIA Director William J. Casey, a University Club member, also addressed one of the noon luncheons. The "top spy" was a familiar face at the Club, where he was a habitué of the steam room. Members always knew when Casey was "in" by the CIA agents who barred the door to the steam room, keeping out any unwelcome or uninvited visitors—friendly or otherwise.

It wasn't all educational activities that year, though. Just for fun, the band "55 Chevy" rocked and rolled the Club at a "Fabulous Fifties Party." As it did throughout most of the decade, the Club held "meet the artist" nights nearly every month, giving members a chance to get to know local artists and their work. The following year, in 1987, members were learning the waltz, fox trot, and cha-cha at Club-sponsored dance lessons, which they put to good use at the Club's fifth annual Mardi Gras Ball, featuring the music of Fred Perry and his Glenn Miller sounds. Others hopped aboard the Club bus on an outing to Wolf Trap Pavilion for a picnic and the Boston Pops. On weekends, members enjoyed the relaxed elegance of the Tides Lodge, one of Virginia's legendary resorts, on Club-sponsored trips.

1988 saw the Small World Series repeat one of its most popular evenings, featuring the Embassy of Greece. The Russian women's tennis team, which was playing in the

Mardi Gras celebration!

Virginia Slims Tournament for the first time, visited the Club. Theater parties took members to see "Les Miserables," while bowlers held a dinner dance.

For St. Patrick's Day, the Club's French chef, Claude Picard, put on an Irish feast, including a raw oyster bar, corned beef and cabbage, lamb stew, and soda bread. Meanwhile, the inimitable Art Carchedi provided his usual wonderful music to go along with Chef Picard's gourmet fare in the Dining Room.

*Members enjoy
St. Patrick's Day
festivities*

The head table took a moment out of the St. Patrick's Day festivities for a group shot. (Seated l to r) Professor George O'Brien, Emcee Bernie Casey, and David Kendall. (Standing l to r) Lee Ellis and Judge Jack Farley.

*Art Carchedi,
pianist
extraordinaire*

While University Club members are frequent recipients of awards, in the summer of 1988, one of the Club's most illustrious members, the Most Reverend James A. Hickey, Archbishop of Washington, received quite a special honor when he was named cardinal by Pope John Paul II. Cardinal Patrick O'Boyle, who served as the first resident archbishop of Washington from 1948 to 1973 and was a former chancellor of Catholic University, was also a Club member. The cardinals were two of a long list of members of the clergy from many faiths who have been special members of the University Club family over the years.

The decade ended with one of the Club's most "colorful" episodes when someone forgot to turn off the swimming pool while renovations were being done over the Christmas holiday break. When swimmers returned ready to work off their Christmas pounds, they found that the water in the pool was 105 degrees and had turned a distinctive orange color. It took eight hundred pounds of ice to put the pool back in operation.

All in all, the '80s proved to be a tumultuous time for the world and the Club, but when the decade ended, this nearly ninety-year-old institution had transformed itself—welcoming women, taking its first steps toward reestablishing itself as one of the city's premier athletic facilities, and moving toward a sounder financial footing. Perhaps the farewell comments of President Reagan, who occupied the White House for much of the '80s, could be applied to the University Club as well: "Not bad. Not bad at all."

President Mike McKevitt and
Vice President Nelson Deckelbaum
enjoying a smile during the
Founders' Day Dinner on February 20, 1993

Chapter Nine

1990s: More Renovations
and a Reenergized Club

he last decade of the twentieth century dawned on an optimistic note as freedom and democracy, long denied, swept out the old Communist regimes of Eastern Europe and the Soviet Union. For the millions who had lived under the yoke of tyranny for more than fifty years, it was a new day. Some claimed it was the end of history. It wasn't. In 1990, the dust had barely settled at the University Club—both literally and figuratively—when America once again found itself at war, this time against Saddam Hussein in the desert sands of Kuwait. Like the Vietnam War, however, Desert Storm had little direct impact on the Club, though members took pride in the fact that the commander in chief, President George H. W. Bush, was a former Club member. By 1992, the political winds were blowing in a different direction, as voters opted for a new president and party with the election of William Jefferson Clinton as the forty-second president of the United States. It would be a decade of economic growth and impeachment; scandal and scientific breakthrough; military victory and failure. Washington seemed to be on a permanent political merry-go-round that began with the election of President Clinton in 1992. In 1994, voters elected the first Republican Congress in forty years. Two years later, impeachment rocked the country, but in 1998, Democrats made gains in Congress. The year 2000 would see the partisan merry-go-round turn again.

Despite the seemingly endless controversies swirling around Washington, the University Club enjoyed years of quiet reinvigoration during the first half of the decade. Two years before the changing of the guard at the White House, the Club made some major changes of its own. First was the election of lawyer Bernard "Bernie" Casey, a senior partner in Reed Smith, as Club president. Casey had already served one year on the Board of Governors and a stint on the Board of Admissions, a position John Beck had initially urged him to seek. After the controversy over the decision to remake the bowling alleys into an expanded fitness center, the Club was ready for a president who could bridge the gap between the older members and the young guard who had pushed for the changes. Casey was the man for the job.

The second major change was the hiring of Albert Armstrong, a highly respected professional club manager, to take over the day-to-day running of the Club as general manager. Armstrong, a graduate of Pennsylvania State University with a BS in Food Service and Housing/Administration, had been the general manager of the Columbia Club in Indianapolis. Under his watch, the Columbia Club undertook a major renovation project, saw a significant increase in membership, and returned to profitability. It was that track record, combined with his visionary plans for the University Club, that earned him the search committee's confidence, and on October 1, 1990, Albert Armstrong began what has been a long and very successful tenure with the Club. For Armstrong, however, the job began as a baptism by fire when local unions tried to organize the Club's 150 employees. The effort failed, and Armstrong turned his attention to the Club's financial problems.

NEW DIRECTIONS

While the renovation battles of the late '80s were over, the financial difficulties they caused weren't. The Club had lost a substantial number of members, but, to their credit, not the bowlers. Sadly, 1991 did see the retirement of Bill Schofield as a board member and treasurer after seven years of extraordinary service to the Club.

*General Manager
Albert Armstrong
with President
George H. W. Bush*

In the early '90s, the board and Armstrong focused on putting the Club's financial affairs in order and, among other things, voted to establish a monthly minimum in the Taft Dining Room. After the contentious '80s, the board realized that the Club needed a new approach to replenish the membership rolls and took several steps to make the Club more attractive to both new and former members. First, it began a series of unobtrusive renovations to spruce up the look of the Club, in order to attract new members. Then the board moved in a more "family friendly" direction by creating activities that would bring members and their children to the Club. At the same time, the Club began sponsoring events and entertainment at a pace not seen in many years. As Bernie Casey puts it, "The Club took on a new feel and a new look."

FOUNDER'S DAY DINNERS—BACK TO THE FUTURE

One of the first events created to help reinvigorate the Club took members "back to the future." With the exception of a few anniversary celebrations, the University Club's famous annual banquets, known for presidents and politics, singing and speechifying, ended in 1913. But in 1991, the Club decided to bring back the tradition with the creation of an annual Founder's Day Dinner that would feature remarks by a prestigious speaker and include the announcement of "Member of the Year." Since then, every year, the president and the Board select a member for special recognition of extraordinary efforts on behalf of the Club. Judge Loren Smith was the first recipient.

Held on February 16, 1991, following the tradition of the original banquets, the reconstituted Founder's Day evening was, as president Bernie Casey put it, "an impresario performance." The dinner featured patriotic music and a replica of the original

UNIVERSITY CLUB MEMBERS OF THE YEAR

1990	Judge Loren Smith	1996	Charles W. deSeve
1991	Ambassador Lev E. Dobriansky	1997	Paul R. D'Armiento
1992	The Honorable Donald Brotzman	1998	Christopher J. O'Shea
1993	Monsignor Peter J. Vaghi	1999	John A. Beck—Member of the Millennium
1994	Leonard A.C. Eiserer	2000	Peter L. Goldman
1995	Susan Neely	2001	John Chandler

2002
Laura Arth

Founder's Day menu from the early 1900s, along with fine champagne and wines. The evening's crown jewel was a multi-tiered birthday cake, complete with pyrotechnics, in celebration of the Club's eighty-seventh birthday. Judge Loren Smith, recipient of what was to become the annual "Member of the Year" Award, turned what was expected to be a serious acceptance into a hilarious performance of magic stunts that had the crowd roaring.

SMOKE GETS IN THEIR EYES

Judge Smith was also behind what has today become one of the Club's most popular events—its cigar dinners. In 1991, Smith, a cigar aficionado, discovered that Windows on the World Restaurant in New York had recently held the first cigar dinner in the United States. He wanted the University Club to be second and went to Albert Armstrong with a proposal. Not long after, the Club could proudly claim itself home of the second cigar dinner ever held in the U.S. The dinners, put on as often as four times a year after that, were black tie affairs. Politicians, Supreme Court justices, television celebrities, and other glitterati showed up for the somewhat raucous affairs, which quickly established several traditions. Among them was the requirement that guests must stand and tell a story or provide entertainment for the members. One evening, Mark Russell leapt from his table to regale members with an impromptu performance of piano and political satire that left the audience howling.

On another occasion, Pierre Salinger, President Kennedy's portly press secretary, shared a little-known story about the Cuban embargo. The embargo was imposed in

Albert Armstrong, Supreme Court Justice Clarence Thomas, Vice President Dan Quayle, and Chief Judge of the Court of Federal Claims Loren Smith attend a Club cigar dinner

February 1962 after Fidel Castro nationalized billions of dollars of American property and businesses. But just before he made it official, Kennedy sent Salinger on a mission— to buy every Cuban cigar he could lay his hands on. The president even provided a White House limousine to cart back the "contraband." Salinger hit most of the good cigar stores in town, buying boxes and boxes of Cubans, no doubt raising a few suspicions in the process. Once Salinger was safely back in the White House, and the president was assured of an ample supply of his favorite smokes, Kennedy signed the embargo. The rest is history.

Loren Smith has been the emcee of every banquet, again by tradition, and his fellow jurist, Richard Leon of the U.S. District Court, has served as the banquet's "poet laureate." At the close of each dinner, Leon would read the famed poem by Rudyard Kipling called "The Betrothed." In it, a young man is given an ultimatum by his new wife: "cigars or me." As Leon would read the final line, the crowd would chime in unison, "A woman is only a woman, but a good cigar is a smoke." Guaranteed to bring down the house every time.

MORE ACTIVITIES

The Founder's Day celebration and the cigar dinners were only two of many new additions to the Club's increasingly busy social scene. Membership Appreciation Day kicked off New Year's Day, 1991, with a "progressive dinner" that took members through the Club for food and drink. It was a thank-you for members held in the tradition of the earlier Governors' Receptions, which had been held for decades on New Year's Day. Membership Appreciation Day became so popular that one year the Club served more than 1,300 people.

In 1991, thanks to the efforts of the Golf Committee, the Club hosted its first annual golf championship at Norbeck Country Club—an event that has become one of the highlights of the sports year at the Club. By 1993, the tournament had found a permanent home at the Bretton Woods Country Club, and its own trophy, the Johnston Lemon Trophy, donated by member Jim Lemon and awarded to the Club champion each year. Proceeds from the championship go to the University Club Foundation to help fund its many charitable projects.

The Club's preeminent swimmer, Blake Clark, then eighty-three years old, won the Athlete of the Year award that year after having won the Corcoran Award in 1985. Clark, who died in 2003 at the age of ninety-four, was one of the Club's most flamboyant characters. With a doctorate in English from Vanderbilt University, he lived a colorful life teaching English at the University of Hawaii in the '30s and '40s. Clark witnessed the Japanese attack on Pearl Harbor and wrote a book, *Remember Pearl Harbor*, about the experience, which became a movie. During World War II, he worked for the OSS and later was an editor for *Reader's Digest*. He once wrote an article for the magazine about a new postwar import, the Volkswagen, which resulted in his ownership of the regional rights to sell the German cars in the mid-Atlantic.

The University Club's swimming team had its own championship moment the following year, when it defeated the Metropolitan Club. Led by captain Richard McBride, the UC team opened the meet with a rousing cheer, "U. Club, U. Club. No blue blood! Swim hard. Drink hard. Cut the rug!"

But sports weren't the only game in town. Agatha Christie would have felt right at home at the Club's murder mystery dinner, held on Friday the Thirteenth in November 1992. Everyone survived the evening. On a more serious note, the UC Capital Breakfast Series brought prominent speakers to the Club to discuss important topics of the day in the context of members' faith. "Meet the Artist" receptions continued to bring members together with some of the area's most talented artists.

About this time, Lee Carlson cooked up what he called the "Dull Men's Club" and invited male members to join up. Women couldn't join, he said, because they weren't dull. While the purpose of the Dull Men's Club remains one of the great mysteries of the ages, Carlson's hilarious sense of the absurd was clearly evident in the flyers he would put up around the Club promoting his dull club "events." One invited members to a Dull Men's Club "bus tour." The excursion, however, entailed parking a bus in front of the Club and then giving tours in and around the bus. In May 1994, another flyer promoted a "Spam Barbecue" promising Spam grilled to perfection and gourmet side dishes like lime Jell-o. The biggest joke of all was the fact that the club was purely a figment of Carlson's wonderful sense of humor. Nonetheless, his "dull" routines entertained more than one Club crowd at cigar dinners and other fun evenings.

A Change in Financial Philosophy

By mid-decade, the Club had stabilized financially, paid off a substantial portion of its $2.6 million debt, and had made a strategic change its fiscal philosophy. Rather than a burden, debt was now seen as a tool to strengthen the Club, to plan for its future, and to focus on capital investment. With the running and financing of the Club becoming a much more complicated business venture, board meetings were no longer held over dinner. Instead, the board decided to begin meeting at 5:30, and only when business was finished would drinks and dinner begin.

The Club had also begun to build membership during these years, under the leadership of a series of Club presidents—Bernie Casey, Mike McKevitt, and Nelson Deckelbaum. As the membership drain turned around and the rolls began to swell, the Club's financial position turned around, too.

UNIVERSITY CLUB BOARDS
AND COMMITTEES

BOARDS

- Board of Governors
- Board of Admissions
- Foundation

COMMITTEES

- Bylaws & Rules
- Centennial
- Communications
- Community Affairs
- Entertainment
- Finance
- Golf
- House
- International
- Literature & Arts
- Long Range Planning
- Membership Development
- Proctor Dougherty Society
- Restaurant
- Sports

MEMBERS GET INVOLVED

As the membership numbers moved higher, the board began to build a much larger committee structure. In 1904, the University Club founders created five committees to oversee the management and planning for the Club and its future. Today, there are sixteen standing committees and three boards: the Board of Governors, the Board of Admissions, and the Foundation Board. Altogether, this new committee structure can boast of 300 to 350 volunteers who help maintain Club morale, encourage Club loyalty and participation, and ensure that the Club reflects the values and preferences of all its members.

In 1992, Bernie Casey's successful term ended and a well-known lobbyist, James "Mike" McKevitt, took the helm. Mike grew up in Spokane, Washington, across the street from Bing Crosby. His older brother and Bing used to entertain the townspeople on Saturday nights at neighborhood theaters—shades of Crosby and Hope. A tireless promoter of the Club, Mike was a former congressman from Colorado, but some of his brother's showmanship obviously rubbed off. No Club president ever concocted more reasons to have an event than Mike McKevitt. There was a party to celebrate the naming of the Taft Dining Room, another to name the Franklin Room, and still another to reopen the Men's Grille after minor renovations and change its name to the Pershing Grille, in honor of the man who had laid the cornerstone of the building in 1920. The portrait of Black Jack Pershing that hangs in the Grille today was a gift of Mike McKevitt. Even bad news couldn't stop Mike. He once threw a bash to dedicate the grand opening of a new first floor bathroom after the pipes burst.

One of the Club's most special evenings took place on September 19, 1992, when Miss Laurence Belanger was recognized for her many years of outstanding service to the Club. More than seventy dedicated "Taft dwellers" commissioned artist Vits Knuble to

1993 University Club Follies participants

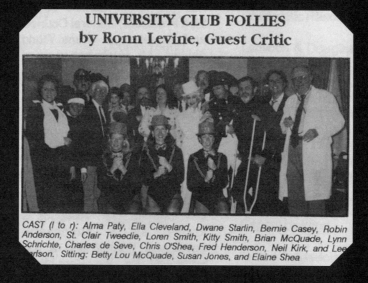

UNIVERSITY CLUB FOLLIES
by Ronn Levine, Guest Critic

CAST (l to r): Alma Paty, Ella Cleveland, Dwane Starlin, Bernie Casey, Robin Anderson, St. Clair Tweedie, Loren Smith, Kitty Smith, Brian McQuade, Lynn Schrichte, Charles de Seve, Chris O'Shea, Fred Henderson, Neil Kirk, and Lee [Ca]rlson. Sitting: Betty Lou McQuade, Susan Jones, and Elaine Shea

paint Miss Laurence's portrait, which was unveiled at a surprise reception just before the Cornerstone Ball held that evening. It hangs today in the room named after her.

The following year the Club "Follies" was the highlight of the social season. The rollicking performance was written and directed by the talented Lynn Schrichte, who also starred in the production. Twenty-five cast members, including Sue Neely, Bernie Casey, and Judge Loren Smith, spent four months rehearsing for the "great performance" which featured singing, dancing, and enough witty dialogue to keep Neil Simon entertained.

MINOR RENOVATIONS

As part of the board's recruitment plan, the Club underwent a paintbrush, low-budget sprucing up in the early '90s that included the Pershing Grille, the Taft Dining Room, the library, and the Franklin Room. The billiard lounge got both a coat of fresh paint and a new top-flight billiard table donated by the members of the Proctor Dougherty Society. On the third floor, the card room was transformed into the Club's administrative offices, and the guest rooms were also redecorated.

A REVITALIZED FOUNDATION

It was on McKevitt's watch that the University Club Foundation got a revamping as well. Earlier, in May 1989, Keith Engel had asked two former Club presidents, Lee Ellis and John Chandler, to join him as trustees of the Foundation. Ellis and Engel nominated Chandler to serve as president, and under his leadership, the newly formed board began to explore ways that the Foundation might better support the Club's charitable activities. When Albert Armstrong arrived at the Club, he, too, was very interested in the Foundation due to his experiences at the Columbia Club, which had used a similar entity to great advantage. So, the Foundation Board and the new general manager joined forces to strengthen what all felt could be a vehicle to advance the Club's mission and activities. The first decision was to change the legal form of the Foundation in order to more effectively carry out its charitable programs and maximize tax advantages to the membership. On June 3, 1992, the reconstituted Foundation was incorporated as a 501(c)3 corporation, with members Mort Caplin and Milt Cerny doing the legal legwork pro bono. They remain advisors to the Foundation today. The first directors of the newly reconfigured Foundation were Ellis, Engel, and Chandler, along with Bernie Casey and former Colorado Congressman Don Brotzman, who was one of the Club's most active and involved members. Over the past ten years, the Foundation Board has expanded to include twelve members, who meet monthly (except during the summer, when president Chandler, an avid golfer, deserts Washington for Maine and gives his colleagues on the board a breather, too). In large part, it has been Chandler's extraordinary leadership and dedication that transformed the Foundation into the integral part of Club life that it has become today.

THE LIBRARY PROJECT

In 1998, the Foundation received a large and continuing endowment from the widow of one of the Club's longtime members, Leona Keefer. Thanks to Dale Jernberg, who worked with Mrs. Keefer, her generous and ongoing contributions, amounting to more than $100,000 a year, help support certain Club activities. Nearly $10,000 a month is allotted to support the library, including the librarian's salary and the cost of books and periodicals. To bring it up to date for the new millennium, the library was renovated again in 2000, adding the latest in computer technology. A century ago, when the Club was founded, the first budget showed an allocation of $75 for books—a lot of money at that time. Today, the Club library is home to more than six thousand books, along with many magazine and newspaper subscriptions. Portraits of Leona and Arthur Keefer, hanging in the library named in their honor, now keep watch over this modern reading room. The beautiful Remington bronzes, also gracing the library for all to enjoy, were a gift of Dr. John Sanders.

2003 UNIVERSITY CLUB FOUNDATION BOARD MEMBERS

John W. Chandler, President
Donald G. Brotzman,
Vice President
Lee T. Ellis, Secretary
William G. Brennan, Treasurer

Laura Arth
Scott E. Beck
Bernard J. Casey
Leonard A.C. Eiserer
Barry Hart
Dale L. Jernberg
Virginia A. McArthur
Douglas K. Spaulding

THE BOOK FAIR DEBUTS

Education, an important part of the Club's beginnings, today remains central to the Club's mission—"to promote science, literature and art, and to maintain a Clubhouse for purposes of social intercourse amongst its members." At the University Club, books have always been an important part of accomplishing that mission. For decades, the Keefer Library has been a quiet haven for members to sink into a comfortable chair and read the day's news or the latest bestsellers—occasionally written by a University Club member. So, in 1991, when Paul D'Armiento, a new member, proposed that the Club begin sponsoring an annual "Book Fair," it was an easy sell. At its inaugural fair, more than sixty authors were "in house" to sign books and sip champagne with members. Today, the fair attracts some of the hottest authors of the day. Writers such as David Brinkley, James Glassman, Chief Justice William Rehnquist, Cokie Roberts, Chris Matthews, Phyllis Richman, Pierre Salinger, Eugene McCarthy, Dick Schaap, and Jim Lehrer are just a few of the many nationally known authors who have headlined the Club's Book Fairs over the last decade.

The Keefer Library was the Foundation's first major undertaking; but throughout the '90s, under president Chandler's direction, the Foundation reached an endowment

Arthur and Leona Keefer

The newly refurbished library

*Members enjoy
the book fair*

of more than $1 million in 1999. As the endowment has increased, so have the Foundation's activities and responsibilities. Today, the Foundation oversees the John Beck Scholarship and the University Club Employee Scholarship Funds, so important to the UC family. Thanks to the Foundation and member Jack Morton's efforts, a beautiful piano now sits in the Taft Dining Room and a wonderful portrait of Benjamin Franklin graces the Franklin Room. Funding for Embassy Nights, the creation of the past presidents' portraits, and this Centennial history are among the Foundation's many philanthropic contributions to the Club. The wheelchair lift in the front vestibule was also financed by the Foundation and sponsored by member Philip Buchen, once counsel to President Gerald Ford.

DISTINGUISHED WASHINGTONIAN AWARD

One of the Foundation's most important projects has been providing support for the Club's "Distinguished Washingtonian of the Year" award and dinner. In 1997, the Club decided to create the award to honor an outstanding Washingtonian associated with the arts. The Board of Governors, with advice from the Literature and Arts Committee, chooses the annual winner. The first recipient was Elizabeth Campbell, founder and first president of WETA, Washington's award-winning public broadcasting television station. Other recipients have included Wilhelmina Cole Holladay, founder and president of the Women's Museum of the Arts; Leonard Slatkin, music director of the National Symphony Orchestra; Michael Kahn, artistic director of the Shakespeare Theatre; internationally known mezzo soprano Denyce Graves; and political satirist Mark Russell.

THE PDS SOCIETY KICKS OFF

In the late 1980s, a group of younger members began holding what became affection-ately known as "Bashes." Twelve members each invited fifty people to these raucous affairs, usually held after work, where beer and a band was the prevailing social scheme. Originally held four times a year, Bashes attracted sizable audiences of half members and half non-members.

The Club had had a Junior Members Committee for many years. By 1990, its most active members, including Peter Farrell, Chris Ambrose, Tom Kirlin, and half a dozen

Ruth Bader Ginsburg along with Distinguished Washingtonian Award winner Denyce Graves and the Becks

Michael Kahn, left, the 2002 Distinguished Washingtonian Award winner, with Mark Russell, the 2001 winner

others, had turned the committee into both a fun group and a force for change in the Club—though occasionally they found themselves in hot water. That year, the group had asked manager Jack Quick for permission to watch the Fourth of July fireworks on the Club's roof. Quick approved the request, but when the group arrived that evening, they found a newly installed padlock on the door to the roof. Not to be deterred, they simply broke the padlock, headed to the roof, and celebrated the nation's birthday in grand style. The board, however, got wind of the "breakout" and called the group on the carpet. Having gotten permission, the gang defended their right to the roof, but in the name of Club harmony, they apologized nonetheless.

While this was a crowd that enjoyed a good time, they were also a very socially conscious group of members who felt deeply that their success in life obligated them to do more to help others. By the early '90s, these younger members were looking for something more than just Bashes, as popular as they were. Many wanted to be involved in both social events designed for a younger set and also activities that would give them an opportunity to help others. And so, in the fall of 1991, the Proctor Dougherty Society was officially formed for members 21–35 years of age, and a portion of every Bash ticket was donated to charitable activities.

TAKING CARE OF THE FAMILY

The Society's first philanthropic venture was the establishment of the University Club Employee Scholarship Fund for the Club's highly valued employees and their families. The Scholarship Fund helps support educational scholarships for qualified Club employees and their children. These scholarships help fund everything from culinary courses to college degree programs.

As time passed and the popularity of the Fund grew, the PDS formed a separate subcommittee to search out new ways to raise money for its support while putting the supervisory responsibility for the scholarships in the hands of the UC Foundation board of trustees. Today, recipients are chosen by the Scholarship Committee. Altogether, the Club has raised more than $100,000 through its various scholarship funds for employees and their children over the past ten years.

PROSPERITY RETURNS

In 1994, Nelson Deckelbaum, a third-generation Washingtonian and senior partner in his own prominent law firm, was elected the forty-seventh president of the Club. During Deckelbaum's tenure, the Club's financial picture brightened considerably. As the economy boomed and the board's strategy to attract members began to pay off, prosperity returned. One of the Club's strongest proponents of women, minorities, and families, Deckelbaum continued to encourage the recruitment of new members throughout his successful term.

The Club also celebrated its ninetieth birthday with the publication of a wonderful new Club history, written by longtime members Ken Reese and Bob Lowenstein.

MEMBERS PUSH FOR COMMUNITY INVOLVEMENT

As the membership changed in the '90s, more and more members were urging the Club to become actively involved in the community. For nearly a century, the University Club had stood as a center of good fellowship, leadership, and intellectual excellence in the hub of downtown Washington. But now, many members believed, it was time the Club recognized that it was also part of a neighborhood and needed to become more involved in helping meet community needs.

So in 1995, Peter Farrell came up with the idea of a Community Affairs Committee to provide members with "an opportunity to give something back to the neighbor-

Tom Walker addresses high school students at College Bound Night

The passing of the presidential gavel: Mike McKevitt leaves the presidency after two years of service, and Nelson Deckelbaum becomes the forty-seventh president

hood—a community of acute social need." At about the same time, D.C. city councilman Jack Evans, a UC member, came to the Club with a problem. It seemed that D.C.'s budget woes had reached such a low point that city parks were no longer being maintained. He asked the Club to "adopt" one of the parks. Before long, Stead Park, located behind Foundry Methodist AME Church on P Street, became the newest addition to the University Club family. The park had soccer and baseball fields, a play area, and an aging "clubhouse," which had once been the carriage house of an estate now long gone. As its first project, a crew of Club members and some of the maintenance staff taped, trimmed, plastered, painted, and generally repaired the deteriorating carriage house while others cleaned up the park. It was a remarkable day. University Club members

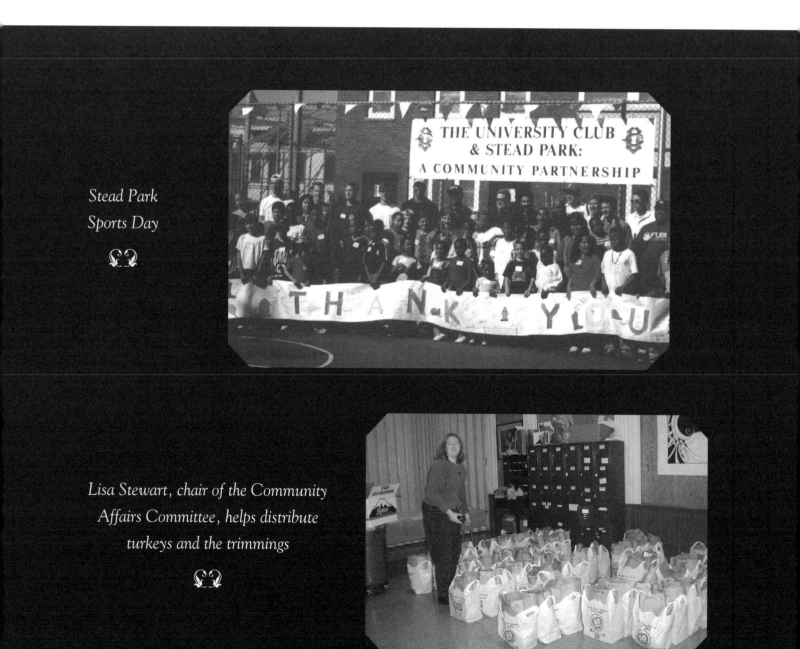

Stead Park
Sports Day

❧

Lisa Stewart, chair of the Community
Affairs Committee, helps distribute
turkeys and the trimmings

❧

were out in force, gardening, tree trimming, weed whacking, sandbox raking, trashcan painting, and blacktop sweeping. Four hours later, Stead Park shined.

The next year, improved landscaping was on the agenda. The year after, the sand box area was refurbished and a shade pergola built by member Michael Wardman's construction company. Next came an automated irrigation system and new grass for the park's field, but the Club hit a small bump in the road with that project. It discovered that rats consider irrigation piping quite a delicacy. Working with other businesses in the area, the Club led a successful effort to reduce the rat population through a community-wide cleanup.

What began as a small rehabilitation project has today turned into a wonderful relationship, capped off every year with the Club's "Sports Day at Stead Park." Two to three hundred children now come to the sports party, which features hot dogs, ice cream, prizes, and "tryouts" in a range of sports and games put on by members of the Club's lacrosse, rugby, soccer, and basketball teams, as well as a few golfers.

Fighting Hunger

With the success of the Stead Park effort, the Community Affairs Committee turned to another neighborhood problem: hunger. Peter Farrell passed the mantle of leadership to Greg Grooms, who expanded the Committee's efforts. Right behind the Club, the Foundry Methodist AME Church already had a "feed the hungry" program in place. So, the Committee joined in a partnership with the historic church that, over the years, has created several programs to help those in need. The first was the "Turkey Triumph." Initially, members' donations provided turkeys to the church for Thanksgiving. Today, the fund has grown into a food donation program that stretches nearly five months, from Thanksgiving to Easter. Next came the Secret Santa program, begun in 1996, with many generous members playing the role of Santa's "helpers" by donating presents to needy children identified by the church. More recently, the Community Affairs Committee has expanded its activities to include an annual winter coat drive and a "professional clothing" drive for the homeless.

The Committee also initiated the "College Bound" counseling program to reach out to inner city kids contemplating college, and the Club now fields a team for the Race for the Cure to raise money for breast cancer research as well.

Renovation Controversy Strikes Again

In 1995, Maurice "Mo" Whalen, Washington managing partner in a national accounting and management consulting firm, took over the Club presidency at a time when many members had had their fill of change. In the previous ten years, the Club had admitted women, gone through several difficult renovations, changed management, and had done so, at times, in an atmosphere of confrontation and controversy. Although Whalen had appointed a special Blue Ribbon Task Force of members to assess the Club's needs, it's hardly surprising that when the task force proposed that the Club redo the athletic facility once more—this time to provide more space for women members, whose locker room was woefully small, the plan was defeated by the membership in a heated meeting. Whalen's vision was recognized a few years later when the Club finally undertook extensive renovations of the athletic facilities, but at the time, Whalen took the heat for what most members would now acknowledge was an idea ahead of its time.

GOING INTERNATIONAL—AGAIN

The University Club's international interests and traditions go back to the Club's earliest days, when members of the diplomatic community were regular guests and speakers, as they often are today. So it was no surprise that Whalen and the rest of the board seriously considered a merger proposal made by the International Club in 1995, as the sister club faced financial difficulties. In the end, the board rejected the proposal and instead took over the lease, changing the facility to the University Club International Center. Two years later, in January 1998, the Center closed when the building's landlord made unacceptable changes in the lease. Happily, 170 former International Club members accepted the University Club's invitation to join its ranks.

But the International Center wasn't the only focus of international activity in the Club during the '90s. The popular Small World Series had ended in the '80s but was brought back to life with a new name—Embassy Nights—which were an immediate hit with members. These entertaining and educational evenings have highlighted a parade of countries, including Argentina, Slovakia, Mexico, Egypt, Turkey, Luxembourg, Bosnia, and Greece. Embassy Nights are only a part of the Club's extensive international program.

Over the years—especially in the '90s and beyond—foreign affairs experts have been regular speakers at the Club, lecturing on a wide range of foreign policy issues. For example, in 1996, members heard Ambassador James Lilley speak on "Peace and Conflict in East Asia." In 1998, member Frank Ahmed was instrumental in arranging a luncheon with Her Excellency Ljubica Z. Aceuska of Macedonia, while John Walker, one of the Club's most influential internationalists and an expert on security issues, held seminars on terrorism at the Club long before the attacks of September 11, 2001. Walker also brought many prominent foreign diplomats to speak, including ambassador Tedo Djaparidze of Georgia.

In the late '90s, Dr. Norman Bailey, a member who has been very active in bringing many national and international speakers and new members to the Club, came up with an idea to make the Club's many international guests feel welcome, especially those from the diplomatic community. Bailey suggested that when an ambassador was scheduled to visit the Club, the flag of his or her home country should be put in the lobby as a symbolic welcome. It was such a good idea that then–president Beck held a reception honoring ambassadors who were Club members and asking them to ceremonially present their nation's flag to the Club, much as they do at the White House. The response was overwhelming, with more than forty ambassadors attending the international affair. Originally, the flags stood in the Governor's Room. Today, they line the vestibule in the Club's front entrance—a perfect symbol for a Club with a long history of interest in international affairs.

STAYING BUSY

In the mid-1990s, as more and more members were added to the rolls, Club activities continued to flourish. A theater party in 1996 saw Jerry Lewis in "Damn Yankees." The Japanese ambassador came to lunch. There was a "Hollywood Night" and a "U.S.O. Night" complete with the "Andrews Sisters." The PDS took bike trips in the summer, and some members were trapped in the Club during the "blizzard of '96." Two of them, Dr. Charles de Seve and Sarah Trott, who met at the Club during the storm, were married a few months later in the Club's library. Still other members danced the night away on a Caribbean Cruise Night held in the Pershing Grille.

On April 16, members were invited to a tongue-in-cheek "Taxpayers Bawl" in the Grille. To help soothe the pain of tax day, beer was only a dollar. That year, members could also opt for "Porterhouses and Martinis Night" or the "Wild Game Dinner."

Club president Susan Neely and her family enjoy the Family Tree Lighting Party

In February 1996, one of the most unusual episodes in the Club's long history with the FBI took place when attorney Tony Bisceglie, a UC member, received a call from David Kaczynski, the brother of the Unabomber who, at the time, was still at large. Kaczynski had begun to suspect that his brother, Ted, could be the notorious terrorist after the Unabomber's "manifesto" was printed in the *New York Times*. Under Bisceglie's protection, the brother flew to Washington to meet with the FBI and stayed at the University Club during his visit. In April, Ted Kaczynski's cabin was raided and news of his brother's cooperation leaked. In a matter of hours, Kaczynski's Schenectady home was surrounded by reporters. In an effort to protect David Kaczynski's privacy, Bisceglie promised the media a news conference on the following Easter Monday. Then, he picked up the phone and called Albert Armstrong. That Monday, more than one hundred reporters crowded into the University Club, where Bisceglie briefed them on David Kaczynski's difficult decision to turn his brother in to the FBI. The rest is history.

In 1997, one of the Club's most energetic and active members, Peter Farrell, moved up to the Club presidency. Farrell, a real estate investment banker at the time, was one of the original founding fathers of the Proctor Dougherty Society. During Farrell's tenure, the Club put even more emphasis on creating family-friendly events and a more welcoming atmosphere in the Club toward children. Offering swimming lessons in the pool and a special kids menu, with favorites like hamburgers and fries, in the dining room are two good examples of the efforts the Club undertook to make families feel at home. In the 1998 holiday season, already a tradition-filled time, the Club added one more: the annual Family Tree Lighting Party, complete with a visit from Old St. Nick. The popular event is still creating wonderful memories for a whole new generation of Club children. The bowling alleys may have been sacrificed to progress, but that didn't stop the bowlers from bowling elsewhere and getting together at the Club for their annual bowling banquets; the group celebrated fifty years of UC bowling in 1998. That year also saw the Club unveil its new website and kick off the Membership Development Committee's Millennium Campaign to spur Club membership.

Under Farrell's leadership, the Club undertook a number of renovation projects, but not the controversial women's locker room renovation. An avid squash player, Farrell got member support for a new ASB international squash court, which helped further solidify the Club's reputation as the preeminent squash center in the city. The new court was the first regulation international court in Washington.

The Pershing Grille also underwent a major renovation during Farrell's term, adding the popular "Humidor Lounge" and an elegant wood bar, but one thing didn't change—the "Club Table" in the back corner of the Grille. Originally, there were two tables at lunch—one for talkers and one for those who appreciated a quiet meal. At night, when the table morphed into the "5:30 Club," only talkers were allowed.

After the renovation, the non-talkers table disappeared into history, but not its counterpart. For more than fifty years, the Club Table has been a center of stimulating conversation for members of every stripe. Admiral Willie Reese, who commanded the aircraft carrier "Enterprise," was a regular at the table from the 1950s almost until his death in 1989. Arriving every evening at precisely 5:25 and leaving at exactly 7:00, the Admiral would drink one beer and one bourbon.

Ken Reese, a Club member since 1960, says the Table is steeped in tradition, with longtime members like Paul Allen, Bryce Rea, and Dick Peterson joining Reese for the nightly bull sessions along with a rotating cast of characters. But it's not just old-timers at the Table. Younger men and, now, women have always been a part of the crowd too, bringing their own spice to the conversations. Regular Peter O'Rourke, who rides a

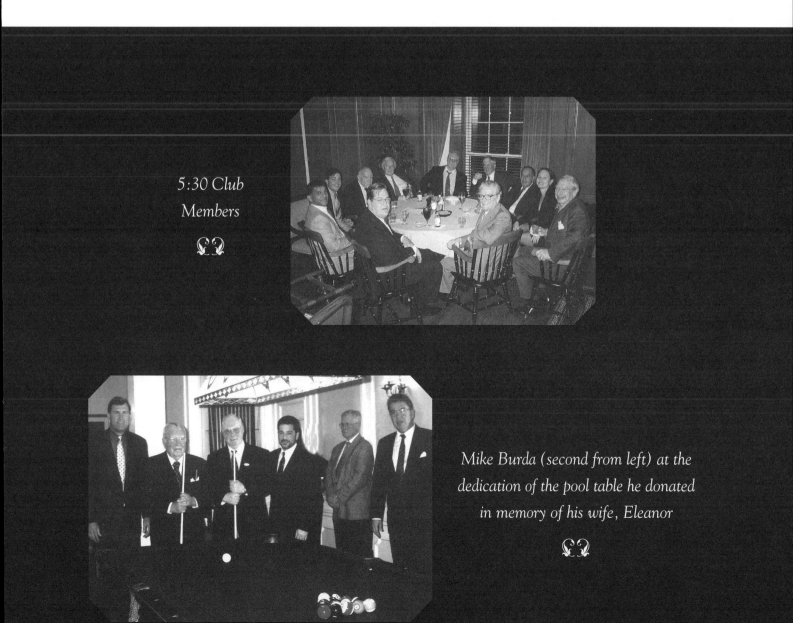

5:30 Club
Members

Mike Burda (second from left) at the
dedication of the pool table he donated
in memory of his wife, Eleanor

Harley, occasionally surfs a hurricane, and just got his pilot's license, says he likes to spend his evenings at the table "trying to set the old guys straight."

The billiard lounge also got a major updating in the late '90s. Member Michael Burda provided the spectacular centerpiece of the lounge renovation—a top-of-the-line, hand-carved Brazilian billiard table donated in memory of his late wife, Eleanor. While a pool table might seem an odd choice for a memorial, in Mrs. Burda's case, it was perfect: her family's company invented and sold the first plastic billiard balls. When her husband wanted a good table, the family connections got him right to the top. He called the president of Brunswick and told him he wanted the best table they had. Anyone who has played a game of billiards in the University Club knows Mike Burda got what he asked for. New chairs, tables, carpeting, and even acoustic panels to minimize noise made the new billiards lounge another fine addition to the Club's growing inventory of first-class rooms.

The Club's front entrance also got a new look, though it wasn't what Farrell expected. Originally, a decision was made to put a canopy over the front entrance to give members some protection from the weather as they exited their cars. As the planning got underway, however, Farrell suggested to manager Albert Armstrong that as long as they were at it, the Club might as well do some landscaping. Then the board decided to redo the driveway, and then came new lights. The entrance looked great, but by the time the external renovations were finished, there was no money left for the canopy. No one seemed to mind.

During Farrell's tenure, the Literature and Arts Committee restored the Club's archives, which were put on permanent display for all the members to enjoy. Farrell also

Custom mantel in the Taft Dining Room

made improved communications with the membership a priority during his presidency, instituting quarterly town hall meetings and a "president's hotline" members could call to voice their opinions. Better communications helped make the renovations go more smoothly than some in the past.

As 1999 began, Maryland and Virginia members got hit with the unexpected as a record ice storm slammed the region in January, much as the blizzard of '96 had done three years earlier. At one point, as the *Washington Post* put it, "230,000 Pepco customers were without electricity in what has been called the worst power outage in the utility's 102-year history. All told, the ice storm left 435,000 Washington areas homes and businesses serviced by Pepco and other companies without power." The University Club came to the rescue for a number of members who took refuge there, enjoying hot showers and hot food. That week, the Taft Dining Room and Pershing Grille were so busy some members said that it felt like a slumber party.

Another Beck Takes Charge

Later that year, investment adviser Scott Beck continued family tradition by assuming the presidency of the Club as his father, John, had done before him. Scott said at the time, "My fondest recollections are of some thirty-five years ago when my father brought me down to work out in the old gym, loft a few bowling balls, swim, and visit Miss Laurence in the Taft Dining Room for dinners and birthdays. How times have changed! Today, we work out in a state-of-the-art athletic facility, swim in the same historic pool, and now I bring my children to see Miss Laurence and celebrate birthdays in the Taft Dining Room."

On July 3, 1999, the Club closed the Taft Dining Room, which was in dire need of a facelift. A little over two months later, Beck reopened the room that held such fond memories for him with a gala birthday celebration in President Taft's honor.

Members saw the original wood paneling stripped and refinished, the carpet and draperies replaced, and the chairs reupholstered. Now adorning the walls were the Club's rare Audubon prints, which had caused a few eyebrows to raise on that first day but before long seemed as much as part of the room as Miss Laurence—well, almost.

The showpiece of the renovation, however, was a custom mantel, which had narrowly escaped a major earthquake in Turkey and, closer to home, Hurricane Floyd, but had come to rest on the east wall of the majestic room. Today, William Howard Taft oversees the comings and goings of the Club's many diners from his lofty perch above the new mantel.

The Keefer Memorial Library, the Franklin Room, the seventh-floor guest rooms, and the presidential and vice presidential suites rounded out the decade's renovations.

CLUBS-WITHIN-A-CLUB

Bridge
Basketball
Bull Moose
914 Club
Chalk & Talk (Billiards)
Classic Cinema Café
Classical Music Club
C.S. Lewis Club

Fur, Fins, & Feathers
Golf
Great Books
Jazz
Port, Cigars, & Politics
Squash
Toastmaster
Trail Mixers

University Club chefs at the Culinary Academy

Port, Cigars, & Politics panel

Bull Moose
swimming awards

C. S. Lewis Club luncheon

914 Club dance

Fur, Fin & Feathers hunt

HAPPY 100TH COMMITTEE

Beck's term may have been only two years, but he was looking five years down the road when he took two major steps that would have a lasting impact on the Club. First, he appointed the Centennial Committee, chaired by Judge Loren Smith, to prepare the way for the Club's one hundredth birthday celebration on February 21, 2004. The ninety-fifth birthday party—the 1999 Founders' Day Dinner—actually got the official festivities underway when speaker Chief Justice William Rehnquist reminded guests of the Club's first president—William Howard Taft, another chief justice. Much more was to follow over the next five years.

A LONG RANGE PLAN

With the Club's space problems still ongoing, especially in the women's locker room, Beck's second decision was to appoint a Long Range Planning Committee to develop a five-year plan for the Club. The new task force was led by its chairman, Barry Hart, and vice chairman, Judge Paul Michel, and included all the chairs of the standing committees. That fall, a member survey was conducted to get input on members' priorities and to better understand what they wanted and what they didn't in terms of Club activities and services. Responses to the survey were due back in January, and the results were made public the following April. The task force's efforts, coupled with the survey results, would form the foundation for the "Second Century Plan," which was to be completed the following year.

CLUBS-WITHIN-A-CLUB PROGRAM

While the Club continued to develop and debate its plans for future renovations, nothing did more during the 1990s to meet the board's goal of expanding Club activities than the many "clubs-within-a club." While the University Club has had a number of small internal clubs for many years, it was in 1999 that the Club formalized this tradition with its "Clubs-Within-A-Club" program. That year, along with some of the more established clubs, members of the Trail Mixers held their first hike. The Treasure Hunters gathered for an "Appraisal Day" luncheon and the Akido crowd took up martial arts. President Scott Beck's wife, Laura, cooked up the idea for the Club's Culinary Academy, where members learned the fine art of preparing gourmet cuisine.

Today, there are more than twenty-two clubs within the Club. One of the oldest is "Port, Cigars, & Politics" which attracts members with an interest in politics and the finer side of a good cigar and a glass of well-aged port. The friendly partisan debate has been on ongoing source of good fellowship for many years.

One of the "youngest" clubs is the "Bull Moose Club," which was formed in the 1980s for the children of Club members and gives the Club a wonderful way to focus on family events. Throughout the year, the BMC hosts holiday parties, cooking classes, swim lessons, and a variety of other activities for children under twelve, including a revival of Billy Whipp's boxing lessons—with a twist. Classes are now taught by a young woman—Lisa "Too Fierce" Foster, a championship professional boxer.

Members can retreat to the past with Bogey and Bacall in the Club's "Classic Cinema Café," or enjoy Beethoven and Bach at special musical performances sponsored by the Classical Music Club. Members who enjoy losing themselves in a good book can join the Great Books Club for monthly discussions or experience the intellectual, cultural, and historical aspects of jazz as part of the Jazz Club. "Fur, Fins, & Feathers" sponsors fishing and hunting excursions, and the Club chef cooks up the catch. There is a "club-within-a-club" for everyone at the University Club, and if not, there's always room for one more.

The End of the Century

The final year of the decade was as active as the first had been. The Club began its "Friday Family Nights," with a child-friendly menu and movies in the President's Room, while mom and dad could enjoy jazz. The cigar lovers held a dinner in honor of the day Texas became an independent republic, featuring an appearance by the outlaw rogue "El Cigaro." There were reports he looked suspiciously like Judge Smith. It was black tie or western wear, although jeans were allowed—with a tuxedo jacket.

There was a St. Patrick's Day singalong and an Easter brunch. The annual golf championship was held in June and Stead Park sports day in October. The PDS Lacrosse and Rugby Midwinter Blowout, which had begun in 1998 to celebrate the end of the playing season, was a rockin' event, with dancing and drinks to the music of the "Totally Confused." The final month of the century was jam-packed with holiday events: the Holly Ball, Sno Ball Slo Ball Squash Tournament, the PDS Bash, Breakfast with Santa, and the Taft Christmas Eve Dinner. Then it was time to break out the champagne and raise our glasses as the clock chimed in the New Year that the world had waited a thousand years to celebrate.

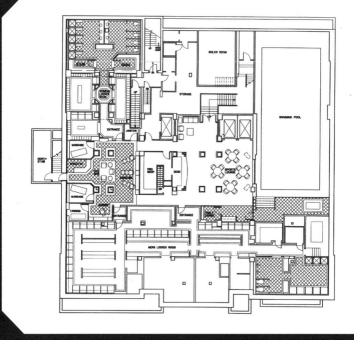

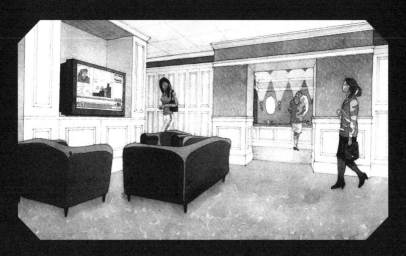

Second Century Plan drawings

Chapter Ten

2000: A New Millennium
The Centennial Countdown Begins

September 11, 2001 was a day unlike any other in Washington. The morning dawned clear and bright—one of those rare fall days without humidity. The kind of day that makes you want to play hooky. And then everything changed in the blink of an eye. At 8:46 a.m., the terror began in New York City, when the first of two passenger jets, piloted by a group of ruthless assassins, hit the World Trade Center. Washingtonians had barely taken in the terrible scenes on their television screens when the terror struck home. A plane that had left Dulles Airport just minutes before had circled the city and taken dead aim at the Pentagon. America would never be the same.

At the University Club, members and staff were stunned as they sat glued to televisions around the Club, watching in disbelief along with millions of Americans and people around the world. Albert Armstrong was still at home when the towers were struck, and immediately raced into the city as most of working Washington headed the other direction.

He remembers that day vividly. "We stayed open. We became a haven of comfort. Members came here, in part because their offices were evacuated; for others, they simply didn't know where else to go. CNN was on every television in the building."

Then–president Doug Spaulding says, "The Grille became kind of a magnet for people who wanted to be with friends and to talk about the experience...and catch up on things."

Members came to the University Club to gather together, much as families do in times of tragedy, where they could sit with others and listen and talk with people in the know about the terrible things going on in the world. The Grille became a hub of activity every evening, with tables full of members engaged in conversation trying to make sense of these senseless acts. Some members, who remembered the attack on Pearl Harbor first-hand, called this attack worse because "it was here," and Washingtonians could actually see the death and destruction.

The Athletic Center was also a busier place, especially in the days immediately following September 11, as members sought to alleviate the stress and anxiety affecting most Americans. In the months afterward, the Club organized several discussions on terrorism put on by the International Committee. Port, Cigars, & Politics took on a new dimension as many members met on September 13 for a special session, with the usual fun and partisanship replaced by deep reflection.

Most businesses in America took a hit as the nation reeled in shock over the double tragedies, and the University Club was no different. While business was booming in the Grille, the Taft emptied to less than half of its normal traffic. Initially, with all the airports closed, people couldn't get out of Washington easily, and the Club's overnight guest rooms were full. Visitors who were in Washington when the tragedy occurred found themselves marooned, but in the weeks after, while Reagan National Airport remained closed, it was difficult for people to get into Washington as well. All banquets originally scheduled at the Club for the weeks following the attacks were cancelled, and many smaller meetings weren't held because out-of-town visitors were involved. So, the occupancy rate was quickly cut in half. September 11 and the weeks following was a time that the University Club, like most of America, will never forget.

Y2K AND MEMBERSHIP APPRECIATION DAY

What happened on that sunny day in September was the most tragic and shocking moment in what has rapidly become a "Decade of Terror." But the new millennium didn't start out that way. When the clock chimed twelve on December 31, 1999, it was only a computer bug nicknamed "Y2K" that was terrorizing the country. The phrase had crept into the popular vernacular in the late '90s as the millennium approached, and people feared that a worldwide computer crash of untold proportions was about to wreak havoc on everything from the national banking system to city stoplights. At the University Club, Membership Appreciation Day had been held on New Year's Day for decades. But with the Y2K threat looming, the Club decided to move the annual celebration to earlier in December to avoid any potential problems. As it turned out, the expected didn't happen. Y2K was a big bust, but in the process, members discovered they liked the earlier date. So, a UC tradition changed to meet the times, and Membership Appreciation Day has been held in December for the past three years.

A little thing like a worldwide computer meltdown, however, wasn't enough to stop the Club's annual New Year's Eve bash. Members rang in the new year, new century, and new millennium with a "Crystal Ball New Year's Eve Gala." Meanwhile, the Club's littlest "members" had their own celebration, a "Y2K Kamp" held to keep the younger set occupied with food, games, and movies while their parents danced the night away upstairs—though 1 a.m. was the "Cinderella hour" for partygoers large and small.

John Beck—Member of the Millennium

The 2000 Founder's Day Dinner in February was special in more ways than one. First, it was an official "Centennial" event—a part of the countdown toward the Club's one hundredth birthday celebration. But it was also the first Founder's Day to be held in a new century and a new millennium. The University Club decided to honor one of its own with an award that comes around only once every thousand years. On Friday, February 25, 2000, John A. Beck was named "Member of the Millennium" at that year's Founder's Day Dinner—a richly deserved honor reflecting his forty-four years of Club service, leadership, and friendship that began when he joined as a young lawyer in 1956.

A member of the prominent law firm of Frost & Towers, Beck was recruited by his good friend and former Club president Jim Johnston. Clarence Pechacek also had a hand in bringing Beck on board.

One of the most popular couples in the Club, John and Helen Beck plunged headlong into the life of the University Club: seeing the world as Club Globetrotters, raising spirits as stalwarts of the mixed Bowling League, and singing along with the fun-loving crowd that made the Peacock Lounge one of the Club's liveliest rooms. But it wasn't all fun. Over the years, Beck served as Club vice president, chairman of the Executive Committee, secretary of the Board of Admissions, and chairman of numerous Club committees, including Entertainment and Long Range Planning. As the most active and title-laden member since Proctor Dougherty, it was no surprise to anyone when John was elected the Club's thirty-third president, serving from 1970 to 1972.

Although John was active in many aspects of Club life in his four decades of membership, perhaps his greatest mark on the Club was the long succession of eleven Club presidents—either law partners or clients of the soft-spoken Beck—who climbed the leadership ladder. Nor is it surprising that his son, Scott, who grew up in the glow of his dad's Club service and good fellowship, would follow in his footsteps to become the Club's first "legacy" president.

"All of the really positive developments of the University Club in the past forty years have shown the influence of John's fine hand," says past president and good friend Dale L. Jernberg. As one Club member put it, "He was the quiet hand behind the scenes

John Beck accepts the Member of the Millennium award, congratulated by his son, Scott, his wife, Helen, and good friend Dale Jernberg

who identified the Club needs and helped find people to fit those needs." John Beck created a legacy of leadership that has spurred nearly four decades of unprecedented change and growth in the Club.

It was Dale Jernberg's idea to create a special "Member of the Millennium" award for the year 2000 Founder's Day Dinner, rather than the Club's usual "Member of the Year." The Club went a step further, however, by also raising money to fund a new John Beck Scholarship for Club employees and their children.

Born in Oklahoma in 1925, Beck grew up in Missouri, served in the Pacific and Japan during and after World War II, and attended law school at George Washington University. His distinguished legal career reflects a lifetime of service. When elected a fellow of the American College of Trial Lawyers, he was the youngest in the country. He also served as president of the Barristers and Lawyers Club of Washington—a reflection of his distinguished fifty-year legal career.

The sold-out 2000 Founder's Day Dinner honoring Beck was also graced by the presence of the learned and always intellectually stimulating Justice Antonin Scalia, who gave the evening's keynote speech to rave reviews. Chief Justice William H. Rehnquist also joined the festivities and introduced his colleague on the Court.

CLUB DOINGS

2000 may have been a new century, but activities at the Club continued at the same dizzying pace that had characterized the '90s. In February, internationalists were treated to Jordanian Embassy Night, featuring Jordanian art and a visit by the country's

Community Affairs Chair Tony Englert, along with Mayor Tony Williams, Club president Scott Beck, and son Will at the 2000 Community Service Awards

esteemed ambassador. Members added beads and boas to their usual party dress for the Club's annual Mardi Gras celebration in March, with music and dancing capping off one of the Club's favorite parties. Lacrosse and rugby players had their own party that month, too, while First Friday Family Nights continued to bring moms, dads, and kids into the Club throughout the year.

Just as they had the previous decade, renovations were still ongoing in 2000. A major updating of the Keefer Memorial Library began over the summer, and members were able to get back to their favorite chairs on September 15, when the newly refurbished library reopened with the latest in computer technology. Also that summer, the Restaurant Committee voted to test a relaxed dress code in the Taft Dining Room and casual attire in the Pershing Grille. In June, the Club once again toasted Miss Laurence with a gala dinner to celebrate her forty years as manager of the Taft Dining Room. A scholarship was also established in her honor.

RECOGNIZING COMMUNITY LEADERS

As part of the Club's ongoing commitment to community involvement, the Community Affairs Committee, under Tony Englert's leadership, decided in 2000 to establish the University Club's annual Community Leadership Award program. Each year, this prestigious award recognizes a deserving Washingtonian who has made an extraordinary contribution to the city's quality of life through community service. The first recipient was Mayor Anthony Williams, followed in 2001 by Virginia Congressman Tom Davis, then the chairman of the House District of Columbia Subcommittee. Next was *Washington Post* publisher Donald Graham. All were honored at ceremonies at the Club,

Club president Doug Spaulding, Donald Graham, CEO of the Washington Post, along with his wife, and Lisa Stewart, chair of the Community Affairs Committee, at the 2002 Community Leadership Award Luncheon

Supreme Court Justice Antonin Scalia, Club president Scott Beck, and Chief Justice William H. Rehnquist celebrate the Club's birthday

attended by many of the Club's community partners. Their many contributions, which make the Club's neighborhood a better place to live and work, were applauded as well.

MORE DOINGS

In October, the Proctor Dougherty Society held a Masquerade Bash, while Bull Moose had its own Halloween party for Club kids. The biggest news that fall was, of course, the hotly contested and eventually historically close presidential election, Topic A at the Club Table and at the meetings of Port, Cigars & Politics. The Club held its traditional election night party in November, but that year members went home in the dark literally and figuratively—not knowing, like the rest of America, who had won the presidency. Once again, University Club members found themselves in a political maelstrom when the Florida recount fight wound up in the U.S. Supreme Court. Chief Justice Rehnquist and Justices O'Connor, Thomas, Scalia, and Kennedy formed the majority opinion that effectively ended the protracted election. Justice Ruth Bader Ginsburg voted with the minority. But all were then and are today active University Club members. Despite the rancorous election, the year 2000 was the happiest of holiday seasons at the Club, with its usual round of parties and festive traditions to liven up even the glummest of politicos.

As the Court and history wrote the final chapter in the controversial election of 2000, the Club closed its books at year's end and proudly showed a modest profit for the sixth year in a row.

THE SECOND CENTURY PLAN

2001, which was to be one of the most tragic in the nation's history, began with a return to an earlier controversy at the University Club. Although the Blue Ribbon Task Force's plan to provide more space for athletic facilities, particularly an expanded and improved women's locker room, had failed in the mid-1990s, the needs, identified in the plan, still existed.

With the results of the members' survey and the Long Range Planning Committee's efforts in hand, the Club's new president, Doug Spaulding, took over where Scott Beck left off and began the process to reconcile the objections that had led to the defeat of the earlier proposal. Spaulding, elected in 2001, was another protégé of John Beck, a senior partner in the prominent law firm of Reed Smith who had joined the Club in 1989. The new president put together a second planning team—the Athletic Center Task Force—to address members' concerns identified in the survey and develop a working concept that reflected their priorities.

The Second Century Plan's Capital Improvements

ATHLETIC CENTER IMPROVEMENTS

- A new 3,000 square foot fitness center on the third floor
- An aerobics/activities studio
- A new enlarged women's locker room with more lockers and space, a steam room, and sauna
- A day spa with massages, body wraps, manicures, pedicures, and facials
- An expanded/upgraded Sports Lounge overlooking the pool
- A second international squash court

UNIVERSITY HALL/GOVERNORS ROOM IMPROVEMENTS

- Upgraded audio-visual equipment
- New carpet and repainting
- Better soundproofing
- New lighting, heating, ventilation and air conditioning

CLUBHOUSE IMPROVEMENTS

- Elevator upgrades
- HVAC upgrades
- Kitchen upgrades, including refrigeration equipment and wine storages
- Phased-in fire alarm and sprinkler protection

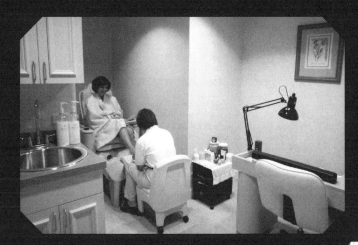

With the addition of the Sage Spa, members can enjoy some much-deserved pampering

Ribbon cutting of the third floor athletic center, April 2003

The Club then brought in two very capable design professionals—Jim Wilson, an expert in the renovation of both private clubs and commercial enterprises like the Hay-Adams Hotel, and Bruce Hayes, who had an impressive record of designing fitness centers in historic buildings. Girard Engineering did the most comprehensive study ever conducted at the Club, analyzing the all-important electrical and mechanical systems. Together, the House Committee and the Task Force developed a set of recommendations for the board's consideration. The Finance Committee then went into action, creating a funding plan for the project. A year later, at a special meeting on March 19, 2002, Spaulding and company presented members with "The Second Century Plan." It was a visionary document, focused on the Club's future success, which maximized Club space while minimizing disruption and dislocation of current space. It was adopted unanimously at a very well attended meeting.

One of the original questions about the earlier proposal to expand Club facilities was whether to convert existing space into a new athletic facility or to construct a new space. The Second Century Plan opted to build the Center in a new space, to be created on the third floor at the back of the building. The facility would have fourteen-foot ceilings and a center for cardiovascular and weight resistance equipment. The existing athletic center would provide the area for the new women's locker room, which would be two and a half times bigger than the current space and would feature a steam room and sauna, designated personal grooming space, additional showers and commodes, a

*The Governors'
Room set up for an
afternoon wedding*

TV lounge, and more lockers. A second international squash court would also be built, with an aerobics studio next door. With the completion of the renovations, members could also enjoy the amenities of a day spa, a new steam room, a sauna and the Sports Lounge.

Under the Second Century Plan, University Hall was to undergo an extensive renovation, along with the Governor's Room and the kitchen. Finally, the plan called for a new, airier stairway to connect the basement facilities with the new Athletic Center on the third floor.

The cost of the entire three-phase project was pegged at $4 million, financed by a small increase in dues and athletic fees beginning in September 2002, a second modest increase the following September, higher new member initiation fees, and debt financing.

THE TEWAARATON TROPHY

The year 2001 was a remarkable year for many reasons—some tragic, others wonderful. Some of the Club's most memorable moments that year came from its athletic programs. The planning for a new athletic center got underway. The annual Sports Banquet featured two of the Club's most prolific sports experts. *Washington Post* sportswriters Tony Kornheiser and Michael Wilbon were the evening's honored guests and Corcoran Award recipients. And a new sports tradition began that year when the University Club awarded the first annual Tewaaraton Lacrosse Trophy, which showcases the Club's long-held commitment to athletics and fitness.

The award was the brainchild of several University Club members: Peter Farrell, Scott Beck, Jim Bond, Tristan Zaia, Brian McQuade, Bill Philips, Jeffrey Mulhall, and Peter Goldman. Today, just three years later, this trophy is now recognized as the country's preeminent lacrosse award, honoring the top female and male varsity collegiate lacrosse players in the United States chosen by the country's college lacrosse coaches. Along with the trophy, a scholarship award is given to the general scholarship fund of each trophy recipient's college or university. An equal amount is also given back to the sport in an effort to support the game, which is one of the oldest team sports played in North America. Rooted in centuries of Native American tradition, lacrosse took on many variations before reaching its present-day form. The name "Tewaaraton" comes from the Mohawk word for the game. In 2003,

Club president Doug Spaulding with 2001 Corcoran Award winners Tony Kornheiser and Michael Wilbon

increasing interest in the award required moving the presentation ceremony from the Club to the National Geographic headquarters across the street. The larger facility accommodates 350 guests and provided a state-of-the-art auditorium for the presentation, which was produced by College Sports TV (CSTV) and broadcast on July 5, 2003.

While athletics at the Club in 2001 were the source of many happy moments, members said their goodbyes to one of the Club's finest athletes and longest-living members that year with the death of Franklin Gould at age ninety-three. Gould, once one of the Club "live-ins," left an indelible mark through his many friendships, his wonderful sense of humor, and his love of squash. It was Gould who first encouraged the young

2001 Tewaaraton Trophy winners: (left to right): male winner Doug Shanahan; Sidney Hill, Chief of Six Nation Confederacy, Onondaga Nation; female winner Jen Adams, and Club president Scott Beck

Ghirma Meres, one of the mainstays of the Club's athletic staff for more than thirty years, to take up squash, and today his memory lives on at the Club through the annual Franklin P. Gould Cup Squash Competition between Baltimore's Maryland Club and the University Club.

A BUSY CLUB

While many events were cancelled after the September 11 attacks, the first eight months of 2001 were busy ones for the Club. Keeping to Dr. Norman Bailey's characterization of the Club as "the premier diplomatic and international club of Washington," the International Committee sponsored a wide range of programs in 2001. Some focused on ethnic conflicts, for example, a luncheon discussion with Ambassador Davorin Kracun of Slovenia was held as tensions along the Macedonian border escalated. Another event featured a panel of ambassadors who discussed the controversial "Summit of the Americas" in Quebec, which had generated so much international coverage and debate. The panel gave members insight into economic trade, immigration, and military cooperation issues. In the summer, the Committee invited Ambassador Nabil Fahmy of Egypt to address a members' luncheon, and still another was held with Pakistani Ambassador Dr. Maleeha Lodhi.

Israeli Ambassador David Ivry captivated a noon luncheon audience, as did a panel featuring former national security adviser Bud McFarlane and former CIA director James Woolsey. Finally, Assistant Secretary of State and Club member Paula Dobriansky spoke to over 120 people, including seventeen ambassadors, on crucial foreign policy issues.

The 2001 Founder's Day celebration was a special event that year, with Justice Scalia scheduled to introduce the evening's speaker, Justice Sandra Day O'Connor. When he was unable to attend at the last minute, Justice Stephen Breyer stepped in to do the honors. As one Club member put it, "Only in this Club do you have spare Supreme Court Justices." A testament to the Club's long relationship with the Court.

In June, members took swing dance lessons and then showed their stuff at the Club's Dinner Dance "Spring Fling." For the more serious-minded, the new Economic Club kicked off its activities with a lecture by Sylvester Scheiber, an expert on the privatization of Social Security and author of *The Real Deal: The History and Future of Social Security*. The musically inclined heard from Pulitzer Prize–winning music critic Tim Page at a noon luncheon. On the Fourth of July, members and their families toasted Independence Day on the Club's roof after the annual birthday buffet—no padlocks were in sight.

In the fall, members were off to Europe on the Club's new Education Tour program, in partnership with the Missouri Athletic Club, the Athletic Club of Columbus, and the Union League Club of Chicago. Fall trips included a "London Escape" and an "Alumni College in Greece" tour which provided an unusual "involvement in the life of one community"—in this case the beautiful Greek Island of Poros.

Saluting Our Vets

On the night after President Bush announced the first allied air strikes in Afghanistan, the Club held its first annual "Veterans' Day Salute"—November 8—to honor the men and women of the military, especially those serving in harm's way. Secretary of Veterans' Affairs Anthony J. Principi, the evening's featured speaker, was introduced by former Attorney General Edwin Meese, a longtime Club member. Chief Justice Rehnquist once again honored the Club with his presence, giving the dinner invocation. It was a bittersweet night for all as American flyers and ground forces joined the first battle in the War on Terror.

2001 ended with many of the Club's traditional round of holiday celebrations, although the spirit that usually characterizes these events was far more reserved than usual, with so many troops overseas and the nation continuing to mourn the losses of September 11.

Justin Thornton reads with a child from the Washington Very Special Arts School as part of the reading buddy program

VIOLENCE STRIKES AGAIN AND MEMBERS RESPOND

A year after the terrible tragedy of September 11, random violence once again struck the Washington area as a sniper pushed the city to the brink of panic. For the Club, the challenge came when the city ordered the sixth annual Sports Day at Stead Park postponed because of the sniper attacks. But there was no stopping Mary Jefferson and her able team of volunteers. Plans were simply changed to move the festivities inside the clubhouse. The city fortunately lifted the ban on outdoor activities when the snipers were caught, and the day was a huge success. That year, the Club's improvement project was a water fountain for the park. In other charitable efforts, the Turkey Triumph, in partnership with the AME Church's food bank, raised $3,900, enough to provide turkeys and all the trimmings for Thanksgiving and Christmas and fresh produce through Easter. The Secret Santa program provided toys for sixty-five children that Christmas, and the Community Affairs Committee relaunched its reading buddy program with the Washington Very Special Arts School.

MEMBERSHIP GROWTH

Despite the economic impact of September 11, the sniper attacks, and a sagging national economy, the University Club bucked the trend in 2002 and saw a small increase in membership. The Club's auditor, Pannell Kerr Forster PC, told the board that most city clubs had lost between five and ten percent of their membership due to the depressed economy. It wasn't just luck that the University Club avoided a membership drain, however. The board had formed a Membership Development Task Force,

Laura Arth, 2002
Corcoran awardee,
Congressman J. C.
Watts, Michael Wilbon,
and Club president
Doug Spaulding at the
2002 Sports Banquet

Frank Ahmed and
Milton Kotler
welcome the
Ambassador of
Turkey at an
International
Committee luncheon

The International
Committee welcomes the
Indian ambassador

headed by Susan Neely, which worked with outside membership marketing consultants to create a winning strategy. That strategy, which focused recruitment efforts on a target eight-block radius of the Club, continued into 2003.

MORE AND MORE ACTIVITIES

In the spring, former congressman and football star J.C. Watts was honored at the Club's twenty-first annual Sports Banquet, where his reputation as one of the country's best speakers was more than evident. The International Committee kept the Club busy with a round of events, including three ambassadorial luncheons featuring India, Turkey, and Germany; and two Embassy Nights, highlighting Brazil and Japan. In the tradition of some of the Club's earlier revues, a Comedy Night was held in March, while in April some of the Club's theatergoers enjoyed a sold-out performance of the musical "Mamma Mia."

The second annual Veteran's Day Salute took place in November, with Chief Justice William Rehnquist and former Attorney General Ed Meese on hand once more to do the honors. This year, the featured speaker was General Al Gray, retired Marine Corps commandant, who inspired the crowd with his moving speech.

Finally, the Centennial celebration moved a step closer when the Communications Committee decided to temporarily rename the quarterly magazine the *Centennial*, in honor of the Club's one hundredth year celebration.

Grand opening of the renovated
Governors' Room

The new third floor finess center

A New Club Emerges

On April 23, 2003, the Board of Governors, with president Doug Spaulding wielding a large pair of scissors, cut the ribbon officially opening the Club's new state-of-the-art Fitness Center. As the celebration began, members were already trying out the latest in cardiovascular equipment while watching the new televisions extended from the ceiling. The Fitness Center staff, under the able leadership of Howard Day and Center Director and star trainer Greg Raleigh, was ready and willing to help members familiarize themselves with the new equipment and explain the many new amenities the Center now offered. The opening of the Center completed Phase II of the Second Century Plan with a minimum of disruption to the Club.

Construction on the last phase got underway in early April, and on September 14, a crowd gathered once again to cheer the opening of the long-awaited women's locker room, Sports Lounge, and Day Spa. This time, however, Susan Neely, the Club's first woman president, cut the ribbon. Ms. Neely, a highly respected communications professional, was elected the fifty-second president of the Club after serving as vice president and on many of the Club's committees since joining the Club in 1991. The University Club can now claim one of the finest private athletic facilities in the city, as well as one of the first women to head a private professional club in Washington.

Sage, a private day spa

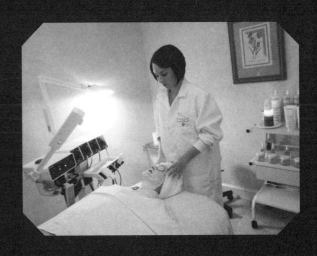

A member is treated to a facial at Sage

While most of the renovations centered on the athletic facilities, the Club also opened "Helen's," an elegant cocktail lounge in the Taft Dining Room, named after former First Lady Helen Taft, wife and confidant of William Howard Taft.

THE UNIVERSITY CLUB GOES PLATINUM

Good news wasn't found only in the Athletic Department that year. In May, the Club was once again selected as a "Platinum Club of America," a testament to the leadership of Albert Armstrong and the talent of the University Club's able and committed staff. More than six thousand of the nation's club managers and presidents are asked for their opinions on clubs throughout the country based on five categories: quality of membership, tradition and heritage, amenities, governance, and professional management and staff. The University Club's selection means that it stands among the top four percent of America's five thousand private clubs in terms of perceived excellence.

YOU BE THE JUDGE

The University Club has always been home to many of Washington's most prominent attorneys and jurists, from Justices Earl Warren, "Whizzer" White, and William O. Douglas of one era to many of the members of the current Court. A new legal tradition was established at the Club, however, on July 16, 2003, when the first annual William Howard Taft Supreme Court Review was held to discuss one of the Supreme Court's most active and controversial terms. The sold-out seminar, an official Centennial event, was the inspiration of attorney Peter Goldman, the Centennial Committee's vice chairman and impresario and one of the Club's most active members. The star-studded panel of legal eagles, moderated by Judge Loren Smith, included two for-

The Supreme Court Review Panel, July 2002

mer Solicitors General, the Honorable Kenneth Starr and the Honorable Seth P. Waxman, L. Michael Sidman, Georgetown University Professor of Law, and Douglas W. Kmiec, Dean of Catholic University's Columbus School of Law. They spoke to a packed house of members and guests, who agreed that the program had been one of the Club's best in recent memory.

A Full Calendar

Throughout 2003, members were treated to a number of outstanding lectures. UC member Thomas Foley, former Speaker of the House and Ambassador to Japan, and Dennis Owens, Washington's best known voice for classical music, were just two of the many prominent speakers who provided insight into the issues of the day. Author Jamie Hume, an international Churchill expert, this time talked to club members about the Gettysburg Address, even going so far as to do his own imitation of what Lincoln's voice might have sounded like.

Judge John Penn and Paul D'Armiento
with Justice Sandra Day O'Connor
at the thirteenth annual book fair

International Committee members
enjoy an evening with Speaker of the House
and Ambassador to Japan Tom Foley

At the annual Sports Banquet that year, Kansas Congressman Jim Ryun, one of the great long distance runners in track history, was the featured speaker and winner of the Thomas G. Corcoran Award. The thirteenth annual Book Fair set new records in sales, attendance, and financial gain for the Club, while Douglas Wheeler, president emeritus of the Washington Performing Arts Society, was the winner of the seventh annual Distinguished Washingtonian Award. In the fall, the PDS's second trip to Virginia's Gold Cup race was a sold-out success.

As the year came to an end, the Club changed its format for the usual New Year's Eve celebration. In order to give members more flexibility, the Club offered two choices that evening. Members could dine in the Taft Dining Room and then head up to the Grille for light refreshments, conversation, and dancing or those dining elsewhere could come just for the cocktails and dancing, making it an evening to suit every member's tastes.

PDS members and guests enjoy Gold Cup, October 2001

Literature Arts Chair Mac Johnston along with the 2003 Distinguished Washingtonian Award winner, Douglas Wheeler and Club president Doug Spaulding

THE CENTENNIAL YEAR

As this history ends, the Centennial Year is poised to begin. The Centennial Committee is putting the final touches on its celebration plans. Albert Armstrong and crew are preparing the menus and sprucing up the Clubhouse. Members are setting aside dates and taking their tuxes out of the closet, all in readiness for February 21, 2004, when the Club will toast its one hundredth year in the grandest of style—a University Club tradition.

One hundred years ago, William Howard Taft wielded a champagne bottle at the Club's first birthday banquet as he and hundreds of other "university" men celebrated in a tradition of fellowship that has come to characterize the University Club throughout its long and prestigious history.

A century later, after wars and peace, after boom and bust, after controversy and camaraderie, the University Club enters its second century strong and sound, ready to restate the bidding of its first banquet program: "Enter All Ye Who Have a Degree of Good Fellowship and Learning."

Boxing instructor extraordinaire Billy Whipp
with the Schiavone family

Chapter Eleven

ATHLETICS AT
THE UNIVERSITY CLUB

*I always turn to the sports pages first, which records people's
accomplishments. The front page has nothing but man's failures.*
—CHIEF JUSTICE EARL WARREN

While exercising the cerebellum may well have been one of the Club's original goals, after the merger with the Racquet Club in 1936, athletics
became and remain one of the mainstays of Club life. But the Club's connections to professional sports go back to its earliest days. Edward J. Walsh, a member
of the Club, was one of three Washingtonians who organized the original American
League Senators baseball team just two years before Proctor Dougherty called the University Club's organizational meeting to order. Walsh and his partners built Griffith Sta-
dium, as it was later known, after the group sold the team to Club manager Clark
Griffith in 1920. Calvin Griffith, Clark's son, moved the team to Minnesota in 1960.
With Washington suffering mightily from a lack of baseball (as it still does today), a
group that included UC member and former Club president Jim Johnston organized a
new Washington Senators expansion team. Eventually, Johnston would own two-thirds
of the team, which was sold to new owners in 1969 and subsequently moved to Texas.

Another longtime UC member and one of the most famous trial lawyers of his time,
Edward Bennett Williams, was an owner of both the Baltimore Orioles and the Washington Redskins. Two former Redskins have served as presidents of the Club as well.
Cliff Battles, a Hall of Fame running back for the Skins for six seasons, retiring in 1938,
was Club president from 1972 to 1974. Pete Larson wore the burgundy and gold during
the 1967 and 1968 seasons after a stint with the New York Giants, and was elected president of the Club in 1989.

143

SQUASH

Squash also became an integral part of the University Club when it moved to its new home in 1936. Originally, the Club had four American standard courts. Today, the Club boasts two regulation international courts. The first opened in 1999 and due to its unique moveable wall can convert to an international doubles court. The second was built in July 2003 as part of the Club's major renovation of its athletic facilities.

In the early years, Otto Glockler, one of the best players in the world in the 1920s, taught squash and spent thirty-three years helping to make the University Club synonymous with the game. Harry Goodheart, another of the country's leading squash professionals, also taught squash, retiring in 1977. Goodheart was not only a great squash player, but also one of the Club's most unforgettable characters. He had a habit of giving members squash lessons while wearing long white duck pants, but his trademark was the cigar he chain-smoked even on the court. Goodheart, a popular figure in the Club for many years, was also a great golfer and fisherman, taking members along in search of the "big one."

Tom Lane, another top notch squash professional, had big shoes to fill when he joined the Club staff as a squash professional in the late '70s. He was followed by yet another excellent squash pro, Howard Day, who now serves as the Club's outstanding Athletic Director. Day, who had been a literature major at the University of Pennsylvania, says he became "addicted to squash at twenty-one." It paid off. Just a year after he came aboard the UC staff as squash pro in 1980, Day defeated Sharif Khan, then the No. 1 ranked squash player in North America, 3–2, in an upset nobody expected. The squash champion got his revenge two years later when he defeated Day 3–1 in a highly publicized return bout.

Over the years, the Club has been involved in many of the country's major squash competitions. In 1982, the Squash Nationals were held in Washington for the second time, and the University Club was the major site for a number of the matches and festivities.

In 1949, the University Club established two major squash competitions of its own. The Woodruff-Nee Invitational, a top-caliber national event, is held every February and attracts 100 to 150 players from across the country. The second tournament—the FitzGerald Cup—pits the squash players of Washington against the best of Baltimore.

Originally, the trophy was sponsored by Ambassador William H.G. FitzGerald, who began playing squash in 1934 in New York City. After his move to Washington in the late '30s, he found there was only one place to play—the Racquet Club on 16th Street.

In an interview with Barry Wood, Ambassador FitzGerald, whose office was just minutes from the University Club, talked about the days when squash was played by a small few.

"I used to play at 6:30 a.m. with Vice President Henry Wallace, who lived at the Wardman Park Hotel," he said. "I'd pull up in front and flash my lights—there was no security—and he would come down." In the late forties, FitzGerald came up with the idea of a Washington-Baltimore competition. Over the years, FitzGerald, who served as ambassador to Ireland from 1992 to 1993, has done more than anyone in Washington to promote the games of squash and tennis. In fact, Washington's Tennis Center was named after the ambassador for his many efforts on behalf of the game. In 2003, the ambassador was one of the honorees at the Washington Tennis and Education Foundation's annual Tennis Ball.

In 2000, the National Capitol Squash Racquets Association created the Annual William H.G. FitzGerald Junior Ambassador Squash Racquets Award to honor an outstanding local junior player for competitive spirit and good sportsmanship.

While the FitzGerald Trophy men's team competition has remained the same for more than fifty years, two more competitions have been added in recent years—a junior team competition for thirteen to eighteen-year-olds in 2000 and a women's competition in 2002.

In the late '80s, then–Squash Committee chairman John Wells tabbed the Club's summer squash competition the "Mosquito Open," and the name stuck. At the time, one of the members, Robert Zimmer, had a summer home in Warrenton, Virginia, which he graciously offered to the players for a barbecue after the competition. The presence of some uninvited pests buzzing around the party gave Wells the idea of calling the competition, which is held the week after July 4 each year, the Mosquito Open. In years past, the Club has also played spirited matches against the Naval Academy and competed for the much-coveted Old Dominion Cup, another event sponsored by Ambassador FitzGerald, against a top-notch Virginia team.

The University Club vies with the Maryland Club every year for the Franklin Gould Cup, established in honor of one of the Club's finest squash players and longest playing members. In 1979, Frank Gould reached the finals of the 70+ age bracket at the U.S. Squash Nationals. In 1990, he wowed squash players young and old when he won the 80+ bracket in the Maine Squash Tournament at Bowdoin College. But Gould's contribution to the University Club's proud history in squash went beyond even his own extraordinary accomplishments. Thanks to Gould, the Club discovered the talents of a twenty-year-old Ethiopian immigrant by the name of Ghirma Meres, who in 1974 was working as an attendant in the Club's athletic facility. Meres knew nothing about squash, but as he went about his duties, he often watched the game being played. One day, he picked up a racquet out of curiosity and started hitting the ball, discovering a natural ability for the game. It wasn't long before Frank Gould discovered it too, and asked the young staffer to be a "sparring partner." Meres says of Gould, "He saw my interest in the game, and he wanted to help me." It was a great partnership for Gould,

Meres, and the University Club. Every morning before Meres began work and on weekends, the pair would play. Before long, Meres's talent was evident, and more and more members were clamoring to play with him. Both Tom Lane and Howard Day helped coach the Club's squash prodigy. By the early '80s, Meres had begun what was to be nearly twenty-five years of squash competition, moving from the C Division up to the A Division. At one point, he was the Mid-Atlantic Champion, reaching the quarterfinals of the nationally known Insilco Tournament. Over the years, Meres has won numerous trophies on behalf of the University Club, including the City Squash Championship, and has also attained the U.S. Racquets Association's highest ranking as a teaching professional, Level II.

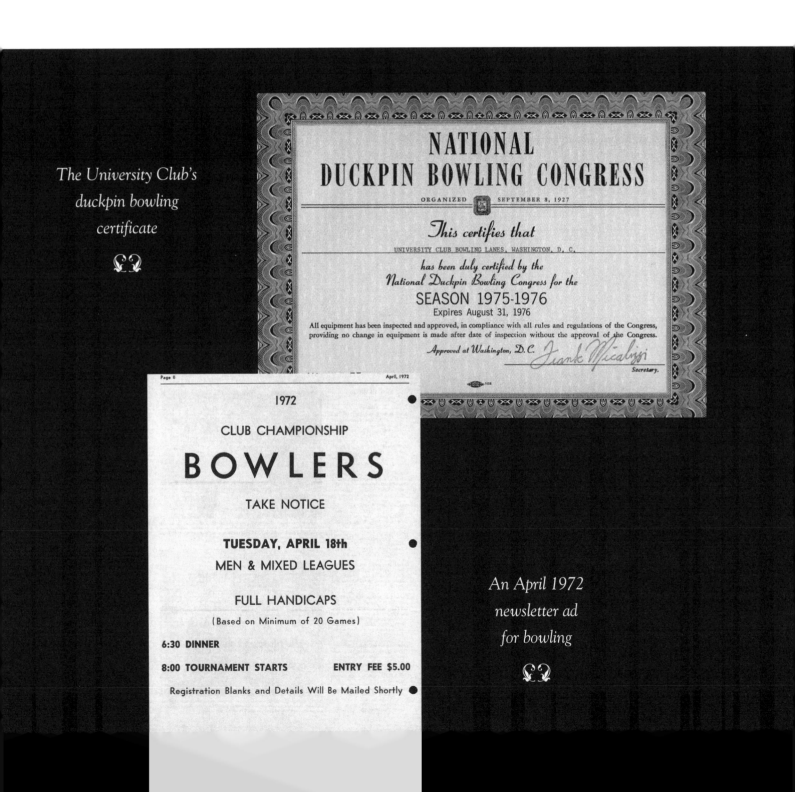

The University Club's duckpin bowling certificate

NATIONAL DUCKPIN BOWLING CONGRESS

ORGANIZED SEPTEMBER 8, 1927

This certifies that

UNIVERSITY CLUB BOWLING LANES, WASHINGTON, D. C.

has been duly certified by the National Duckpin Bowling Congress for the

SEASON 1975-1976

Expires August 31, 1976

All equipment has been inspected and approved, in compliance with all rules and regulations of the Congress, providing no change in equipment is made after date of inspection without the approval of the Congress.

Approved at Washington, D. C. Frank Micalizzi

Secretary.

Page 8   April, 1972

1972

CLUB CHAMPIONSHIP

BOWLERS

TAKE NOTICE

TUESDAY, APRIL 18th

MEN & MIXED LEAGUES

FULL HANDICAPS

(Based on Minimum of 20 Games)

6:30 DINNER

8:00 TOURNAMENT STARTS   ENTRY FEE $5.00

Registration Blanks and Details Will Be Mailed Shortly

An April 1972 newsletter ad for bowling

Today, more than seventy-five members, men and women, are regular squash players. The Club can also boast of having had some of the country's best "senior" squash players, with members like Frank Gould, Phil Brown and Charles Smoot playing competitively into their eighties and nineties.

BOWLING

For more than half a century, bowling was an important part of the sports and social life of the University Club. Bowling was already in place at the Racquet Club when the merger took place in 1936, and the University Club members took to it with relish. In Cecil Wilkinson's history of the Club's first fifty years, he writes, with his usual sense of humor, "Up from the subterranean caverns...during the winter come tremors which send the seismograph at Georgetown University a-fluttering. The intra-club duckpin bowling league is in progress!"

Bowlers from the 1930s through the 1980s took to the Club's four lanes in friendly competitions. From fall to spring, men's league bowling was held on Mondays and Tuesdays, with UC teams named after Big League baseball teams—the Red Sox, Dodgers, Yanks, Cubs. Wednesdays through Fridays, the ladies were invited and mixed teams vied for the Club championship. A bartender, usually LeRoy Harper, was on duty to keep spirits up. The Peacock Lounge was often the site of jolly drinks and dinners "après bowling," as members enjoyed the fellowship of good friends and friendly competitors.

Many of the bowlers became the nucleus of the Club's leadership structure for more than three decades and were behind many of the Club's liveliest social events over the years. From John and Helen Beck to Randy and Patty Donavan, from Lee and Paula Ellis to John and Helen Chandler, from Don and Joan Baldwin to Gene and Mary Ann McCoy—the list goes on and on of bowlers who made the Club a center of fun and fellowship for many years.

After the alleys were removed in the late '80s, the Club's bowlers continued their league play at Kenwood Country Club but still held their annual Bowling Banquets at the University Club. In 1998, this lively group celebrated fifty years of bowling at the Club.

THE POOL

When the University Club moved into its new building, it was the only Club in downtown Washington with a pool—and what a pool it was, measuring 60 feet by 25 feet with five lanes and holding 78,000 gallons of water. Hundreds of members over the years have taken advantage of the pool, including some of Washington's most prominent. On a given day, a swimmer might have found John F. Kennedy or Whizzer White in the next lane. Today, it might be Chief Justice William Rehnquist or former Veterans Affairs Secretary Togo West.

In the late '70s, Sports Committee chairman General Charles Cogswell came up with the idea of creating an incentive for members to swim and an athletic tradition—the "Swimathon"—began. Initially, the Swimming Committee set a fifty-mile target that participants were required to swim within one year—from May to May. When members reached that target fairly easily, the Committee raised the bar to sixty and then seventy-five and eighty miles. Finally, the Committee decided upon a permanent number—113 miles, which translated into 10,000 lengths. When vying in the Swimathon, swimmers are racing against both themselves and the calendar. The member who finishes the 113 miles first wins the "Annual Blake Clark Swimathon Award," honoring the Club's legendary swimmer. When it came to swimming, no one in the Club's history has been able to match Blake Clark for his endurance and determination. He won the Swimathon trophy from 1980–86, in 1991, and again in 1995 when in his eighties. His extraordinary dedication to physical fitness earned him the Club's first "Athlete of the Year" Award in 1991, along with the Corcoran Award. Clark, described as a remarkable individual by nearly everyone who knew him, died in 2003 at the age of ninety-four.

Between thirty-five to fifty members participate in the Swimathon every year—each logging in his or her laps on a board posted in the pool area and all done through an honor system.

Today, the pool has become home to both men and women; once it was only the purview of men, who enjoyed the freedom of their daily swims "au naturel." One guest of a member staying at the Club called his friend the next day and said, "I was so embarrassed. I went swimming with trunks on."

The addition of women swimmers may have changed the dress code but not the dedication of the many members whose week or workout isn't complete without a swim in the UC pool. And that includes a long list of members over the years who have been pool regulars well into their seventies and even eighties. In fact, one senior member actually lost his dentures there.

GOLF

Club bulletins going back decades highlight members' many golf outings and tournaments, which began with the Club's first field day in August of 1922 at the Columbia Country Club. UC members have always had an affinity for the sport. In 1991, however, the tradition was made official with the Club's first annual Golf Championship at Norbeck Country Club. The following year, the tournament moved to Springfield Country Club, but Bretton Woods became the Club Championship's permanent home.

In 1995, Jim Lemon, a member since 1977, generously offered to donate a trophy for the annual event—now called the Johnston Lemon Golf Trophy. The beautiful crystal obelisk can be found today in the Club's new trophy room, where it provides inspiration and incentive for many a UC golfer vying to win the competition. Each tournament champion receives a smaller glass replica of the original Clubhouse trophy.

BOXING

Boxing at the Club can be traced back to the 1920s, when Bill Whipp began a tradition at the Racquet Club that continues today. Whipp, a professional boxer himself who once coached Jack Dempsey, spent the better part of fifty years teaching both members and many of their sons the fine art of boxing. From 1929–1932, he also taught physical education at the University of Maryland and had his own health program on WDON radio. In 1956, the *Washington Star* did a feature story on Whipp called "Boys Are Taught to Box Without Losing Tempers":

Billy Whipp, Club Physical Director, puts on display 1972's crop of aspiring pugilists, sons of members taking boxing on Saturday mornings at the Club

A couple of boys were really mixing it up. Suddenly they stopped slugging each other and grinned. Nearby, their fathers were beaming. What halted the fight was a toot from the whistle of William R. Whipp, now in his 34th year as Physical Director of the University Club. . . . "I try to develop character through sports," says Mr. Whipp. "I carefully explain to the boys that loss of temper means loss of control or judgment."

The article went on to point out that many of the boys were the sons of some of Washington's most prominent citizens, including FDR confidant Tommy Corcoran and former Atomic Energy Commission Secretary Roy Snapp as well as several members of the diplomatic corps.

Today, boxing is still taught at the Club in the new Athletic Center—to men, women and the children of members—by two boxing professionals, including Lisa "Too Fierce" Foster, a former women's welterweight champion. With the renewed popularity of boxing, a number of members have banded together to form the UC "Boxing Club" which offers boxing classes as well as outings to local boxing events.

THE SPORTS BANQUET

This year the Club will celebrate not only its one hundredth birthday, but the twenty-fifth anniversary of one of its premier events—the University Club Sports Banquet. The dinner is held each year to honor both the Club Athlete of the Year and the annual winner of the Thomas Gardiner Corcoran Award, which honors an individual for scholarship, athleticism, and public service. Members have heard from a range of distinguished speakers over the years, from Chief Justice William Rehnquist to former Congressman J.C. Watts. Other recipients have included former Senators Al Simpson, George Mitchell, and Howell Heflin, House Speaker Thomas Foley, and Congressman Jim Ryun. George Washington University basketball coach Michael Jarvis and University of Maryland coach Gary Williams, along with *Washington Post* sportswriters Michael Wilbon and Tony Kornheiser, have also received this prestigious award. This banquet is truly a celebration of the athletic spirit that has come to characterize the University Club as it enters its second century.

THE TEWAARATON TROPHY

Just three years ago, a group of members, spearheaded by Peter Farrell, Tristan Zaia, Scott Beck, Peter Goldman, Jim Bond, Brian McQuade, Bill Philips, and Jeffrey Mulhall, decided it was time college lacrosse players got some national recognition, much as the Heisman Award honors the top college football player every year. This idea spurred the creation of the University Club's Tewaaraton Trophy, which honors the top female and male varsity collegiate lacrosse player in the United States. To help create the trophy, the University Club members formed the 501(c)3 Tewaaraton Foundation and worked with a number of outstanding lacrosse coaches that included Dave Urick and Kim Simons of Georgetown University; Don Starsia, of the University of Virginia; and Richie Moran, the former head coach at Cornell.

Lacrosse is one of the oldest team sports played in North America. Rooted in centuries of Native American tradition, the game took on many variations before reaching its present-day form. The Foundation's trophy, "Tewaaraton," is the Mohawk name for their game and the progenitor of present-day lacrosse. The Tewaaraton Trophy has received the endorsement of the Mohawk Nation Council of Elders.

The bronze trophy, featuring a Mohawk native, was designed and created by Frederick Kail, a distinguished sports sculptor and the pre-eminent lacrosse sculptor. To assist with historical authenticity, Thomas Vennum, Jr., the renowned Native American lacrosse historian, and author of "American Indian Lacrosse: Little Brother of War," served as a consultant to Kail through the development stage of the trophy.

The awards ceremony has grown each year, attracting national media coverage and moving in 2003 to National Geographic's auditorium to accommodate the growing crowd. Today, the Tewaaraton Trophy is bringing a new prominence and recognition to the Club, much as its squash competitions have done in years past.

OUTSIDE SPORTS

Along with its many in-house athletic activities, the Club also sponsors a number of team sports and sporting activities outside the building. Today, the Club can claim a

TEWAARATON AWARD WINNERS

lacrosse team; basketball team; rugby team; a runners' club; a billiards club, "Chalk and Talk;" a hunting and fishing club, "Fur, Fins, & Feathers;" a Sailing Club; and a hiking group, "Trail Mixers."

THE NEW ATHLETIC CENTER FOR THE "SECOND CENTURY"

April 23, 2003, was another historic day for University Club sports when the new state-of-the-art Athletic Center opened for business, marking the end of the second phase of the Club's Second Century Plan. As Club president Doug Spaulding cut the ribbon, members were ready to try out the more than $85,000 in top-notch fitness equipment filling the bright and airy room with its cathedral ceiling and ten foot high windows. An audio-cardio theater, stocked with televisions and headphones, keeps members on top of the news during their cardiovascular fitness workouts with stair machines, tread-mills, upright and recumbent bikes, and elliptical machines. The Center also has first-rate circuit weight training equipment and free weights. Members can also take advantage of aerobics, Pilates, yoga, and spinning classes in the new 15 by 30 foot Exercise Studio. For boxers, the Center has both a speed bag and a heavy bag located down-stairs next to the squash courts.

The Athletic Center's staff of twelve includes five personal fitness trainers, two squash professionals, and one swimming instructor. They help members reach their health and fitness goals of weight loss, body toning, or sport-specific needs for golf, squash, swimming, tennis, skiing, or other sports. Greg Raleigh, a former football player who first joined the Club's athletic staff in 1989 as a trainer, has been director of the Fitness Center since 1995. It's not difficult to find members who would tell you that Greg's training regimens are behind their newly toned physiques. Former House Speaker Tom Foley is a perfect example. Working closely with Greg, Foley lost more than ninety pounds while learning to lift ninety-pound free weights.

MEMBERS OF THE SECOND CENTURY COMMITTEE

The Construction Committee
President Doug Spaulding
Vice President Susan Neely
Board Member Steve Peer
Sports Committee Chair Laura Arth
House Committee Chair Sue Wegrzyn

The other major element of the Athletic facility renovation was a new women's locker room and Sports Lounge complemented by a full-service day spa, which officially opened on September 14, 2003. Susan Neely, the Club's new president and the first woman to hold the post, cut the ribbon on a day chosen to also celebrate William Howard Taft's birthday—September 15. Laura Arth, the first woman chair of the Sports Committee and a member of the Second Century Committee, was also on hand to celebrate the long-awaited women's locker rooms.

Today, thanks to the Second Century Plan renovations, the University Club's Athletic Center ranks as one of the city's finest fitness facilities. The University Club's outstanding Athletic Center is a testament to the many long hours of pro bono work and creative thinking provided by the membership during the planning and renovation process. But it is also a reflection of the Club's rich traditions of athleticism and fellowship that will take the University Club into its second century.

Supreme Court Chief Justice William H. Rehnquist addresses the Club

Supreme Court Justice Sandra Day O'Connor

Supreme Court Justice Antonin Scalia, Club president Scott Beck, and Supreme Court Chief Justice William H. Rehnquist

Supreme Court Chief Justice William H. Taft

Chapter Twelve

THE CLUB OF THE COURTS

Few clubs can claim the membership of such a distinguished line of judges stretching from President and Chief Justice William Howard Taft to Chief Justice William Rehnquist today.

Back in the 1950s and '60s, Chief Justice Earl Warren was a Club regular, often seen on Friday evenings in the Taft Dining Room with his wife, Honey Bear. The couple, along with their children, were always seated at the same table—in the corner by the American flag. Warren also loved to swim and was a regular in the Club's steam room—making more than one young member of the bar stop in his tracks upon seeing the Chief Justice "au naturel." Being a little intimidated by the man who headed the Court when the historic *Brown v. Board of Education* was handed down is somewhat understandable, but Club members who knew him say he was really just a "regular guy."

Justice William O. Douglas was another member often seen at the Club. In fact, he lived at the club off and on—usually when going through a rough spot on the home front. Douglas was a fan of the Taft Dining Room as well, where he ate on a regular basis and even celebrated when wife, Cathy, graduated from law school.

Justice Byron "Whizzer" White was a squash aficionado and could be seen tearing up the squash courts on a regular basis. And Chief Justice Warren Burger used both the athletic facilities and the dining room. One evening, Miss Laurence remembers, both Warren and Burger dined in the Taft at the same time—one the former Chief Justice and the other the current Chief Justice. A coincidence that could only happen at the University Club.

Today, a number of Supreme Court justices are University Club members, with none more active than Chief Justice William Rehnquist. The Chief Justice has emceed dinners, sat on the Centennial Committee and the Literature and Arts Committee, sold his books at the Book Fair, and swum more lengths of the pool than the rest of the Supreme Court put together. He graciously added his thoughtful words to this book in the preface.

Justice Antonin Scalia, one of the most active UC members on the Court, is a man who loves a good cigar and is a regular at the Club's cigar dinners. At one of these smoke-filled events, comedian Mark Russell sat next to the conservative jurist at dinner. Afterwards, Russell was expected to make a few remarks, and he began by telling the crowd, "I'm delighted to be here tonight sitting to the left of Justice Scalia." He then asked with a sly grin, "But, then, isn't everybody?" Scalia's life of public service also earned him the prestigious Corcoran Award, presented at the Club's annual Sports Banquet. Like Rehnquist, Scalia is a familiar face at Club dinners and events.

Justice Clarence Thomas shares Justice Scalia's passion for a good cigar—or at least he used to. When the cigar dinners were first held at the Club, Thomas was often seen at the slightly raucous affairs. He was asked to tell a story one evening, and he recounted the tale of the first cigar he ever smoked. It belonged to his grandfather. Just a boy at the time, young Clarence sneaked into his grandfather's bedroom and filched a tiparillo from the dresser. He had smoked nearly the entire cigar when his grandfather caught him in the act.

Although at the time he had feared the worst, Thomas told the dinnergoers that his grandfather hadn't punished him at all. "Smoking that whole cigar is far worse than anything I can do to you," his grandfather told him. He was right. The young justice-to-be promptly turned green, and it was a long time before he smoked another cigar.

Today, he doesn't smoke at all, thanks to an important promise he made. A few years ago, Thomas was speaking to a group of Chicago schoolchildren, urging them to make a commitment to stay off drugs, study, and stay in school. One of the kids told the Justice, "only if you promise to quit smoking." He did and so the cigar dinners lost a favorite son.

University Club member Justice Anthony Kennedy, a Lincoln historian, was once asked to give a thirty-minute talk at the Club on the Gettysburg Address as part of a remembrance on Lincoln's birthday. The Justice agreed and, with a wry smile, told the crowd on the appointed day that, "The Gettysburg address is two minutes long. That means I can give it fifteen times, or I can give it once and talk about it."

Justice Sandra Day O'Connor was the special guest for the Club's St. Patrick's Day Celebration one year, along with her husband, John, who was for many years a daily swimmer at the Club. Justice O'Connor also joined her fellow authors at the annual Book Fair after the publication of her bestselling memoir, *Lazy B: Growing Up on a Cattle Ranch in the American Southwest.*

Justice Ruth Bader Ginsburg has also been a special guest at Club activities and events. An opera buff, she did the honors with a wonderful introduction of Denyce Graves when the talented mezzo-soprano was named Distinguished Washingtonian of the Year. The Justice is endowed with an obvious sense of humor. When invited to join the Club, she sent a short note stating that she would be happy to join but only if the misspelling of Chief Justice Rehnquist's name in that year's directory was corrected.

There's no doubt that the Club can claim a majority opinion on the Supreme Court for UC membership.

While the University Club is honored that so many justices of the Supreme Court have joined in the fellowship that is the University Club, jurists have always been drawn to the Club on 16th Street, perhaps because of its historic connection with Chief Justice William Howard Taft. In the 1920s, Judge Martin Knapp of the Commerce Court was a member; in the '50s and '60s, so were Marvin Jones of the Court of Claims and Judge Godfrey Munter of the D.C. Superior Court. In the '70s, Judge John Sirica of Watergate fame was a Club regular, along with George Neilson of the D.C. Superior Court. Neilson could also claim the title of television's first on-air judge after sitting on the "bench" of the NBC show "Traffic Court" in the '50s.

Today, there are still a number of active UC members who come from the judicial community. Judge Loren Smith, the Club's Centennial Committee chairman, sits on the U.S. Court of Federal Claims along with its Chief Judge, UC member Edward Damich. Long Range Planning Committee chairman Paul Michel is a member of the U.S. Court of Appeals for the Federal Circuit, while John Terry is a judge of the D.C. Court of Appeals. Gregory Carman, Chief Judge of the U.S. Court of International Trade; John "Jack" Penn, Judge of the U.S. District Court; and former judge Kenneth Starr add to the Club's illustrious judicial heritage.

Even this partial list clearly shows why the University Club proudly claims the title the "Club of Courts."

"Miss Laurence," Laurence Belanger

LeRoy Harper

Chapter Thirteen

IT WOULDN'T BE THE UNIVERSITY CLUB WITHOUT THEM

When it comes to a first-rate staff, no club can claim a better one than the University Club of Washington. More than 150 dedicated and experienced men and women keep the club humming and its members happy as they do their jobs with professionalism and spirit. They are an outstanding group of talented individuals who help make this Club the remarkable place that it is today. Trying to tell the reader about each of them would take another century, but there are a few whose extraordinary service to the Club has earned them a special mention.

ALBERT ARMSTRONG: GENERAL MANAGER

General Manager Albert Armstrong began his successful tenure with the University Club on October 1, 1990, joining a long list of club managers going back one hundred years. A graduate of Pennsylvania State University with a BS in Food Service and Housing/Administration, Albert came to the Club from the Columbia Club in Indianapolis, where he had also been general manager. Indiana's loss was Washington's gain. During his twelve years at the helm, the University Club has returned to a sound financial footing while greatly expanding both activities and services for members. Albert's special touch can be seen throughout the Club, which has taken on a new, livelier atmosphere under his highly respected leadership. Albert's ability to balance the needs of the members with the future needs of the club ensured a smooth transition as the Second Century Plan renovations were completed successfully and with a minimum of disruption. Working closely with the Board of Governors, Albert has been a major force in turning the Club into the first-class home of good fellowship and fun that it has become.

MISS LAURENCE: MANAGER OF THE TAFT DINING ROOM

On May 3, 1960, Miss Laurence Belanger, a young French-Canadian woman, crossed the threshold of the building that would be a second home to her for more than forty-four years. Although she never intended the University Club to be her life's work, members stretching over four decades are glad she did. Her welcoming smile, gracious personality, and ability to remember the smallest detail has endeared her to more than one generation of Club members. In 1992, more than seventy fans of Miss Laurence honored her many years of outstanding service to the Club, commissioning artist Vits Knuble to paint her beautiful portrait, which now hangs in the "Miss Laurence" Room in the Taft Dining Room. In 2000, members applauded her a second time, celebrating her forty years of service to the Club with a gala dinner. A scholarship has also been named in her honor.

LEROY HARPER: BARTENDER IN THE PERSHING GRILLE

LeRoy Harper is as much a fixture in the Pershing Grille as the portrait of the old general himself, although LeRoy didn't start out in the Grille. When he first came to the University Club in 1963, he started out serving food and setting pins in the bowling alley. Later, he moved up to the Taft Dining Room, where he was a busboy, and then was promoted again to the Billiard Lounge to wait tables. It took ten years for LeRoy to find what has become his permanent home behind the beautiful wood bar in the Grille, where he presides as one of the city's best and most discreet bartenders—so discreet that he even refused to talk shop with this author as a matter of principle. He did share one memory, however, with another staff member. On September 11, he recalled that there were two groups in the Grille who had been stranded in Washington, one from New York and the other from Indiana. The Midwest gang hired a cab to drive them home. The New Yorkers, he says, hired a limo. During interviews for this book, many members spoke fondly of LeRoy and, to a person, sang his praises as one of the most beloved staff people in the history of the Club.

HOWARD DAY: ATHLETIC DIRECTOR

Howard Day didn't start out to be an athletic director. He was a literature major at the University of Pennsylvania who, as he says, "became addicted to squash at twenty-one." Actually, he learned to play the game as a kid and then later, became a tournament player and teacher. Howard came to the University Club in 1980 as squash pro from the Berwyn Club, where he was squash director. The Club has come a long way from its original athletic facility with only a handful of training machines, squash courts, and a pool. Today, Howard's vision of a state-of-the-art athletic center that can meet the needs of a diverse membership has now become a reality, and this top-notch sports professional oversees one of the finest private athletic centers in the city. Howard and his talented and energetic staff of twelve are always there to help members "be what they can be" with the kind of personal attention that has earned Howard and company the thanks and friendship of many members.

GHIRMA MERES

In 1974, Ghirma Meres was a young Ethiopian immigrant working as an attendant in the University Club athletic center. He'd never picked up a squash racquet, but every day as he worked, he watched UC members play the game. Finally, curiosity got the better of him. He picked up a racquet and found his sport. Franklin Gould was the first to recognize the young player's talent, but it didn't take long for other members and the Club's squash pros to see that Ghirma Meres was in a league by himself. Howard Day and former squash pro Tom Lane coached Meres as he became a popular playing partner for members. By the early '80s, he had begun to play in tournament competition, moving from the C Division up to A. For twenty-five years, Meres has played squash competitively, winning many trophies for the Club. Over that time, many members have benefited from a game or a lesson with the well-liked Meres, who all would agree is a true pro.

GARTH "BRAD" ELMORE

When Albert Armstrong headed east to the University Club, he brought more than just his own talent and vision. He brought along one of his most able fellow staff members at the Columbia Club, Brad Elmore, who had been clubhouse manager. Elmore began his service with the University Club as rooms manager, but his interest in international affairs led him to become the clubhouse manager for the University Club's International Center. For the past eight years, he has held the post of clubhouse manager for the University Club, serving as Albert Armstrong's right-hand man. Brad holds one other very special honor. For the past three years, he has served as president of the Cherry Blossom Festival, bringing the University Club's connection with one of Washington's most famous attractions full circle from Mrs. William Howard Taft's original acceptance of the beautiful trees from the mayor of Tokyo in 1911.

PRESIDENTS OF THE UNIVERSITY CLUB

WILLIAM H. TAFT
1904–1906

GEORGE B. CORTELYOU
1906–1907

CHARLES D. WALCOTT
1907–1910

STEPHEN B. ELKINS
1910–1911

GARDNER F. WILLIAMS
1911–1913

MYRON M. PARKER
1913–1921

MARTIN A. KNAPP
1921–1923

DANIEL W. SHEA
1923–1925

LEWIS H. TAYLOR
1925–1927

OLIVER METZEROTT
1927–1929

GEORGE F. SNYDER
1929–1939

PROCTOR L.
DOUGHERTY
1931–1933

CHARLES A. DOUGLAS
1933

T. HOWARD DUCKETT
1933–1936

STANLEY P. SMITH
1936

SPENCER GORDON
1936–1938

STANLEY P. SMITH
1938–1940

GEORGE S. WARD
1940–1942

FREDERICK R. GIBBS
1942–1944

DEAN HILL STANLEY
1944–1946

STERLING ELY
1946–1948

CECIL J. WILKINSON
1948–1950

H. STEWART
MCDONALD
1950–1952

CHARLES E.
PLEDGER, JR.
1952–1954

JAMES M. JOHNSTON
1954–1956

ARTHUR L. WINN
1956–1958

MARCUS H. BURTON
1958–1960

HARVEY G. GRAM, JR.
1960–1962

CARL A. PHILLIPPS
1962–1964

FRANK H. CARMAN
1964–1966

HOWARD A. DONALD
1966–1968

JOSEPH L. WHYTE
1968–1970

JOHN A. BECK
1970–1972

CLIFF BATTLES
1972–1974

GEOFFREY CREYKE, JR.
1974–1976

ARTHUR F. M. HARRIS
1976–1977

GENE E. McCoy
1980–1982

DALE L. JERNBERG
1982–1984

JOHN W. CHANDLER
1984–1985

G. MONTGOMERY
SPINDLER
1985–1987

LEE T. ELLIS, JR.
1987–1989

H. PETER LARSON, III
1989–1990

BERNARD J. CASEY
1990–1992

JAMES D. "MIKE"
McKEVITT
1992–1994

NELSON DECKELBAUM
1994–1995

MAURICE J. WHALEN
1995–1997

PETER J. FARRELL
1997–1999

SCOTT E. BECK
1999–2001

DOUGLAS K.
SPAULDING
2001–2003

SUSAN K. NEELY
2003

MEMBERS OF THE UNIVERSITY CLUB

Mr. Herschel Lee Abbott, Jr.	2001	Mrs. Betty E. April	2002
Ambassador Farid Abboud	1999	The Hon. Glenn L. Archer	1996
Dr. Walid Mahmoud Abdelnasser	2002	Dr. Nicolas Ardito-Barleta	2000
Mr. Edward H. Able, Jr.	1983	Mr. Hadley Philip Arkes	2002
Dr. Amir Abouelnaga	1998	Mrs. Brooks A. Armandroff	2001
Mr. Robert J. Abraham	2000	Dr. Frank Maurice Armbrecht	2001
Mr. Carlos A. Acevedo	1997	Mr. William S. Armistead	1993
Dr. Thomas S. Acker	1996	Ms. Anne C. Armstrong	1993
Mr. David Morgan Adams	1989	Mr. Geoffrey Kenneth Armstrong	2002
Dr. Joan Fiske Adams	2002	Mr. Timothy K. Armstrong	2000
Mrs. Judith Duff Adams	2001	Mr. Michael Deane Arny	2004
Mr. Matthew T. Adams	1968	Ms. Laura E. Arth	1994
Mr. Russell Theodore Adams	2002	Mr. John H. Arundel	2000
Mr. Terrence B. Adamson	2003	Mr. William Charles Arzt	1985
Mr. Errol M. Adels	1997	Mr. Benedict Aspero, Jr.	2003
Mr. Steven E. Adkins	1998	Dr. Nabil J. Asterbadi	1983
Mr. M. Peter Adler	1992	Ambassador Hatem Atallah	2001
Mr. Edward L. Aduss	1995	Mrs. Bernard J. Atchison	1947
Mrs. William C. Affeld, Jr.	1985	Dr. Bettina H. Aten	2003
Mrs. Joan Affleck-Smith	1994	The Hon. Chester G. Atkins	1993
Mr. James F. Agnew, III	2001	Mr. Susumu Awanohara	1995
Mr. Francisco Aguirre-Baca	1962	Dr. Amadou Lamine Ba	2003
Mr. Aakif Kazi Ahmad	2001	Mr. Demba Ba	2002
Ambassador Syed Hasan Ahmad	2002	Mr. Schuyler J. Baab	1991
Mr. Frank Ahmed	1995	Mr. Jon C. Babb	1997
Mr. Truett E. Airhart, Jr.	2000	Mr. William Arnold Babb	1970
Ambassador Abdulwahab Al-Hajjriai	1998	Mr. Faton Alain Bacaj	2003
Dr. Rostom Al-Zoubi	2003	Mr. Richard L. Bacon, Jr.	1999
Dr. Damian P. Alagia, III	1989	Ms. Sandra M. Baer	2002
Mr. Alexander Albert	2003	Dr. Norman Alishan Bailey	1984
Dr. John M. Albertine	1992	Mrs. Pamela G. Bailey	1999
Dr. Judith E. Albino	1993	Mrs. Patricia B. Bailey	1974
Mr. Harry Lyle Albrecht	1963	Ms. Robin Baker	2001
Mr. Eloy Alfaro	2002	Mr. Donald Baldwin	1966
Ambassador Roberto Alfaro	2003	Mr. Neal Ball	1974
Mr. Robert L. Allbritton	1999	Dr. Louis B. Balla	1974
Mr. Paul Shearman Allen	1980	Ms. Debra T. Ballen	1991
Mr. Richard V. Allen	1970	Mr. Charles V. Baltic, III	1992
Mr. Stephen E. Allis	1994	Mr. Jacques D. Bambling	1995
Mr. Jim Allison	2002	Ambassador Donald Bandler	1994
Mrs. Rana H. Altenburg	1998	Ms. Anne C. Banner	2001
Mr. Christopher M. Ambrose	1986	Mr. Russel A. Bantham	1994
Mr. Myles J. Ambrose	1979	Ms. Katherine W. Bantleon	1996
Mr. Harry C. Ames, Jr.	1954	Mr. Mark R. Baran	2000
Dr. Leo David Amorosi	1971	Mr. David Barca	2000
Mr. Carl A. Anderson	1949	Mrs. Tamara S. Barclay	2000
Mr. Douglas G. Anderson	2002	Mr. Terrance A. Barkan	2004
Mr. Norman F. Anderson	1999	Mr. Thomas A. Barnes	2000
Mr. Cliff W. Andrews	1999	Mr. A. Vernon Barnett, IV	2002
Mr. Robert F. Andrews	1997	Mr. Curtis H. Barnette	1992
Mr. Robert Louis Andrews	1970	Mr. Robert Everette Barr	1990
Mr. Anthony Anikeeff	1999	Fr. Ignacio Barreiro	2002
Mr. David Vincent Anthony	1967	Mr. George Edward Barrett	1998
Mr. Peter A. Anthony	2000	Mr. James Warren Barrett	1965
Mr. Frank A. Anton	1999	Dr. Robert Wesley Barrie	1974
Mr. Dominic F. Antonelli	1964	Mr. Thomas E. Barron	2001
Mr. Peter Antonoplos	2001	Mr. Doyle C. Bartlett	1994
Mr. D. Lee Antton	1994	Mr. Richard V. Basch	2001

Mr. Patrick F. Bassett	2001
Mr. Paul W. Bateman	1995
Mr. William B. Bates	1992
Mr. Stephen R. Bathon	1998
Mr. Michael J. Battles	2000
Cardinal William W. Baum	1974
Mr. Michael S. Bearse	1995
Mr. John A. Beck	1956
Mr. Scott E. Beck	1989
Mr. William B. Becker	1947
Mr. Edgar F. Beckham	1998
Mrs. Robert L. Beckwith	1985
Mr. Chess Bedsole	1999
Mr. R. Carey Beer	1983
Mr. Mark S. Begeny	1997
Mr. Falk W. Beindorff	1994
Mr. John Martin Belcher	2002
Mr. Alfred F. Belcuore	1994
Mr. M. Wendell Belew, Jr.	1986
Mr. James L. Bell	2003
Mr. Stephen Bello	2003
Ms. Rebecca J. Benge	1997
Ms. Dawn J. Bennett	1990
Mr. Steven Alan Bennett	2000
Mr. Gary T. Berberian	2000
Ms. Lori A. Berger	2003
Mr. Michael Jay Berger	1995
Mr. Robert Kern Bergman	1957
Mr. Andrew T. Bergstein	1986
Dr. Ida M. Bergstrom	2000
Mr. Alan J. Berkeley	1994
Mr. Donald M. Berlin	2002
Dr. Peter G. Bernad	2003
Mr. Brian A. Bernstein	1986
Mr. Patrick Bernuth	1993
Mr. Luis Berrios-Amadeo	2000
Mr. David J. Berry	1998
Mr. Luis L. Bertorelli	1999
Mr. Rajendra Bery	1995
Mr. Kirk Howard Betts	2003
Dr. Christopher T. Bever	1967
Ambassador Andres Bianchi	2001
Mr. Mark F. Bielski	1990
Dr. Roger R. Bilboul	1994
Mr. Arthur Henry Bill	1963
Mr. Kevin Billings	1995
Mr. Anthony P. Bisceglie	1993
Mrs. Judith Heisley Bishop	1992
Mr. John G. Black	1992
Mr. William Oxford Black	1999
Mr. John Anthony Bladen	1995
Mr. Richard K. Blatt	1996
Mr. David Cooper Blee	2001
Mr. Philip E. Blevins	1979
Mr. Stuart Marshall Bloch	1980
Judge Lawrence J. Block	2003
Dr. Gary Burl Blodgett	2000
Mr. Mark A. Bloomfield	1979
Mr. David Alan Bockorny	2001
Mr. William Herbert Bode	1973
Ms. Helen E. Bodron	1994
Mr. Leopold B. Boeckl	2003
Mr. Robert S. Boege	1991
Mr. Mark Boekenheide	1999

Dr. Judith V. Boettcher	1998
Dr. John William Boettjer	1989
Mrs. Mary P. Bogan	1955
Mr. J. Caleb Boggs, III	1992
Mr. James Edward Boland, Jr.	1998
Mr. James E. Boland, III	2004
Dr. Elizabeth Mary Boles	2002
Mr. Kenneth A. Bolles	2001
Mr. Thomas Newton Bolling	2002
Mr. Paul P. Bollinger, Jr.	1992
Ms. Frances Bolton	2001
Mr. Steven M. Bonavita	2003
Mr. James D. Bond	1974
The Hon. Niles Woodbridge Bond	1947
Col. Richard Laughlin Bond	2003
Mr. Douglas G. Bonner	2000
Mr. Francesco F. Bonomolo	1998
The Rev. David Randell Boone	2001
Mr. Robert Henry Boorman	1948
Ambassador Jose Octavio Bordon	2003
Mr. George Thomas Borger	1985
Mr. William H. Borghesani	1967
Mr. Kevin E. Borland	1998
Ambassador Eric J. Boswell	1994
Mr. Rodrigo Botero	1964
Mr. Joseph W. Bow	1958
Ms. Ginger W. Bower	2003
Mr. David Bowers	1997
Mr. Winston Hammond Bowman	1998
Ms. Mary E. Boyd	2000
Mr. Carlo Bozino	1998
Mrs. John Brabner-Smith	2002
Mr. John R. Braden	1996
Dr. James Peyton Brady	1952
Mr. Phillip Joel Braff	1979
Mr. Stuart John Brahs	1980
Mr. Gregory Alton Brake	1996
Mr. Dan S. Brandenburg	1984
Mr. David M. Braun	1997
Mr. Michael Breen	2000
Mr. Bruce J. Brennan	1966
Mr. William G. Brennan	1991
Mr. Richard S. Brent	2000
Mr. William W. Bride, III	2000
Mr. Steven L. Briggerman	1970
Capt. Jim Brincefield	1995
Mr. Timothy M. Broas	1998
Ms. Angela Brock	2003
Dr. Eric Brodin	1980
Dr. Andrew Bronin	2003
Mr. Luke Aaron Bronin	2002
Mr. Gilbert T. Brophy	1959
Mr. Raymond C. Brophy	1964
The Hon. Donald G. Brotzman	1977
Mrs. Brooks G. Brown	1955
The Hon. Clarence Brown	1993
Mr. Gregg Allen Brown	2004
Mr. James P. Brown	1991
Mr. Kwame R. Brown	2002
Mr. Leland S. Brown, Jr.	1948
Mr. Omer Forrest Brown, II	1988
Dr. Philip Stoddard Brown	1964
Mr. Russell James Brown	2001
Mr. Scott F. Brown	1979

Mrs. Sommers T. Brown	1958	The Hon. Gregory W. Carman	1983
Mr. Miguel D. Browne	1997	Dr. George S. Carnett	1958
Mr. Edmund B. Brownell	1966	Mr. Jorge E. Carnicero	1950
Mr. Roy E. Brownell, II	2000	Mr. Kenneth S. Carpenter	1977
Mr. William T. Browning, Jr.	1998	Mr. Christopher K. Carr	2000
Lt. Col. Stephen G. Brozak	1989	Dr. Ronald R. Carrier	1997
Mr. Alan Lee Brubaker	2002	Mr. James Michael Carroll	2002
Mr. Thomas W. Bruce	1995	Mr. Rodolfo Casasola	2000
Dr. Karen L. Brugge	2000	Mr. David Randall Case	1977
Ambassador Diego Abente Brun	2000	Mr. Bernard J. Casey	1976
Mr. Carl A. Brunetto	1998	Mr. James J. Casimir	1993
Mr. Ronald B. Brunetto	1994	Mr. Alejandro Luis Casiro	2002
Ms. Anne L. Bryant	1993	Mr. Michael J. Caslin, III	1988
Mr. David A. Bryant	2000	Ms. Joan Walsh Cassedy	2001
Mr. James S. Bryant	1995	President John T. Casteen, III	1993
Mrs. Mary C. Buchanan	1941	Mr. Fernando A. Castillo	2000
Mr. Patrick J. Buchanan	1969	Ambassador Hernan R. Castro	1998
Mr. Thomas M. Buchanan	1999	Mr. Frank G. Caterinicchio	2000
Ms. Judith A. Buckalew	1992	Mr. Joseph J. Cattaneo	1993
Mr. Thomas L. Buckmaster	1993	Dr. Michael Robert Cave	2002
Mr. William E. Bucknam	1998	Mr. John J.R. Cavendish	2003
Mr. Robert R. Budway	1995	Mr. Frederick Ulysses A. Cedoz	2002
Dr. James Bundschuh	2001	Mr. Donald Cefaratti, Jr.	1948
Mr. Jessie Thomas Bunn	1985	Mr. Benny Frankie Cerezo	1990
Mr. Michael Burda	1996	Mr. Milton Cerny	1992
Ms. Barbara Ann Burgess	1995	Mr. Mark P. Chadason	2001
Dr. Guenter Oatwin Burghardt	2003	Mr. Shu-Ping Chan	2000
Mr. Gerard P. Burke	1995	Mr. John W. Chandler	1968
Mr. John G. Burke	2000	Mr. Armando C. Chapelli, Jr.	1983
Mr. Phillip C. Burnett	1990	Mr. L. William Chapin, II	1995
Mr. Larry D. Burton	1993	Mr. Bruce K. Chapman	2001
Mr. Chris R. Bury	1994	Mr. Colin A. Chapman	1993
Ambassador Martin Butora	1999	Ms. Elizabeth M. Chapman	1998
Rev., Dr. Charles Gregory Butta	2002	Dr. Steven Edward Chapman	2002
Mrs. Diana Byfield	1942	Ms. Meg Charles	2003
Mr. S. John Byington	2000	Mr. Derwood S. Chase, Jr.	2001
Mr. Lloyd G. Byrd	1964	Ambassador Luis Enrique Chase	2002
Mr. Gregory R. Byrnes	1999	Mr. L. Stanley Chauvin, Jr.	2000
Rev. William J. Byron, S.J.	1997	Dr. H. H. Chen	1995
Mr. Robert J. Cabelly	1996	Mr. Gerard Le Chevallier	1999
Mr. Cesar B. Cabrera	1990	Ms. Anne Richmond Chitwood	2003
Mr. Michael R. Calabrese	2002	Mr. David C. Chou	2003
Mr. Robert A. Calderisi	1995	The Hon. Jack C. Chow	2003
Mr. James Neely Caldwell	1955	Rev. Ronald F. Christian	1993
Mr. William J. Callahan	2001	Mr. John C. Christie, Jr.	1989
Mr. Kevin R. Callwood	1992	Mr. Thomas Matthew Cicotello	2003
Mr. Generoso G. Calonge	2001	Mr. Tom Clancy	1993
Mr. Charles A. Camalier, III	1982	Mr. Michael K. Clare	1986
Mr. F. Davis Camalier	1979	Mr. Andrew Clark	2003
Mr. Carl Capper Campbell	1956	Mr. Harry L. Clark	2000
Mr. Willard D. Campbell, Jr.	1972	Dr. John FJ Clark	1995
Mr. Robert P. Canavan	1994	Mr. John O. Clarke, Jr.	1986
Mrs. Daniel W. Cannon	1952	Mr. William Clarkson, V	2001
Mr. Fred Cannon	2000	Mr. Don Richard Clay	1970
Mr. Santiago A. Canton	1999	Mr. Kenneth J. Clayton	1997
Mrs. Marianne S. Cantwell	1994	Ms. L. Jane Clement	2003
The Hon. Mortimer Caplin	1969	Mr. Thomas E. Clement	1997
Mr. Frank S. Capozza	2003	Mr. Robert S. Clements	1954
Mr. Michael R. Caputo	1996	Mr. David L. Cleveland	1991
Mr. John Ariel Cardon	1958	Mr. Harlan Cleveland	1995
Mr. Thomas A. Carey	1999	Mr. David Palmer Close	1947
Mr. Joseph A. Cari	1995	Dr. G. Wayne Clough	1993
Mr. Leland V. Carlson, V	1991	Mr. Robert Watson Cobb	1984
Ms. Nancy Beth Carlson	2003	Mr. Ronald N. Cobert	1976

Mr. Robert James Cocchiaro	2002
Dr. Elizabeth A. Cocke	2001
Mr. Mark William Coe	1991
Mr. Matthew B. Coffey	1999
Mr. Harvey B. Cohen	1999
Mr. Marcus Reuben Cohen	2002
Mr. Mark A. Cohen	1996
Ms. Michele Coiron Swartz	1994
Mr. Irvin Delano Coker	1995
The Hon. Joseph V. Colaianni	1984
Mr. Edward George Coleman	2003
Mr. Herbert H. Coleman	1991
Mr. Justin S. Colin	1956
Mr. Patrick D. Coll	1999
Mrs. Philip R. Collins	1950
Mr. Richard L. Collins	1998
Mrs. Warren C. Coloney	1985
Mrs. John W. Connelly, Jr.	1988
Mr. Robert F. Connelly	1995
Mr. Jimmy Hoyt Conner	1980
Mr. John Davis Conner	1946
Ms. Annemargaret Connolly	2000
Mr. Gregory M. Connors	1997
Rev. David John Conway	1965
Mrs. Anita Cook	1966
Mr. Gary M. Cook	1979
Ms. Catherine Joanna Cooke	2003
Ms. Catherine Nixon Cooke	2003
Mr. Joseph T. Cooke	1959
Ms. Kiersten Todt Coon	2002
Mr. Christopher A. Coons	1998
Mrs. Ben H. Cooper	1954
Mr. Benjamin S. Cooper	1997
Mr. Thomas G. Corcoran, Jr.	1964
Mr. Neil Raymond Corey	1970
Mr. Richard J. Cornish	1959
Mr. Philip S. Corwin	1998
Mrs. Benedict C. Cosimano	1963
Mr. Roger Cossack	1996
Mr. Michael E. Costello	1992
Mr. Nicholas P. Cotroneo	1996
Mr. William J.G. Cottam	2002
Mr. Joaquin A. Cottani	2000
Mr. James A. Couter	1991
Mr. Christopher Paul Cowie	2003
Mr. Denis M. Crane	1962
Mr. Thomas J. Craren	1997
Mr. Charles S. Crawford	2003
Mr. Ray T. Crescenzo	1997
Mr. T. Kenneth Cribb, Jr.	1990
Mr. Garrett N. Crichton	1997
Mr. Thomas M. Crimmins	1998
Mr. Robert Worth Crolius	1980
Ms. Amy S. Cropp	2000
Ms. Susan L. Crown	2001
Mr. Rafael E. Cuellar	2003
Mr. K. E. Krispen Culbertson	2002
Dr. Leon R. Culbertson	1950
Mr. David Andrew Culver	2002
Father Charles L. Currie	1998
Mr. L. Rodger Currie	2000
Mr. Timothy Brian Curry	2003
Ms. Marika M. Cutler	1994
Mr. James Madison Cutts	1970

Mr. Richard Lee Cys	1970
Mr. Grover Edward Czech	1979
Mr. Jonah Jennings Czerwinski	2003
Mr. Alexander D'Amico	2003
Mr. William S. D'Amico	1991
Mr. Paul D'Armiento	1990
Mr. William Kay Daines	1970
Mr. Dack W. Dalrymple	1994
Dr. William Dalston	2000
Mr. Ole B. Dam	2002
Mr. Alan A. Dambrosio	1993
The Hon. Edward J. Damich	2002
Mr. Thomas J. Dammrich	2001
Mr. C. F. Damon, Jr.	1961
Mr. M. Doug Damron	2001
Mr. Andrew Michael Danas	2001
Dr. William H. Danforth	1993
Mr. Scott M. Daniels	2002
Ms. Beverly B. Danielson	1999
Ambassador Roberto Danino	2002
Mr. Jean Louis R. Danis	1993
Mr. David W. Danjczek	1972
Ambassador Jaime Daremblum	1998
Mr. Steven M. Darien	1997
Mr. Thomas D. Darlington	1999
The Hon. Hal Daub, Jr.	2001
Mr. Thomas M. Davidson	1993
Mr. Conyers Davis, II	2003
Mr. Floyd E. Davis, III	1979
Mr. John Gilbert Davis	1986
Mr. Joshua Michael Davis	2003
Mr. Stephen C. Davis	1996
Mr. Timothy Gary Davis	1989
Mr. William E. Davis	1983
Mr. Calvin Davison	1959
Mrs. Adelaide B. Dawson	1979
Ambassador Leila T R De Cowles	2000
Ambassador Albert Borg Olivier de Puget	1996
Dr. Charles de Seve	1985
Mr. Ronald O. Deabler	1995
Mr. Charles L. Debrunner	1994
Mr. David A. Deckelbaum	1983
Mr. Nelson Deckelbaum	1979
Dr. Robert Deckelbaum	1997
Ms. Colleen Anne Deegan	2003
Mr. Haskin U. Deeley, III	1994
Mr. C. Stanley Dees	1971
Mr. C. Michael Deese	1995
Mr. Thomas Michael DeFrank	2002
President John J. DeGioia	2002
Mrs. Joseph A. Degrandi	1995
Mr. Makarand V. Dehejia	1995
Ambassador Edmund T. DeJarnette	1995
Mrs. Sarah Carter Delaney	1990
Dr. W. Morgan Delaney	1939
Mr. Timothy Delany	2002
Mr. Jairo Delgado	2003
Mr. John J. Dempsey, III	2000
Mr. Joseph J. Dempsey, Jr.	1999
Mr. William L. Dennis	1992
Ms. Janet S. Denny	1999
The Hon. Butler C. Derrick	1994
The Hon. Edward J. Derwinski	1989
Dr. Malcolm M. Desouza	1995

Dr. Denis Detzel	2001
Mr. John J. Devine	2000
Dr. Wolfgang Dexheimer	1997
Mr. Robert M. Diamond	1987
Mr. Alvaro Diaz De Vivar	2000
Mr. Ben H. Dickens	1989
Dr. Chester T. Dickerson, Jr.	1982
Mr. B. Gordon Dickey	1955
Mr. Iannis D. Dikos	2002
Mr. Frank W. Dillow	1999
Mr. Fabio Paolo Diminich	2003
Mr. Francis E. Dimond	1983
Mr. Thomas A. Dine	1999
Ms. Patricia Dinger	2001
Mrs. Margaret Dinneen	1962
Mr. Brent Parker Dinsdale	2003
Mr. Anthony E. Diresta	2000
Dr. Ralph R. Disibio	1993
Ambassador Lev E. Dobriansky, Ph.D.	1957
The Hon. Paula J. Dobriansky, Ph.D.	1991
Dr. John Dodds	2003
Dr. Richard L. Doege	2001
Mr. Steven Paul Doehler	1983
Mr. Peter F. Doherty	2004
Mr. Robert F. Domagala, Jr.	1988
Mr. Matthew E. Donahue, III	1971
Mrs. Howard A. Donald	1950
Mr. Stephen G. Donches	2001
Mr. Raymond Edward Donnelly, III	2002
Mr. Patrick J. Donovan	2000
Mr. Richard Carl Donovan	2003
Mr. Timothy G. Donovan	1978
Mr. Devin John Doolan	1969
Mr. Wayne Elliot Dorman	1961
Mr. John Dougherty	1970
Mr. Frederick A. Douglas	1993
Mr. J. Richard Dowell	1993
Mr. Arthur T. Downey, III	1993
Mr. Thomas M. Downs	2000
Mr. J. Andrew Doyle	1988
The Hon. John Frances Doyle	1967
Mr. Paul Dragoumis	1979
Dr. John Warren Drake	1977
Mrs. Patricia H. Dresser	2000
Mr. Scott T. Driscoll	1997
Mr. Timothy S. Driscoll	1999
Mr. Andrew J. Dubill	2000
Mr. Louis M. Dubin	1988
Ambassador Sorin Dumitru Ducaru	2002
Mr. Daniel Levon Dudas	1986
Mr. Robert Arthur Dufek	1990
Dr. Dick Duffey	1949
Ms. Erin E. Duffy Conaton	2000
Ms. Elizabeth A. Duffy	2000
Mr. Stephen C. Duffy	1998
Mr. Francis Duggan	1999
Mr. Charles E. Dujon	1996
Mr. William F. Dunbar, IV	1988
Dr. Mary Ellen Duncan	1997
Mrs. Tricia E. Duncan	2001
Mr. Wallace Lamar Duncan	1986
Mrs. Lucy M. Duncan-Scheman	1993
Mr. Dorsey C. Dunn	1999
Mr. William John Dunn	2002

Mrs. Patricia B. Dunnavant	1964
Ms. Elizabeth Van Orman Dupree	2002
Mr. Michael E. Durkin	1988
Mr. Jan Dvorak	1999
Mrs. William S. Dwinnell	1986
Mr. John W. Dykes, Jr.	2000
Mr. Robert Lee Eacho	1954
Mrs. William C. Eacho, Jr.	1952
Mr. Bryan R. Earl	1997
Mr. Stephen J. Easley	1998
Mr. David K. Easlick, Jr.	2001
Ms. Sarah Jane Easlick	2001
Mr. Samuel Ewer Eastman	1959
Mr. Lawrence S. Ebner	1980
Mr. Clifford C. Eby	1999
Dr. Oscar A. Echevarria	1997
Mrs. W. Bradley Edelblut	1939
Ms. Courtney R. Eden	2001
Mr. Roy C. Edgerton	1970
Mr. James Warren Edmondson	2003
Mr. Thomas B. Edsall	1993
Mr. Bert Tvedt Edwards	1970
Judge Harry T. Edwards	1994
Mr. Macon T. Edwards	1998
Mrs. Thelma Edwards	1944
Mr. Collins C. Ege	2001
Dr. Steven A. Eggland	2001
Mr. Leonard A. C. Eiserer	1956
Mr. Ashraf A. Elattar	2000
Mr. Eduardo Elejalde	1996
Mr. Akram Elias	2002
Ms. Molly A. Elkin	1997
Professor Marc S. Ellenbogen	1997
Dr. Lloyd H. Elliott	1979
Mr. Lee Thomas Ellis, Jr.	1973
Ms. Pamela Kathleen Ellis	2003
Brother Patrick Ellis	1992
Mr. Raymond S. Elman	2003
Mr. Thomas W. Elwood	1997
Ms. Charity C. Emeronye	2000
Mr. Christopher Emerson	2003
Dr. Robert C. Emling	2000
Mr. G. Raymond Empson	1994
Mr. Carl F. Emswiller, Jr.	2002
Ambassador Roland Eng	2000
Mr. Vincent A. Eng	2000
Mr. W. Keith Engel	1957
Mr. Preston A. Englert, Jr.	1987
Mr. William Lloyd Ensign	1978
Mr. Xavier FCO Equihua	1994
Mr. Bulent Erdemgil	2002
Mr. Harvey F. Ernest, Jr.	1992
Ms. Susan C. Ervin	2001
Mr. Gregory L. Evans	1999
The Hon. Jack Evans	1993
Mr. James G. Evans	1995
Rev. John Miles Evans	1978
Mrs. Rae Forker Evans	1991
Mr. Ralph Bayard Evans	2001
Mr. G. Stimson Eveleth	1980
Mr. Anthony H. Ewing	2003
The Hon. Thomas W. Ewing	2003
Mr. Ralph K. Eyster	1963
Mr. Bernard M. Fagelson	1991

Ambassador Mohamed N. Fahmy	2000
Mr. F. Peter Falcone	2001
Mr. R. Scott Faley	1977
Ms. Alexandra Falzon	2001
Mrs. Joseph J. Fanelli	1995
Mrs. Tisha Fang	1993
Mr. Chester W. Fannon, Jr.	2003
Mr. Joseph M. Farrell	1965
Bishop Kevin J. Farrell	1996
Mr. Peter Justin Farrell	1983
Mr. Richard T. Farrell, Jr.	1989
Mr. Connor Keating Faught	2003
Mr. Saul Feder	2001
Ms. Kirsten Ann Fedewa	2002
Mr. L. John Fedewa, Jr.	1997
Dr. Craig F. Feied	1994
Mr. John W. Feist	1979
Mr. Timothy P. Feldman	1990
Dr. Alvin S. Felzenberg	1991
Mr. David W. Fenstermaker	1979
Mr. Frank Fenton	1980
Mr. Nicholas M. Ferguson	1995
Mrs. Joyce S. Fernando, RN	2003
Mr. Lionel Shane Fernando	2001
The Hon. Andrew B. Ferrari	1954
Dr. Eduardo Ferrero-Costa	2002
Mrs. Margaret J. Ferrin	1997
Ms. Margaret A. Ferry	1999
Mr. Hart Fessenden	1987
Mr. Robert G. Fichenberg	1995
Mr. Reid M. Figel	2000
Mr. John Kahl Figge	1988
Mr. Thomas John Filep	2002
Ambassador Edward R. Finch	1941
Dr. Elizabeth Finch	1984
Mr. Jimmie Finkelstein	1992
Mr. Chester E. Finn, Jr.	1989
Ambassador Juan Enrique Fischer	2002
Mr. L. Richard Fischer	1990
Mr. Paul W. Fish	1993
Ms. Donna Jeanne Fisher	2000
Mr. Eric K. Fisher	1999
Mr. Joseph A. Fisher, III	1969
Mr. Peter C. Fisher	1997
Dr. Richard P. Fishman	1990
Mr. Matthew J. Fitzgerald	2000
Ambassador William H. G. FitzGerald	1935
Mr. Christopher C. Flaesch	1990
Dr. Martin P. Fleming	1999
Mr. Harold K. Fletcher	1964
Mr. Lawrence G. Flick	2002
Mr. Thomas M. Flohr	1999
Mr. John A. Flood	2000
Mr. Edward M. Fogarty	1974
The Hon. Thomas S. Foley	1988
Mr. Clayton S. Fong	1997
Mr. Peter D. Forbes	2001
Mrs. James David Ford	1988
Mr. Randy Ford	2001
Mr. Richard Edwin Ford	1962
Mr. John R. Fornaciari	1972
Ms. JuliAnne H. Forrest	2003
Mr. Douglas R. Forrester	1995
Mr. Robert J. Forrester	1999

Mr. John G. Forsythe	1999
Mr. Albert J. Forte	1995
Mr. Francesco Forte	2003
Mr. Stephen Patrick Forte	2002
Ms. Amy E. Fortenberry	1997
Col. H. Minton Francis	2003
Mr. Peter A. Frank	1993
Mrs. James Denny Franklin	1985
Mr. Mark A. Franz	1992
Ms. Suzon W. Franzke	1995
Mr. Donald Ross Fraser	1954
Mr. James W. Fraser	1999
Mr. Douglas Freberg, II	2002
Mr. James Carlton Free	1981
Mr. Anthony G. Freeman	1995
Ms. Paula A. Freer	1991
Mr. John A. Frekko	2003
Mr. Oliver P. R. Fremond	1999
Mr. Alvin Friedman	1995
Dr. Aharon Friedman	2000
Mr. Allen R. Frischkorn, Jr.	1995
Ambassador Claudia Fritsche	2001
Dr. Howard C. Froehlich	1994
Ms. Susan Frost	2002
Mr. David E. Frulla	1991
Dr. William F. Fry	1993
Mr. Todd J Frye	1999
Mr. Hugh Nevin Fryer	1983
Mr. Harold W. Furman, II	2001
Mr. Toshihiko Furuya	2000
The Hon. Bohdan A. Futey	1992
Mr. James S. Gable	2002
VADM Paul G. Gaffney, II	2001
Mr. Philip A. Gagner	1998
Mr. Benito Gaguine	1937
Mr. Robert F. Gair	2002
Ms. Jatrice Martel Gaiter	1999
Mr. James E. Gale	1995
Mrs. Elizabeth F. Gallagher	1995
Mr. Peter A. Gallagher	2001
Dr. Harvey Galper	1993
Mr. Charles A. Gambrill	1958
The Hon. Raul Gangotena	2003
Dr. John Anthony Gans	1989
Dr. Ernest Garcia	1954
Mr. Michael O. Garcia	1996
President Antonio R. Garcia-Padilla	2002
Mr. James L. Garde-Meader	2000
Mr. Syed Zulfiqar H. Gardezi	2003
Mr. Bryant Everett Gardner	2002
Mr. James F. Gardner	1997
Mr. James Franklin Garver	1950
Mr. Bruce A. Gates	2003
Mr. Brian X. Gaul	1999
Mr. Damien Joseph Gaul	2001
Ms. V. Anne Gehrett	1992
Mr. Michael D. Gehrisch	2002
The Hon. Samuel Gejdenson	2000
The Hon. J. Russell George	2000
Mr. Leo I. George	2002
Mr. Richard W. George	2001
Father William L. George, S.J.	1992
Mr. Jack Noel Gerard	2001
Mr. James Watson Gerard, V	1984

Mr. Mark L. Gerchick	1985		Mrs. Faye Anne Graul	2001
Mr. James W. Geriak	1979		Ms. Denise Graveline	1997
Mr. Ahmad Ghassabeh	1980		Ms. Denyce Graves	2000
Ms. Maria C. Ghazal	1994		Ltg. Ernest Graves	1995
Ambassador S. A. K. Ghazzali	1999		Mr. Gordon T. Graves	1999
Mr. Andrew A. Giaccia	1994		Mr. Alan Gibson Gray	1974
Mrs. Megan Diane Gianchetta	2002		Ms. Carolyn D. Gray	1991
Mr. David F. Giannini	1997		Mr. Michael T. Gray	2004
Mr. Petch Gibbons	1984		Mr. Robert Reid Gray	1955
Mr. Jeffrey J. Gibbs	2001		Ms. Victoria Gray	1998
Mr. Monte Gibbs	2002		Mr. George G. Green	1995
Mr. Robert F. Gibbs	1977		Ms. Sheila Frances Green	2001
Mr. Brian B. Gibney	1988		Mr. William A. Green	1999
Mr. Alan B. Gibson	1999		Mr. Jeffrey L. Greenblum	1990
Judge Reginald W. Gibson	1993		Ms. Nancy Deale Greene	1999
Dr. Richard Scott Gibson	1998		Mr. Randall Ashley Greene	1990
Dr. Anne Grace Giesecke	2002		Mr. Mark A. Gresham	1995
Ambassador Rodolfo Hugo Gil	2002		Mr. Dennis C. Griesing	1993
Monsignor James G. Gillen	1965		Mr. Mark Gerard Griffin	1971
Mr. Neal P. Gillen	1991		Col. Leonard Griggs	1990
Mr. James S. Gilliland	1994		Mrs. Marilyn J. Grimm	1993
President Malcolm Gillis	1993		Mr. John Farrar Grissom	1992
Mr. Peter Ladd Gilsey	1955		Mr. Charles L. Grizzle	1991
The Hon. Douglas H. Ginsburg	2002		Mr. Louis L.I. Grossman	1983
The Hon. Ruth B. Ginsburg	1993		Mr. John Henry Grover	1954
Mr. Joseph Michael Gionfriddo	2001		Ambassador Przemyslaw Grudzinski	2002
Mr. Carl Edward Girth	1971		Ambassador Kostyantyn Gryshchenko	2000
Mr. Thomas M. Gittings	1957		Ms. Lee B. Guerry	2000
Mr. Joseph C. Giuliani	1972		Dr. Donald L. Guertin	1994
Mr. Scott Glabman	1995		Mr. Gaurang Mitu Gulati	2001
Mr. Herbert Alexander Glaser	2003		Mrs. Virginia W. Guldi	1994
Ms. Sharon Kay Glickman	2002		Mr. James B. Gurley	2001
Mr. Maurice O. Glinton	1993		Mr. John W. H. Gushee	1993
Mr. Gerd F. Gloeckle	1999		Mrs. Frances M. Gwin	1957
Dr. Harold Jerome Goald	1998		Mr. Charles Thomas Haag	2002
Mr. Gregory Gerald Godbout	2003		Mr. Theodore J. Hadraba	1996
Mr. Constantine B. Gogos	2000		Dr. Joseph H. Hagan	1965
Mr. Sherwood "Woody" D. Goldberg	1986		Mr. W. Eugene Hagar	1969
Mr. Cornelius J. Golden	1993		Mr. J. K. Hage	1996
Mr. Peter L. Goldman	1994		Senator Chuck Hagel	1987
Mr. Charles Frank Goldsmith	2004		Mrs. Arthur C. Hagen	1943
Mr. Ira Goldstein	1993		Ms. Colleen M. Hahn	1993
Mr. Robert E. Goldsten	1994		Mr. James F. Haight	1965
Mr. Michael J. Goltzman	1998		Mr. John J. Haley	1993
Mr. Martin J. Golub	1985		Dr. Carl W. Hall	1995
Mrs. Rudolph E. Gomez	1996		Mr. Richard P. Hall	2001
Mr. Martin Gomez-Bustillo	1997		Mr. William N. Hall	1993
Mrs. Alice C. Goodman	1998		Mr. Robert Halligan	1995
Mr. David Lewis Goodman	1979		Mr. David R. Halperin	1972
Mr. Gary R. Goodweather	1997		Ms. Andrea Mead Halverson	2003
Mr. John D. Goodwin, Jr.	2001		Mr. Shinya Hamano	2003
Ms. Amanda Hughes Gordon	2002		Mr. J. Craig Hamilton	1974
Mr. Spencer Gordon, Jr., M.D.	1951		Mr. Palmer C. Hamilton	1995
Mr. Donald Michael Gore	2003		Ms. Sally Elizabeth Hamlin	2001
Mr. Neil M. Gorsuch	2003		Ms. Jennifer H. Hamm	2000
Mr. Kingdon Gould, Jr.	1962		Ms. Carole D. Hamner	2000
Mr. C. Marshall Graham	1998		Ms. Jenny Nova Han	2000
Mr. Duncan Graham	1995		Dr. Jady G. Handal	1999
Ms. Amanda Rhea Grainger	2003		Dr. Gay. P. Hanna	2003
Col. Wallace D. Gram	1992		Mr. Richard L. Hanneman	1987
Mr. Patrick Clifford Graney, IV	2002		Mr. Mark C. Hansen	1994
Mr. Theodore M. Grannatt	2001		Mr. Michael L. Hansen	1995
Mr. John M. Grau	2001		Mrs. Robert L. Hansen	1993
Mr. John D. Graubert	1997		Mr. Terry L. Hansen	2001

The Rev. Bruce Edward Harbert	2003		Ms. Kimberly Elizabeth Hippler	2002
Mr. John T. Hardisty	1995		Mr. Richard Henry Hirsch	1979
Mr. Stan M. Harrell	1998		Mr. D. Jeffrey Hirschberg	1992
Ms. Patricia McLauglin Harris	2003		Mr. Robert L. Hirshberg	1995
Col. John W. Harrison	1974		The Hon. Peter J. Hoagland	1995
Mr. Orrin L. Harrison	2000		Mr. Henry E. Hockeimer	1991
Mr. Barry J. Hart	1993		Mr. John Carl Hockenbury	1998
Mr. Benson Hambleton Hart	1965		Mr. John R. Hocker	1996
Monsignor Kevin Thomas Hart	1986		Dr. Emory F. Hodges	1960
Dr. Donald H. Harter	1991		The Hon. Robert H. Hodges	1994
Dr. A. Howland Hartley	2001		The Hon. Thomas F Hogan	2002
Ms. Nancy Hartzenbusch	1995		Mr. Thomas H. Hogan	1998
Mr. Brian S. Harvey	2002		Mr. Peter W. Hoguet	1942
Mr. Robert Glenn Haskell	1990		Mr. George E. B. Holding	1999
Mr. Scot T. Hasselman	2003		Mr. James H. Holl	1999
Ms. Holly Hassett	2003		Mrs. Wilhelmina C. Holladay	2000
Mr. Jace C. Hassett	1993		Mr. J. Timothy Holland	1978
Dr. Hussein Hassouna	N/A		Ms. Carolyn Hollander	1999
Ms. Cary Collins Hatch	1981		Mr. Russell A. Hollrah	1999
Mr. Robert Neil Hatch	1972		Mr. Bryan L. Holmes	2000
Mr. John Jude Hathway	2002		Mr. Mark S. Holmes	1998
Mr. Martin J. Hatlie	1994		Mr. Stephen G. Holowesko	1996
Mrs. Grace B. Hawken	1991		Ms. Lynn F. Holstein	2002
Mr. James W. Hawkins	1990		Mr. Peter Hong	2001
Mr. Ashraf Mohammad Hayat	2003		Mrs. Sally Ann Hooks	1987
Mr. John W. Hayden	2003		Mr. Gregg Ross Hopkins	1978
Mr. James P. Head	1992		Mr. Stephen A. Hopkins	1977
Ms. Laura E. Head	1997		Mr. Robert Jack Horn	1978
Ms. Joan Saenz Healey	1997		Mrs. Martha B. Hossman	2000
Mr. Brian Keith Heard	1989		Mr. David G. Houck	1994
Mr. William Herbert Hecht	1976		Mr. Robert F. Housman	1995
Mr. John M. Heckler	1990		Mr. Frank J. Howard	2001
The Hon. Margaret M. Heckler	1992		Mr. Gerald M. Howard	2001
Mr. L. Eugene Hedberg	1943		Mr. Matthew C. Howard	1989
Dr. Edward Joseph Heiden	1989		Mr. Curtis Joseph Hoxter	1988
Mr. John I. Heise	1959		Mr. Clark Hoyt	2000
Mr. Jon E. Heisler	2002		Ms. Claudia A. Hrvatin	1998
Mr. Milton Heller	1990		Mr. Michael Stuart Hubbard	2002
Mr. Robert W. Helm	2000		Mr. Laverine Hubert	1990
Ms. Cynthia C. Henderson	1998		Mr. Daryl J. Hudson	2000
Mr. Douglas B. Henderson	1966		Mr. Ernest Boyd Hueter	1984
Dr. Fred B. Henderson	1979		Mr. John Boston Huffaker	1950
Mr. James G. Hendrickson	1990		Mr. Patrick Arthur Huge	2001
Dr. G. Ronald Herd	1962		Mr. Charles Scott Hughes	1990
Mr. Louis Hering	1994		Mr. Evan G. Hughes	1990
Mr. Mauricio Herman	1995		Mr. George J. Hughes	1961
Mr. Sylvan Herman	1991		Lt. Gen. Harley A. Hughes	1989
Mr. Richard A. Herold	1996		Mr. James R. Hughes	2003
Ambassador Marcelo Hervas	2003		Dr. John J. Hughes	1962
Dr. Walter John Hesse	1960		Mr. Thomas G. Hughes	1998
Mr. Stephen O. Hessler	1994		Mr. Cameron R. Hume	1994
Mr. Henry Lewis Heymann	1971		Mr. Charles A. Hunnicutt	1995
Cardinal James Hickey	1980		Major Gen. Milton Hunter	2003
Mr. Christopher Hicks	1996		Mrs. Thomas W. Hunter	1979
Mr. J. Thomas Higginbotham	1975		Ms. Mary Ann Huntington	1989
Mr. James F. Higgins	2002		Col. Frank K. Hurd	2004
Mr. Michael J. Higgins	2000		Mr. James D. Hurd	1948
Dr. Patrice LR Higonnet	1998		Capt. Robert C. Hurd	2000
Mr. Kazuo Higuchi	2000		Archbishop Francis T. Hurley	1959
Mr. Sanford JA Hill	1994		Ambassador Lionel A. Hurst	2002
Mr. Vada Hill	2000		Mr. Kenneth Gene Hurwitz	1991
Mrs. W. M. Hill	1944		Mr. John D. Hushon	1990
Mr. Willard I. Hill	1994		Mr. James S. Hutchinson	2002
Mr. Van D. Hipp	1995		Mr. James F. Hyde	1949

Mr. Richard W. Hynson	1949		Ms. Nawal Kamel	2001
Dr. Joseph Anthony Imler	1984		Mr. Ronald P. Kananen	1975
Mr. Arthur E. Imperatore	1983		Ambassador Tony Kandiero	2000
Mr. Kenneth Ingram	1992		Mr. John J. Kane	2001
Mr. Fred Israel	1976		Mr. Tai S. Kang	1998
Mr. Charles S. Iversen	1989		Mr. Jeffrey John Kanne	2002
Mr. William J. Ivey	2002		Ambassador Mary M. Kanya	1997
Mr. Alfred Jackson	1995		Mr. Jacob J. Kaplan	1995
The Hon. Alphonso Jackson	2003		Mr. Jeffrey Kaplan	1999
Mr. Christopher R. Jackson	1999		Mr. Michael H. Kappaz	1995
Mr. James John Jackson	2002		Mr. Anil Kapur	1997
Mr. Neal Andrews Jackson	1976		Mr. Nuhad E. Karaki	1998
President Thomas Humphrey Jackson	1998		Mrs. Sargent Karch	1987
Mr. Thomas H. Jackson	2000		The Hon. David K. Karnes	1981
Ms. Madeleine Jacobs	2004		Mr. Hrishi Karthikeyan	2004
Mr. Timothy C. Jacobson	2000		The Hon. Robert W. Kasten	1993
Mr. David Bruce Jaffe	2003		Mr. Hans C. Kastensmith	2003
Mr. Armiger Louis Jagoe	1953		Mr. Alexander N. Kasuya	2003
Mr. E. Allen James	1992		Mr. Joel R. Kaswell	1981
Mr. Gregory Lee James	2003		Mr. Harry J. Katrichis	2004
Monsignor W. Ronald Jameson	2000		Amb. Theodore H. Kattouf	2003
Mr. Robert Byrd Jamison	1978		Mr. Robert N. Katz	1986
Mr. Frank Jao	2003		Mr. John L. Kaufman	2000
Dr. Charlene Drew Jarvis	1999		Mr. Yoshihiko Kawamura	1996
Mr. Michael D. Jarvis	1993		Mr. Robert F. Kay	1997
Mr. Joshua M. Javits	1990		Mr. Frederic Gould Kayser	1990
Mr. David C. Jeanes	1995		Mr. J. Patrick Kearns	1997
Ms. Mary Louise Jefferson	1996		Mr. Kevin L. Kearns	2002
Ms. Elvira Jeffrey	1983		Mr. Perry E. Keating	1998
Mr. Joshua Nicolas Jeffries	2003		Mr. James Keats	1999
Mr. Leo J. Jennings	1992		Ms. Suzanne E. Kecmer	2003
Dr. William A. Jennings	1994		Mr. Eugene Adams Keeney	1970
Dr. Donald Norman Jensen	2002		Mr. Herbert B. Keil	1997
Mr. Dale L. Jernberg	1965		Mr. R. Bruce Keiner	1967
Mr. Joe L. Jessup	1984		Mr. Mark Richard Kelley	2002
Dr. G. Griffith Johnson	1950		Mr. Oliver N. E. Kellman	2003
Mrs. Helen L. Johnson	2003		Mr. Michael K. Kellogg	2000
Mr. James W. Johnson	1993		Mr. Charles Brian Kelly	1998
Dr. James Dean Johnson	2003		Mr. Dennis Peter Kelly	2003
Mr. Michael Jan Johnson	1998		Dr. John T. Kelly	2002
Mr. Nicolas Charles Johnson	2002		Mr. Michael S. Kelly	1987
Mr. Paul Richard Johnson	1998		Mr. Stan Kelly	1996
Mr. Richard Clark Johnson	1969		Mr. W. Thomas Kelly	2001
Mr. Roderick L. Johnson	2003		The Hon. Jack F. Kemp	1999
Mr. Theodore M. Johnson	1967		Mr. Thad S. Kemp	1991
Mr. Felton "Mac" Johnston	1975		Professor Reinhard K. Kempa	2001
Mr. Christopher M. Jones	2000		Mr. Jackson Kemper	1985
Mr. Wiley Newell Jones	1982		Mr. Jonathan L. Kempner	1987
Ambassador William B. Jones	1995		Mr. Coleman S. Kendall	2003
President I. King Jordan	1988		Mr. Alfred P. Kennedy	1997
Mr. John E. Jordan	1995		The Hon. Anthony M. Kennedy	1989
Mr. Allen T. Joseph	1977		Mr. John Patrick Kennedy	1962
Ms. Michele F. Joy	1994		Ms. Judith A. Kennedy	2003
Mr. Paul M. Joyal	1998		Fr. Robert T. Kennedy	2000
Mr. Thomas Michael Joyce	1965		Mr. Robert G. Kennedy	2002
Mr. Moises E. Juliao	2003		Mr. William D. Kenworthy	1999
Mr. Charles P.E. Junet	1996		Mr. Thomas L. Kenyon	1990
Dr. Hans U. Juttner	1996		Mr. Floyd Kephart	1997
Dr. Gopal Kadagathur	1998		Mr. Breene Mitchell Kerr	1966
Mrs. Rose L. Kadan	1950		Mr. William Owen Kerr	1999
Mr. Ely J. Kahn	2003		Ms. Karen A. Kerrigan	2002
Mr. Michael P. Kahn	2002		Mr. Sean Richard Keveney	2003
Mr. Steven C. Kahn	1990		Mr. John F. Kevill	1995
Mrs. Harry R. Kain	1981		Mr. G. Chandler Keys	1998

Ms. Astrid Helen Khayat	2002	Mr. Edward R. Kump	1993
Mr. Edward Walker Kidd	2002	Ms. Yoncha Kundupoglu	2000
Mr. Douglas C. Kiker	2002	Dr. Sachiko Ueno Kuno	2002
Mrs. Ruth A. Kile	1999	Dr. James A. Kushlan	1995
Dr. Robert A. Kilmarx	1995	Ambassador Alan John Kyerematen	2002
Mr. Thomas J. Kim	2000	Mr. Thomas F. Kyhos	1980
Mr. James Verlin Kimsey	1972	Mr. John Anthony Lacey	1987
Ms. Jessica Jean King	2002	Ms. Pamela A. Lacey	1994
Mr. John C. King	2003	President Benjamin Ladner	1994
Mr. Robert J. King	2001	Dr. George Madison Lady	1966
Mr. Richard J. Kinney	1994	Mr. Pierre J. LaForce	1969
Mr. Joseph M. Kipp	1980	Mr. William N. LaForge	1991
Mr. Clarence T. Kipps	1995	Mr. Mario S. Lagdameo	1995
Mr. Peter M. Kirby	1992	Reverend Paul Terrence Lamb	1960
Mr. Karl S. F. Kirchner	1995	Mr. James H. Lambright	2004
Ms. Beverly K. Kirk	2000	Dr. W. Henry Lambright	1976
Mr. Neil Jamison Kirk	1990	Mr. John James Lampros	2001
Mr. Edwin P. Kirkpatrick	1966	Mr. Robert Raymond Lane	2002
Mrs. Rowland F. Kirks	1950	Dr. Michael D. Langan	1997
Mr. John P. Kirlin	1989	Dr. Mark D. Lange	2003
Mr. Thomas John Kirlin	1989	Mr. Chiswell D. Langhorne	1967
Dr. William Kirwan	1989	Col. John V. Lanterman	1995
Mr. John Daniel Kiser	1997	Dr. Michael F. Lapadula	1962
Mr. David W. Kistler	1993	Mr. Nicholas Lardy	1995
Mr. H. Donald Kistler	1937	Mr. William R. Large	2001
Mr. David Armin Klaus	2003	The Hon. Larry P. LaRocco	1999
Mr. Andrew Manning Klein	1990	Mr. Peter M. Larsen	1975
Mr. Gary J. Klein	1991	Mr. Richard Gary Larsen	1990
Mr. Martin A. Klein	1979	Mr. Charles F. Larson	1994
Ms. Teresa L. Klein	2000	Mr. H. Peter Larson	1971
Mr. George D. Kleinfeld	1992	Mrs. Roberts B. Larson	1986
Mr. C. Fred Kleinknecht	1973	Mr. Claude William LaSalle	2002
Mr. Lawrence Lee Klumpp	2002	Mr. John N. Lauer	1995
Mr. Leon Thomas Knauer	1970	Ambassador Luis Lauredo	2001
Mr. Richard M. Knauff	2003	Mr. William J. Lauttamus	1961
Mr. John M. R. Kneuer	2002	Mr. Anthony Leo Lawless	1985
Mr. Albert Baker Knoll	1995	Mr. Charles R. Lawrence	1999
Rev. Bernard P. Knoth	1999	Mr. George H. Lawrence	1965
Mr. James Burbank Knowles	2003	Mr. Stanton T. Lawrence	1996
Mr. Kent F. Knutson	1995	Mr. Belford Vance Lawson	2001
Major Victor H. Koch	2001	Mr. Richard C. Lawson	1999
Dr. Leslie W. Koepplin	1979	General Richard L. Lawson	1987
Dr. Israel Kogan	1976	Mr. Erik J. Laykin	2004
Mr. Charles E. M. Kolb	1998	Mr. Kenneth A. Lazarus	2001
Mr. Glen Franklin Koontz	2000	Mr. Richard C. Leahy	1997
Dr. Jeffrey P. Koplan	1999	Mr. Robert D. Leahy	1986
Mr. Donald R. Kornblet	2003	Dr. William Richard Leahy	1978
Mr. Tony Kornheiser	2001	Rev. William P. Leahy	1996
Mr. Milton Kotler	1994	Dr. Linda J. Lear	1997
Mr. Charles J. L. T. Kovacs	1995	Mr. Ronald H. Leasburg	1997
Ms. Kasia O. Kozinski	1999	Mr. Jeff S. Lee	2002
Ambassador Davorin Kracun	2000	Ms. Katharine K. Leeson	2003
Ambassador Sakthip Krairiksh	2002	Mr. Edward Leftwich, Jr.	2000
Mr. Theodore Keil Kral	2002	Mr. Willie L. Leftwich	1993
Rev. Philip J. Kratovil	1989	Mr. Carroll H. Leggett	1986
Mrs. Margery Kraus	2002	Mr. Matthew H. Leggett	2001
Mr. Harvey J. Krauss	1998	Ms. Dana Lehmer	1999
Mr. Richard S. Kraut	1998	Mr. Chrys D. Lemon	1992
Mr. Frederick Krebs	1991	Mr. James H. Lemon, Jr.	1977
Ms. CeCe Kremer	1992	Mr. Glenn Brian LeMunyon	2003
Mr. John W. Kropf	1995	Dr. Marjorie Peace Lenn	1999
The Hon. Kevin H. Kruke	1988	Mr. Gerald I. Lenrow	1991
Mr. Pedro Pablo Kuczynski	1962	Mr. Terry F. Lenzner	1995
Mr. Shylendra Kumar	2002	Mr. Earl T. Leonard, Jr.	1989

Ms. Eileen N. Leonhardy	2000	Ambassador Princeton N. Lyman	1995
Mr. Donald G. Lerch, Jr.	1967	Mr. Anthony John Lynch	1988
Mr. Francis A. Lesieur, III	2000	Mr. Joseph Patrick Lynch	1962
Mrs. Kirsten A. Leslie	1989	Mr. Michael Lynch	1970
Mrs. Cynthia W. Lett	1997	Mr. Richard Potter Lynch	2003
Mr. Charles F. Lettow	1989	Mr. Robert E. Lynch, Jr.	1973
Mr. Arthur David Levin	1979	Mr. John W. Lyon	1986
Mr. David F. Lewis	2002	Mr. Gary R. Lytle	1992
Mr. Flint H. Lewis	2002	Mr. Peder Maarbjerg	1997
Mr. Howard Lewis, III	2002	Mr. Gordon P. MacDougall	1990
Mr. R. Brian Lewis	1995	The Hon. Ronald K. Machtley	1995
Mr. Stuart M. Lewis	1995	Mr. Charles S. Mack	1995
Mr. W. Brad Lewis	2003	Mr. James Edward Mack	1950
Mr. Mark L. Lezell	1998	Mr. Colm Mackernan	1991
Ms. Meredith A. Light	2000	Mr. Edward R. Mackiewicz	1978
President Peter W. Likins	1993	Mr. Jeffrey M. MacKinnon	1993
Dr. Alfred M. Lilienthal	1981	Ms. Wendy M. MacLeod	2001
Mr. Clifton E. Lind	2001	Mr. Thomas J. Macpeak	2000
Ms. Teresa C. Lindsey	1998	Ms. Marian Macpherson	1997
Ms. Paddy Link	2000	Mr. H. Cabell Maddux, Jr.	1947
Mr. John J. Linnehan	1973	Mr. Alan M. Madison	2000
Professor David F. Linowes	1995	Mr. Gary K. Madson	1997
Mr. Harry Michael Linowes	1975	Mr. Edward Charles Maeder	1974
Mr. Marc R. Lippman	2001	Mr. James T. Magee	1995
Mr. Harry Joseph Lister	1986	Mrs. Warren E. Magee	1957
Mr. Basil R. Littin	1970	Mr. William F. Magner, III	1989
Mr. John J. Lively	1998	Mr. Dadi Mahlouji	1999
Mr. Robert W. Lively	1995	Mr. William G. Mahoney	1966
Mr. Nicholas Lloreda	1994	Mrs. Elizabeth Malarkey	1956
Mr. Henry Malcolm Lloyd	1976	Mr Steven Malevich	2001
Capt. Wallace H. Lloyd, Jr.	1964	Mr. Richard A. Maloney	1993
CDR. Wallace H. Lloyd, III	1981	Ambassador Charles T. Manatt	1994
Mr. William Atkinson Lobb	1978	Mr. Jeffery Manber	1996
Mr. James A. LoBosco	2001	Dr. N. Bhushan Mandava	1995
Mr. Brian A. Lobuts	2002	Mr. Robert Alton Mangrum	1976
Mr. Robert Hugh Loeffler	1980	Ms. Jennifer M. Manly	1996
Mr. Stephen Edward Loflin	2003	Mr. Frank Ernest Manning	1963
Ambassador Osman Faruk Logoglu	2001	Ambassador Lalit Mansingh	2002
Mr. Steven P. Lombardo	1996	Mr. J. Eugene Marans	1986
Mr. Joshua E. London	2002	Mr. Albert John Marchetti	2002
Mr. Charles R. Long	1988	Mr. Stanley M. Marcuss	1980
Ms. Heather E. Long	2004	Mr. Stanley V. Margolin	1982
Mr. John Robert Longenecker	2003	The Hon. Lawrence S. Margolis	1993
Mr. Edward J. Longosz, II	1990	Mr. Gregory J. Marich	2001
Mr. Kevin L. Lorenz	2000	Mr. Luther A. Markwart	1998
Mr. Robert E. Losch	1961	Dr. Albert Edward Marland	1956
Mr. Thomas C. Louthan	1994	Mrs. F. Hal Marley	1995
Mr. Nash M. Love	1960	Mr. Michael R. Marsh	1999
Ms. Alexandra Noelle Lowe	2002	Mr. Daniel V. Marshall	2003
Mr. J. William Lowe	1995	Ms. Susan Marshall	2001
Mr. John Gordon Lowe	2002	Ms. Susanne T. Marshall	2003
Mr. William Douglas Lowe	1998	Dr. William E. Marshall	1984
Mr. William Webb Lowe	1957	Mr. Harry Martens, Jr.	1949
The Hon. John Lowell	2003	Mr. Clarence E. Martin, III	2000
Mr. Robert Lowenstein	1975	Mr. James L. Martin, Ph.D., M.D.	2000
Mr. Harry Lucas, Jr.	1969	Dean Joseph Martin	1993
Father Gregory Lucey, S.J.	2000	Mr. Ralph D. Martin	1991
Mr. John F. Lucey	1992	Mr. Tobey B. Marzouk	1978
Rev. George F. Lundy, S.J., Ph.D.	2000	Mr. Frank E. Mason, III	1996
Ms. Cecily U. Lupo	2001	Dr. Alfonso D. Massaro	2003
Mrs. J. Gerald Lustine	1996	Mr. Albert L. Massoni	1997
Mrs. Barbara Luther	1943	Mr. Marcelo A. Massoni	1999
Mr. James Reindert Luyten	2002	Mr. Richard D. Mathias	1967
Mr. Martin E. Lybecker	1986	Mr. Michael Matteo	2003

Mr. Derek James Maurer	2001
Mr. James Collins May	1989
Mr. Eddie R. Mayberry	1997
The Hon. H. Robert Mayer	1998
Mr. H. Albert Mayorga	1999
Mr. Albert S. Mazloom, III	1996
Mr. Julian I. Mazor	2003
Dr. Sean D. McAlister	1998
Ms. Virginia A. McArthur	1998
Mr. Richard J. McBride, Jr.	1990
Mr. William C. McCahill, Jr.	2001
Mr. Douglas F. McCallum	2001
Mr. John D. McCallum	1997
Mr. Thomas L. McCally	1998
Cardinal Theodore E. McCarrick, Ph.D., D.D.	2001
Mr. James A. McCarthy	1995
Mr. James R. McCarthy	1986
Mr. Howard G. McClintic	1981
Rev. C. John McCloskey, III	1998
Mr. Frederick Donald McClure	2002
Mr. William E. McClure	1996
Mr. Jesse T. McCollum	2001
Mr. Leander McCormick-Goodhart	2003
Mr. Gene E. McCoy	1962
Mr. Todd O. McCracken	1999
Mr. Thomas O. McCraken	2000
Mr. Ian F. McCredie	1999
Mr. John E. McCullough	1997
Mr. John A. McCullough	1974
Ms. Carol A. McDaid	1997
Mr. John P. McDaniel	1983
Mr. Daniel J. McDermott	1993
Mr. Terrence M. McDermott	1997
Dr. Daniel F. McDonald	2000
Mr. John Lee McDougal	1966
Dr. Gerald N. McEwen, Jr.	2001
Mr. Douglas B. McFadden	1972
Mr. Jere D. McGaffey	1986
Mr. Gregory K. McGillivary	1995
Mrs. Ruth Ann McGrail	1954
Mr. Jerome James McGrath	1954
Mr. John Adams McGraw	1971
Mrs. Marie J. McGroary	1944
Rev. Martin McGuill	1999
Mr. Martin E. McGuinness	2001
Mr. Joseph M. McGuire	2001
President Patricia McGuire	1999
Mr. William D. McGuth	1999
Mr. William J. McHale	1969
Mrs. Samuel D. McIlwain	1953
Mr. Stephen B McKanna	2001
Mrs. Arnold McKee	1995
Mr. Paul W McKee	2001
Mrs. James D. McKevitt	1979
Mr. James Thomas McKinlay, III	2003
Dr. Donald H. McKnew, Jr.	1956
Mr. Timothy P. McKone	2000
Mr. Bruce M. McLane	1999
Mr. Thomas Anthony McLaren, Jr.	2002
Mr. Donald W. McLaughlin	2003
Mr. Francis X. McLaughlin	1992
Mr. Christopher Michael McLean	2003
Very Rev. Daniel McLellan, OFM	2003
Mr. Michael G. McManus	2003
Mr. Kay McMurray	1973
Mrs. Frederick V. McNair, III	1966
Mr. James E. McNair	1997
Mr. J. Paul McNamara	1996
Mr. Christopher M. McNulty	1981
Mr. James F. McNulty	1991
Mr. Paul E. McNulty	1995
Mr. Gary R. McNutt	1997
President M. Peter McPherson	1998
Mr. Robert Brian McPherson	1993
Mr. William C. McPike	1976
Mr. Brian D. McQuade	1979
Dr. John McShefferty	1994
Mr. James Patrick McVaney	1999
Mr. Grady Edward Means	1990
The Hon. Edwin Meese, III	1993
Mr. Thomas Fleetwood Mefford	2002
Dr. Michael E. Melich	1970
Ms. Ronnie Mae Melnick	2003
Mr. Paul A. Meloan	2002
Mr. M. Edward Melton	1964
Ambassador Jerome Mendouga	1998
Mr. Adolfo Menendez	1995
Mr. Russell C. Merbeth	2000
Ms. Lisa Downey Merriam	1993
Mr. Philip Merrill	1995
Dr. Alan G. Merten	1997
Ms. Linda G. Messersmith	1995
Mr. Alfred Mark Messina	2003
Mr. Douglas W. Metz	1989
The Hon. Howard M. Metzenbaum	1996
The Hon. John C. Metzler	1994
RADM Wayne E. Meyer, USN	1994
Mr. Gerald Edward Meyerman	1999
Mr. Khaled M. Mezran	1996
Mr. Matthew N. Mezzanotte	1963
Mr. David Phillip Michaels	2000
Judge Paul R. Michel	1993
The Hon. Robert H. Michel	1981
Mr. Buxton S. Midyette	1990
Mr. Tetsuhide Mikamo	2003
Mr. Stacey Milam	2003
Mr. Edward D. Miles	1991
Mr. William W. Millar	2001
Ms. Debra A. Millenson	2003
The Hon. Christine O. C. Miller	1991
Mr. David J. Miller	2003
Ms. Elizabeth Smith Miller	1996
Mr. Richard Charles Miller	1997
Mr. Rollins W. Miller	1954
Mr. Todd Adam Miller	2002
Mr. W. Todd Miller	2003
Mr. William T. Miller	1980
Mr. William A. Milligan	1995
Mr. Roger K. Minami	2001
Mr. Yoichi Mineo	1999
Mr. Thomas H. Miner	1995
Mr. James Robert Minter	2001
Mr. Alexander V. Mirtchev	1995
Dr. Luis Mispireta	1990
Mr. Peter K. Mitchell, Jr.	1991
Mr. Louis Mitler	1997
Mr. John F. Mizroch	2001
Mr. Robert L. Moberly	2000

Mr. David Thomson Mohler	2001	Mr. Whitney Myrus	2000
Mr. Samuel T. Mok	1998	Mr. Frederick P. Nader	1994
Mr. Jose D. Molina	1999	Ms. Laura J. Nafis	2003
Dr. Jayhun Mollazade	1995	Mr. Richard W. Naing	1981
Mr. Robert Thomas Molloy	1959	Mr. Osamu Nakayama	2003
Mr. Chester Manly Molpus	1974	Mr. J. Christopher Nassief	1998
Mr. Joseph A. Monaghan	2002	Mr. Vincent M. Nathan	1997
Mr. Thomas Patrick Monaghan	2004	Mr. John F. Natoli	1999
Mr. Carl C. Monk	1992	Mr. Stephen L. Neal, Jr.	1997
Mr. W. Kirk Monroe	1993	The Hon. Susan K. Neely	1991
Ms. Lois H. Montaigne	1998	Amb. John D. Negroponte	1989
Mr. Kevin P. Montgomery	1991	Ambassador Charles J. Nelson	1995
Mr. Larry Dean Montgomery	1980	Mr. Daniel W. Nelson	1996
Mr. Mario G. Montoto	1999	Dr. Douglas T. Nelson	1995
Mr. Warren K. Montouri	1970	Ms. Lynn C. Nelson-Paretta	1997
Mr. Thomas Y. Moon	1998	Dr. Mark Richard Nemec	2001
Mr. Adrian Wallace Moore, Jr.	1955	Mr. Alexander Lloyd Nerska	2001
Mr. Carlos F. J. Moore	1982	Mr. Roger Alan Neuhoff	1956
Mr. Francis B. Moore	1993	Mr. Edward John Neumann	1979
Ms. Jennifer Alice Moore	2002	Mr. Andrew Christian Neville	2001
Mr. Peter O'Bannon Moore	2002	Mrs. Hal Harker Newell	1968
Mr. Walter K. Moore	1991	Mr. Jack R. Newman	1975
Mr. James Olaf Moorhouse	2003	Mrs. Henry S. Newport	1995
Mr. Thomas P. Moran	1999	Ms. Lisa Michelle Newport	2001
Mr. Philip Moreau	1996	Mr. Bruce C. Nichols	1991
Ambassador Luis Moreno	1999	Mr. Daniel A. Nichols	1991
Mr. Richard Alan Morgan	2003	Mr. Christopher Nicholson	1995
Mr. James F. Moriarty	1996	Mrs. David Brown Nicholson	1947
Mr. Peter Ford Moriarty	1984	Ambassador James Nicholson	1998
Dr. Richard Morrill	1997	Mrs. Margaret T. Nicholson	1947
Ms. Elizabeth R. Morrissey	2000	Ms. Marlene N. Nicholson	1994
Mr. Gerald A. Morrissey, III	2003	Mr. Richard K. Nobbe	1995
Ms. Rebecca Morter	2003	Ms. Diane Z. Noble	1997
Mr. Jack Morton	1945	Mr. David A. Norcross	1994
Mr. William L. Morton	1999	Mrs. Bernard I. Nordlinger	1966
Ambassador Peter Moser	2000	Mrs. Patricia Marie Normile	2001
Mrs. Robert Sheriffs Moss	1950	Mrs. Mary Kathleen Norris	2003
President C. Daniel Mote, Ph.D.	1999	Dr. Herbert R. Northrup	1971
Mr. William E. Mouzavires	1983	Mr. Charles D. Nottingham	1992
Dr. Jack H. Mower	1981	Mr. Aleksandr V. Novoselov	1997
Mr. Hussein Abol Kirim Mubarak	2002	Father Alan Novotny, S.J.	1998
Mr. Philip J. Mudd	1972	Mr. Howard Nusbaum	2002
Mr. Ronald O. Mueller	1997	The Hon. Bernard Nussbaum	1994
Mr. Charles A. Muldoon	2003	Mr. Eugene Nyambal	2000
Mr. Joseph Muldoon, III	1990	Mr. Michael J. O'Bannon	1992
Mr. Jeffrey B. Mulhall	1986	Mr. Anthony Nicholas O'Brien	2003
Major Timothy James Mulholland	2003	Archbishop Edwin O'Brien	1997
Rev. Richard A. Mullins	2003	Dr. Gregory M. St. L. O'Brien	1997
Mr. Gregory Allen Munford	2003	Very Rev. David M. O'Connell, C.M.	1998
Mr. L. Manning Muntzing	1995	Mr. Brian T. O'Connor	1999
Mrs. Dorothy Bell Murgolo	1949	Mr. Charles A. O'Connor, III	1971
Ms. Diane W. Murphy	2003	The Hon. Sandra D. O'Connor	1988
Mrs. Mary Ann Murphy	1984	Ms. Victoria Aine O'Connor	2003
Mr. Sean Patrick Murphy	1998	Dr. Timothy O'Donnell	2003
Mr. Timothy M. Murphy	1993	Dr. Mary J. O'Driscoll-Levy	1997
Mr. James Milton Murray	1958	Ms. Catherine C. O'Farrell	1995
Mr. James M. Murray	1993	Mrs. Jean O'Hanlon	1946
Mr. Samuel Haines Murray	1977	Mr. Daniel F. O'Keefe, Jr.	1960
Ms. Suzanne M. Murrin	1999	Ms. Grace D. O'Malley	1995
Ms. Mary Ursula Musacchia	2003	Mr. Robert S. O'Neil	1992
Mr. Carter Breland Myers	2002	Mr. C. Larry O'Rourke	1995
Mr. Daniel N. Myers	1995	Mr. Peter E. O'Rourke	1993
Mr. Donald J. Myers	1999	Mr. James F. O'Sullivan	1986
Mr. Carl Steere Myrus	2000	Mr. John Denis O'Toole	1976

Mr. Claudio Godinez Ochoa	2003	Mr. Clarence G. Pechacek	1938
Mr. Robert C. Odle, Jr.	1986	Mr. Steven M. Peer	1996
Mr. Clint Edward Odom	2002	Ms. Ann Pelham	2003
The Hon. Neil H. Offen	1994	Dr. Richard G. Pellergrino	2000
Mr. Eric M. Oganesoff	1995	Mr. Emil T. Pena	2001
Ms. Yoshie Ogawa	1995	The Hon. John G. Penn	1993
Mr. Yasunaga Ohara	1994	Mr. A. Rhodes Perdue	1998
Ms. Theresa M. Ojakli	1996	Mr. Enrique F. Perez	1998
Mr. Robert Andrew Okun	2001	Mr. Edward M. Peters	1996
Mr. John W. Olcott	1993	Mr. John Henry Peterson, III	2003
Mr. William C. Oldaker	1994	Mr. Marshall R. Peterson, III	2002
Ambassador Roble O. Olhaye	1997	Mr. Peter G. Peterson	1971
Mr. Alvin Earl Oliver	1954	Mr. Richard W. Peterson	1977
Mr. Van Roger Olsen	1976	Mr. Richie Petitbon	2003
Mr. Michael A. Olshonsky	2003	Ms. Monika F. Petter	2001
Mr. John Frederick Olson	1986	Mr. Brian T. Petty	1992
Mr. Michael Sanders Olson	1998	Mr. Hugo M. Pfaltz	1998
Mr. Nels B. Olson	1996	Mr. Christopher Leland Philbrook	2003
Mr. Timothy Olson	1993	Mr. Donald W. Phillips	1988
Ms. Diann K. Onsted	1986	Mr. Howard Phillips	1990
Mr. Peter Louis Oppenheim	2003	Mr. Howard W. Phillips, Jr.	1981
Mr. Vance K. Opperman	1991	Mr. Walter C. Phillips, III	1999
Mr. Brian J. Orbell	1993	Mr. William D. Phillips	1990
Mr. Allen H. Orenberg	1989	Mr. James Kade Pickard	1957
Mr. David Osnos	1999	Mr. Lee A. Pickard	1984
Mr. Christopher Anthony Ott	2002	Mr. Stanley F. Pickett	1978
Mr. Gregg D. Ottinger	1987	Mr. William R. Pierangeli	1999
Mr. Josh Kelly Overbay	2003	Mr. Steven J. Piguet	1994
Mr. Charles L. Overman	1996	Mr. Douglas G. Pinkham	1997
Mr. Douglas H. Paal	1993	Mr. John G. Pinto	2003
Mr. Richard Pacheco, Jr.	1999	Mr. Gordon Russell Pipe	1961
Dr. Edward A. Padelford, Jr.	1956	Mr. Herman R. Pirchner	1996
Mr. Keith Owen Palmer	2002	Dr. John Pisarkiewicz	1996
Ambassador Martin Palous	2001	Mr. Nicholas J. Pittas	1999
Mr. Joseph C. Palumbo	1965	Minister Diego Pizano	1995
Mr. Jack J. Pannell, Jr.	2000	Mr. Daniel Jeffrey Plaine	1976
Mr. Peter S. Pantaleo	1990	Mrs. Susann W. Plair	1982
Ms. Carolyn Panzer	1995	The Hon. Donald J. Planty	2002
Dr. Dimitri B. Papadimitriou	1996	Mr. Stephen B. Pociask	2001
Mr. Duane A. Parde	2000	Dr. William Lawrence Pollard	2003
Mr. Lawrence R. Paretta	2000	Mr. David B. Pollin	1997
Mr. Donald L. Park	1995	Mr. Alex J. Pollock	2002
Mr. James A. Parker	1981	Mr. Carl F. Pompei	2000
Mr. Kevin M. Parker	2003	Mr. Daniel John Popeo	1989
Mr. Robert P. Parker	1997	Ambassador Elena Borislavova Poptodorova	2002
President Stephen D. Parker	1996	Mr. Alexander Ellsworth Porteous	2003
Mr. M. Everett Parkinson	1946	Mr. William Lane Porter, Jr.	1968
Mr. Lewis W. Parks	1997	Mr. Lendell W. Porterfield	1997
Mr. David T. Parry	1997	Mr. Michael J. Poston	1999
Mr. Leonard Edward Pasek	1952	Mr. James Craig Potter	1988
Ambassador Hafiz Pashayev	1995	Dr. Aemil Pouler	1974
Mr. Barry A. Passett	1980	Mr. Edward J. Poutier	2001
Mr. Alfred A. Patnaude	1999	Ms. Erin Elizabeth Powell	2002
Mr. James H. Patterson	1973	Mrs. Pauline Doyle Powell	1990
Dr. Jonathan L. Patterson	1999	Mrs. Elina H. Pratt	1999
Major Gen. George S. Patton	1991	Mr. Stuart K. Pratt	2002
Mr. Charles W. Paul	2003	Mr. Robert A. Prenner	2000
Mr. Christopher S. Paul	1992	Mr. R. Edward Price	1999
Mr. Anthony T. Pavel, Jr.	2001	Secretary Anthony J. Principi	2001
Mr. Malcolm E. Peabody	1977	Mr. John E. Prominski	1991
Mr. David F. Pearce, Jr.	1999	Mr. Peter Davis Prowitt	1989
Mr. Steven R. Pearlstein	1993	Mr. Arthur Jay Pugh	1977
Mrs. Jed W. Pearson	1989	Ltc. Norman A. Pugh-Newby	2003
Ms. Mary Frances Pearson	1992	Mr. George H. Purcell	2001

Ms. Terry L. Purkable, Ph.D.	2000	Mr. Stephen F. Riley	1996
Mr. Raymond S E Pushkar	1975	Dr. Auguste E. Rimpel, Jr.	1995
Mr. Thomas Oakley Pyle	2002	The Hon. Matthew J. Rinaldo	1993
Mr. John Pyles, III	1967	Mr. William K. Ris, Jr.	1996
Ambassador Ashraf Jehangir Qazi	2002	Mr. Harvey Rishikof	1999
The Hon. Dan Quayle	1992	Mrs. Louise B. Risk	1963
Mrs. Virginia C. Quigley	1984	Mr. C. Willis Ritter	1973
Mr. Harold P. Quinn, Jr.	1994	Mr. David B. Rivkin	1991
Mr. James L. Quinn, Jr.	2000	Mr. Christopher S. Rizek	2001
Mr. T. Anthony Quinn	1997	Mr. Philip Joseph Rizik	1970
Mr. Marc Harding Radasky	2003	Mrs. Susan Morgan Rizik	1954
Dr. Paul M. Rader	1999	Mr. Jack R. Roadhouse	1999
Mr. Charles A. Ragan	1948	Mr. David H. Robb	1997
Mr. Michael Patrick Rahill	2002	Major Gen. Earnest O. Robbins, II	2003
Ms. Anneli H. Rahn	1992	Dr. Paul H. Robbins	1950
Mr. Alan Taylor Rains, Jr.	1984	Mr. Edwin S. Roberson	1999
Ms. Maile P. Ramzi	1995	Mr. Thomas W. Roberson	1998
Mr. Christopher Rand	2003	Mr. David H. Roberts	1995
Mr. D. Michael Rappoport	1974	Mr. Lee Harris Roberts	1993
Mr. John C. Rasmus	1995	Mr. W. Wesley Roberts	1949
Mr. Joshua B. Raynolds	1992	Mr. William A. Roberts	2002
Mr. Bryce Rea, Jr.	1948	Mr. Fraser Robertson	1998
Ms. Celina Realuyo	1990	Mr. Bernard M. Robinson	2000
Mr. Pompeyo Roa Realuyo	1977	Mr. Edward M. Robinson	1997
Mr. Roger R. Ream	1991	Dr. Prezell R. Robinson	1995
Mr. Thomas J. Reckford	1977	Mr. David A. Roby, Jr.	2004
Mr. Robert E. Redding	1953	Mr. Andres F. Rodriguez	1998
Mr. Michael A. Redisch	1983	Mr. Jesus Rodriguez-Montero	1998
Mr. Robert Redpath	2002	Mr. Mario Rodriguez-Montero	1999
Mr. Charles D. Reed	1978	Mrs. Eugene F. Roesser	1954
Mr. Kenneth M. Reese	1960	Mr. Carl Roeth	2000
Mrs. Robert H. Reeside	1984	Mr. Douglas A. Rogers	2000
Mr. John A. Regan	2000	Ms. Martha P. Rogers	1994
Mr. Alfred S. Regnery	1988	Mr. Richard R. Roldan	2000
Mr. Eric Rehfeld	1995	Mr. Emil A. Romagnoli	1994
The Hon. William H. Rehnquist	1971	Ms. Cynthia Cox Roman	2002
Col. Robert Newton Reid	1939	Mr. Zvi Steve Rome	1991
Mr. William H. Reigeluth	1998	Ambassador Aivis Ronis	2000
The Hon. William Kane Reilly	1977	Dr. Linwood H. Rose	1999
Mr. Gary B. Reimer	1995	Mr. Richard J. Rosenthal	2001
President Jehuda Reinharz	1994	Ms. Eve Ross	2000
Mr. James Edgar Reinke	1971	Mr. Gray Dunnington Rosse	1994
Mr. Robert A. F. Reisner	1993	Mr. Mark T. Rossini	1999
Dr. Peter D. Relic	1995	Ms. Mary Patricia Roth	2000
Mr. Pablo Andrew Renart	2000	Mr. Andrew J. Rotherham	2000
Mr. John O. Renken	1995	Mr. James E. Rottsolk	2000
Dr. Judith A. Renyi	1998	Mrs. Frances Rotwein	1990
Mr. M. Riley Repko	1990	Mr. Malcolm D. Rowat	1981
Mr. John M. Reskovac	2002	Mr. James A. Rowland	1997
Mr. Barclay T. Resler	1989	Mr. Avik S. A. Roy, M.D.	2000
Mr. Jeffrey Michael Revis	2003	Mrs. Cora G. Rubenstein	1986
Mr. George Dewey Reycraft	1963	Mr. Michael Eric Rubin	2004
Mr. Joseph A. Reyes	1999	Mr. Ross N. Rubin	2000
Ambassador Jesus F. Reyes-Heroles	1997	Mr. Nicholas C. Ruffin	2001
Pres. Emer. Frank H. T. Rhodes	1993	Mr. Kurt Rumsfeld	1999
Mrs. Paul Miller Rhodes	1950	Mr. Richard N. Runes	1995
Dr. L. Lawrence Riccio	1999	Dr. George Rupp	1993
Mr. Ralph S. Richard	1966	Mr. Wayne H. Rusch	1987
Ms. Patricia Richards	1990	Mr. John W. Ruser	1999
Mr. Daniel E. Richardson	1994	Mr. Barry Russell	1996
Mr. Donald H. Richardson	1947	Mr. Mark Russell	2001
Mr. Stephan G. Richter	1998	Mr. McKinney H. Russell	1995
The Hon. Donald Wayne Riegle	2002	Mr. Timothy M. Rutten	1999
Mr. Kenneth C. Rietz	1995	Mr. Luis Ruvira	1999
Rev. Vincent J. Rigdon	1999	Dr. James A. Ryan	1960

Mr. Jay T. Ryan	1997		Mr. Peter M. Scott	1995
Mrs. Maria L. Ryan	1953		Dr. Yvonne Scruggs-Leftwich	2000
Mr. Stephen Michael Ryan	2002		Ms. Jennifer A. Scully	1993
Ms. Pamela Jo Rypkema	1993		Dr. Edward D. Scura	1994
The Hon. Jim Ryun	2003		Mr. Raymond S. Sczudlo	1981
Mrs. Gladys Sabin	1953		The Hon. Ronald A. Seale	2003
Mr. Federico Jose Sacasa	2002		Mr. Scott H. Segal	1996
Mr. Stephen K. Sacks	1992		Mr. Jorge F. Segura	2001
Mrs. Victor Sadd	1980		Mr. Charles N. Seidlitz	1986
Mr. Jonathan Leo Sade	1986		Ms. Suzanne M. Seipel	1999
Mr. Mohammad Sadiq	2002		Mr. Robert A. Sellery, Jr.	1982
Mrs. Marvin P. Sadur	1994		Mr. William C. Sellery, Jr.	1979
Mr. Thomas Locke Saidy	1991		Mr. Peter M. Seremet	1996
Mr. Jonathan S. Saiger	1998		Ambassador Horacio Serpa	2003
Ms. Therese Marie Saint Hilaire	2003		Mr. Miguel Angel Serrano	2003
Ms. Leslie B. Salba	2003		Mr. Steven M. Servidio	1995
Mr. Franklin Salisbury, Jr.	1997		Mr. John R. Seward	2000
Mrs. Tamara C. Salisbury	1938		Mr. Brian J. Sexton	1993
Ms. Marguerite W. Sallee	2003		Mr. Thomas G. Shack, III	1991
Mr. Nadim E. Salti	1997		Mr. Thomas G. Shack, Jr.	1965
Mr. Joseph E. Samora, Jr.	1997		Mr. Parks D. Shackelford	1991
Mr. John Alan Sanders, Jr.	1985		Mr. Virginius Shackelford, IV	2002
Ms. M. Claire Sanders	1994		Mr. Howard J. Shakespeare	1997
Mr. John Alan Sanders, M.D.	1960		Mr. James R. Shanahan, Jr.	1987
Commander Randy Sandoz	2002		Admiral John J. Shanahan	1995
Mr. Joseph M. Sandri, Jr.	2000		Mr. James R. Shappell	1981
Mr. Bruce William Sanford	1983		Mr. Donald B. Shea	2002
Mr. Andrew C. Sankin	1991		Ms. Catherine E. Sheehan	1999
Ms. Joan K. Sansbury	1998		Mr. Shaun McGill Sheehan	1986
Mr. Donald E. Santarelli	1992		Mr. Robert Arthur Shelton	1971
Mr. Albert J. Santorelli	1968		Mr. John E. Sheridan	1998
Mr. Lewis J. Saret	2000		Mr. David Bell Sherwood, Jr.	2003
Dr. Walter James Sarjeant	2002		Mr. Harvey G. Sherzer	1978
Ms. Ann Sarkes, R.N.	2003		Mr. Jonathan A. Shimer	1998
Mr. E. Antonio Sarrge	1998		Rev. Richard J. Shmaruk	1975
Mr. Thomas J. Saunders	1994		Mr. Larry G. Shockley	2000
Mrs. Katarina Olivia Savino	2003		Mr. Peter Joseph Shudtz	2001
Mr. Savvas P. Savopoulos	1995		General Lewis F. Shull	1957
Mr. Logan Everett Sawyer, III	2003		Mr. Joseph D. Sica	2001
Ms. Paula L. Scali	2001		Mr. Simon Sidamon-Eristoff	1993
The Hon. Antonin Scalia	1988		Mr. Allen G. Siegel	1991
Dr. Thomas J. Scanlan	1989		Dr. Evan Bennett Siegel	1981
Mr. Terrence M. Scanlon	1983		Mr. John Scott Sietsema	2001
Mr. Ralf A. Scherschmidt	2001		Mr. Andrew Siff	2001
Mr. Barry A. Schiffman	2003		Chancellor John R. Silber	1993
Mr. Scott Schirmer	2000		Mr. Gordon Bruce Silcox	1967
Mr. Christian Schlect	1997		Mr. John O. Sillin	1989
Ms. Lyn Schlitt	1992		Mr. David Silver	1984
Mr. Charles E. Schlumberger	1998		Mr. Kenneth H. Silverberg	1982
Mr. Robert Louis Schmidt	1966		Mr. Gary J. Silversmith	1999
Ms. Susan M. Schmidt	1999		Major Gen. Frank J. Simokaitis	2002
Mr. Alan J. Schmitz, III	1993		Ambassador Andras Simonyi	2002
Mr. Herbert Kurt Schmitz	1973		Mr. Ralph A. Simpson	1997
Mr. Michael R. Schmitz	1986		Mr. Patrick J. Sims	1997
Mr. Kai-Niklas Anton Schneider	2003		Mrs. Robert J. Sinnenberg	1996
The Rev. Theodore F. Schneider	2002		Mr. Mark K. Sisitsky	1991
Mr. Abraham L. Schneier	1991		Mr. Theodore Sitkoff	1995
Mr. Stephen C. Schott	1995		Mr. James C. Sivon	1984
Mr. A. Kolbet Schrichte	1978		Adm. William G. Sizemore	1989
Mr. Christopher Schrichte	1985		Mrs. Mary M. Sjoquist	2003
Mr. Russell J. Schriefer	1993		Mr. Laurence E. Skinner	2000
Mr. Brian E. Schutrumpf	1969		Mr. Frank Sklaris	1988
Dr. David Lee Schutt	2001		Mr. Francis Skrobiszewski	1986
Mr. William E. Schuyler, Jr.	1953		Mr. Joseph Charles Skroski	2002
Mr. Theodore A. Schwab	1997		Mr. Leonard Slatkin	1999

Mr. David P. Sloane	2000	Mr. William T. Stephens	1967
Dr. Harvey Sloane	1961	Mr. G. Philip Stephenson	1993
Mrs. Diana M. Smallridge	2001	Mr. David R. Stepp	1996
Mr. A. W. Pete Smith, Jr.	1992	Dr. Richard L. Sterling	1999
Mr. Allen Thomas Smith	1966	Mr. Ernest Max Stern	1975
Mr. Christopher Smith	1986	Mr. James Y. Stern	2003
Mr. David L. Smith	2000	Mr. C. Joseph Stetler	1966
Mr. Edward Delmer Smith	1960	Ms. Virginia Leggett Stevenson	1999
The Hon. Fern M. Smith	2000	Mrs. Deborah B. Stewart	1999
Mr. G. Wayne Smith	1995	Ms. Lisa A. Stewart	1997
Mrs. Harry J. Smith, Jr.	1995	Mr. Raymond C. Stewart	1991
Mr. James R. Smith	1982	Mrs. Susan H. Stewart	2002
Ms. Kathryn Smith	2001	Mr. Walter Joseph Stewart	1982
The Hon. Loren Allan Smith	1987	Mr. Perry J. Stieglitz	1995
Mr. Michael D. Smith	1997	Mr. B. J. Stiles	1998
Mrs. Mildred Smith	1986	Mr. Robert D. Stillman	1994
Mr. Robert Smith, III	1975	Mr. Lee J. Stillwell	1988
Mr. Robert Gerard Smith	2003	Mrs. Cari N. Stinebower	2001
Mr. Rodney A. Smith	1985	Mrs. Deborah Jane Stirling	2003
President Samuel H. Smith	1993	Mrs. Ralph Nelson Stohl	1959
Mr. Sean C. Smith	2003	Mr. Laurence Storch	1982
Mr. Stuart Alan Smith	1977	Mr. R. Jon Stouky	2002
Dr. W. Lamar Smith	1993	Mr. Keith A. Strubhar	2000
Dr. William S. Smith, Jr.	1999	Mr. A. Scott Sudduth	1996
Mr. William C. Smith	1979	The Hon. Eugene R. Sullivan	1989
Dr. Mary Frances B. Smoak	1990	The Hon. Louis W. Sullivan	1989
Mrs. Thomas Smull	1943	Mr. Mark A. Sullivan	1999
Mr. Thomas Marshall Sneeringer	2003	Mr. Mark O. Sullivan	2000
Mr. James J. Snyder	1992	Dr. Patrick K. Sullivan	2001
Mr. Robert Neil Snyder	1989	Mr. Timothy Sullivan	1978
Mr. Peter B. Sobol	1979	President Timothy J. Sullivan	1992
Mr. Stephen Sohn	1981	Mr. William M. Sullivan, Jr.	1999
Mr. Marshall D. Sokol	1995	President Lawrence H. Summers, Ph.D.	2001
Mr. Michael F. Solomon	1993	Mr. Thomas M. Susman	1994
Mr. Garrick J. Solovey	2001	Mr. Geoffrey I. Suval	1997
Dr. Kyung S. Song	1999	Mr. John Philip Suval	1999
Mr. David N. Southard	2002	Mrs. Shannon L. Suydam	2003
Dr. Kenneth R. Sparks	1974	The Hon. Margaret M. Sweeney	2003
Ms. Christine Ann Spaulding	2003	Mr. R. Michael Sweeney	1995
Mr. Douglas K. Spaulding	1989	Mr. David M. Sweet	2001
Mrs. Sylvia G. Spear	1957	Mr. Philip E. Swink	2000
Mr. Daniel E. Speilman, III	2002	President Haywood Patrick Swygert	2003
Mrs. Solveig B. Spielmann	1991	Mr. Ronald P. Szabat	1994
Mr. Charles R. Spies	2000	Mrs. George C. Tagg	1992
Mrs. M. Christina Spilhaus Shioutakon	1997	Ms. Angelica Oleg Tang	2003
Mr. Robert H. Spratt, Jr.	1989	Mr. Henry S. Tang	2001
Mr. Peter D. Spyke	1995	Mr. Gordon O. Tanner	2000
Ms. Janet G. St. Amand	1995	Mr. Peter J. Tanous	1994
Mr. Keith R. St. Germain	2003	Mr. Robert A. Tappan	1990
Amb. Salvador E. Stadthagen	2003	Mr. C. Michael Tarone	2003
Mr. Connell C. Stafford, Jr.	2001	Mr. Morton S. Taubman	2003
Mr. Peter Vincent Stanton	2003	Mrs. Frances J. Tausig	1941
Mr. Walter J. Stanton, III	2000	Mr. C. William Tayler	1957
Mr. Kenneth G. Starling	1998	Mr. Dwight D. Taylor	1954
The Hon. Kenneth W. Starr	1992	Mr. Louis Taylor	1998
Mr. Philip A. R Staton	1991	The Hon. Richard P. Taylor	1995
Mr. Ricky Leonard Staton	2002	Mrs. Russell Willis Taylor	2002
Ms. Anne R. Stauffer	1998	Mr. Randal C. Teague, Jr.	2001
Dr. Thomas R. Stauffer	1973	Mr. Randal C. Teague, Sr.	1983
Mr. Edward M. Staunton, III	1988	Mr. Sten E. Tegner	1992
Mr. Douglas L. Steele	2002	Mr. Riley K. Temple	2002
Mr. Jeffrey L. Steele	2000	Mr. Fred S. Teng	1999
Mr. Malaku J. Steen	1995	Mr. Joshua P. Tenuta	1995
Mr. Lawrence Othmar Stein	2003	The Hon. Edgar Teran	1992
Mr. C. Don Stephens	1995	Judge John A. Terry	1970

The Hon. Lee Terry	2003	Ms. Susan M. Valaskovic	1993
Mrs. Shahira Hamed Tewfik	2002	Mr. Luis Daniel Valdes	2002
Mr. Henry Laynell Thaggert, III	2003	Dr. Anthony D. Valente	2001
Mrs. Virginia R. Theberge	1983	Mr. Eduardo Vallarino	2000
Mr. Alan D. Theriault	1998	Mr. Frans Christiaan van der Lee, Jr.	2003
Dr. Abigail Thernstrom	2002	Father John D. Van Dooren	1998
Maj. Gen. Lucius Theus	1995	Dr. Richard J. Van Loon	1997
Dr. Siva Thiagarajah	2002	Mrs. Betsy G. Van Orman	1957
Ms. Susan B. Thigpen	2003	Mr. James C. Van Story, Jr.	1954
The Hon. Clarence Thomas	1991	Dr. Caroline Van Vleck	1995
Mr. Henry A. Thomas	1957	Mr. Craig Geoffrey Veith	1989
Mr. John W. Thomas	1996	Mr. Matthew Francis X. Veneri	2002
Mr. Dan King Thomasson	1989	Mrs. Millicent Adams Vesper	1998
Mr. Gordon Ellef Thompson	1986	President Charles M. Vest	1993
Mr. J. Timothy Thompson	2003	Mrs. George E. Viereck	1948
Mr. Joe M. Thompson	1999	Mr. G. Duane Vieth	1957
Mr. Louis M. Thompson, Jr.	1983	Mr. Alfred R. Villalobos	1993
Ms. Marilyn W. Thompson	2001	Mr. Scott Glenn Villanueva	2001
Mr. Richard E. Thompson	1978	Mr. Carlos C. Villarreal	1964
Mr. Tom R. Thoren	1996	Mr. Robert C. Virden	1998
Dr. David C. Thornton	1991	Mr. Fernando S. Virgolino	2001
Mr. Justin A. Thornton	1990	Mr. Paul Charles Vitrano	2003
Mr. James E. Thrash	2002	Mr. George Nicholas Vogelei	2002
Mr. Christopher D. Thuma	2001	Ambassador Knut Vollebaek	2001
Mr. Eugene Edwards Tibbs, Jr.	2002	Mr. Robert M. Volmer	1999
The Hon. Moody R. Tidwell	1997	Mrs. Joseph Volpe	1958
Mr. Robert P. Tiernan	1972	Mr. William R. Voltz	1966
Mr. Joseph B. Tockarshewsky	1986	Ms. Dominique C. Von Planta	2001
Mr. Martin Tolchin	1998	Mr. Eric A. Von Salzen	1994
Dr. John S. Toll	1979	Mr. M. Jon Vondracek	1965
Mr. Gregory P. Tomasso	2000	Mr. Dominic G. Vorv	2003
Ambassador Esteban Tomic	2000	Mrs. Helen P. Vournas	1940
Mr. James E. Tompert	1997	Ms. Alisha Rae Waid	2001
Mr. Michael A. Tongour	1994	Mrs. Gardner H. Wales	1936
Mr. Richard C. Tonner, Jr.	1987	Mr. Barton F. Walker, Jr.	1989
Mr. Brian C. Toohey	2000	Dr. David J. Walker	2003
Mrs. T. Murray Toomey	1955	Ms. Diana S. Walker	2002
Col. Allan C. Torgerson	1964	Mr. John C. Walker, III	1958
Mr. Christopher Torgerson	1993	Mrs. John Denley Walker	1958
Mr. Leonard Tousignant	1965	Mr. Kenneth Thomas Walker	1998
Mr. John M. Townsend	1990	Mr. Merrill B. Walker, Jr.	1986
President Stephen Trachtenberg	1988	Mr. Ronald P. Walker	1995
Ms. Lori L. Trautwine	2003	Mr. Steven S. Walker, Jr.	1995
Ms. Susan E. Trees	1998	Ms. Madeleine Elizabeth Wall	2002
Dr. Quan Trinh	1992	Mr. John R. Waller	1967
Mr. Konrad Trope	1990	Mr. Robert Daniel Wallick	1964
Mr. Nathaniel Reeve Trott	1975	Mr. David James Walsh	1977
Dr. John B. Tsu	2002	Mr. Alan S. Ward	1966
Mr. Michael E. Tucci	1993	Ms. Carolyn A. Ward	2000
Mr. William Tucker	1995	Mr. Joe Henry Ward, Jr.	1971
Mr. James P. Tunkey	2000	Mr. Thomas Joseph Ward	1973
Mr. James B. Tunny, Jr.	1958	Mr. Michael J. Wardman	1993
Mr. Mark H. Tuohey, III	1981	Mr. H. Hudnall Ware, IV	1992
Mr. William J. Turenne	1991	Mr. Benjamin S. Warren, III	1972
Mr. Randall J. Turk	2001	Mr. George Lewis Warren	2001
Ms. Cynthia Turner	1995	Mr. John A. Washington	1956
The Hon. James Turner	1991	Mr. John A. Washington, Jr.	2000
Mr. Paul B. Turner	1999	Mr. S. Kevin Washington	2001
Mr. Stephen Jay Ubl	2002	Mr. Glen D. Wasserstein	1998
Mr. Halil Ugur	1996	Mr. Barry Conway Watkins	2002
Mr. Francis S. Urbany	1995	Mr. Roland Watkins	2000
Ambassador Vygaudas Usackas	2001	Mr. Jack H. Watson, Jr.	1994
Ambassador Yuri V. Ushakov	2000	Mr. Thomas C. Watson, Sr.	2001
Mr. Carl Lee Vacketta	1970	Mr. Robb Watters	2001
Rev. Monsignor Peter Vaghi	1977	The Hon. J. C. Watts	2002

Ms. Kathleen C. Waugh	1997	Mr. Lewis I. Williams, IV	2000
Mr. Clyde N. Wayne	1996	The Hon. Mary Ellen Coster Williams	2003
Ms. Robin Weaver	2000	Mr. Michael F. Williams	1999
Mr. Frederick L. Webber	1984	Mr. Mikel Howard Williams	2003
Mr. Jeffery D. Weekly	2002	Mr. Roger J. Williams	1999
Dr. Kent R. Weeks	1996	Mr. Wesley S. Williams, Jr.	1977
Ms. Susanne R. Wegrzyn	1996	Mr. John R. Williford	2003
Mr. Hans M. Weichsel, Jr.	1955	Mr. Matthew Willis	1999
Mr. Matthew C. Weider	1996	Mr. Mason Willrich	1972
Mr. Steven Jiro Weidman	2001	Ms. Kathryn Berry Wilson	2002
Ms. Shauna Christine Weiler	2003	Mr. Otis D. Wilson, Jr.	1957
Mr. John B. Weiner	1999	Mr. Padgett R. Wilson	2003
Ms. Olivia Shannon Weiner	2003	Mr. Thomas Edward Wilson	1973
Mr. Ronald H. Weiner	1982	Mr. James Patrick Winner	2001
Mrs. Shirley Weinschel	1995	Mr. Mark E. Winter	1998
Mr. Arnold H. Weiss	1989	Mr. Solomon L. Wisenberg	2000
Mr. David Weiss	1986	Mr. Samuel J. Wohlstader	1997
Mr. Todd M. Weiss	1999	Mr. Alan F. Wohlstetter	1995
Mr. Peter T. Welle	1998	Mr. John C. Wohlstetter	2001
Mr. Milton T. Wells	1996	Mr. M. Craig Wolf	2000
Mrs. Margaret Wendt-Webster	2001	Mr. William B. Wolf, Jr.	1981
Mr. John Joseph Wertzberger	2002	Mr. Richard E. Wolfe	2003
Mr. Jacobus P. Wessels	2000	Mrs. Robert A. Wolff	1999
The Hon. Togo D. West, Jr.	1981	Mr. Michael A. Wolyn	1996
Ms. Molly Lynn Westrate	2003	Mr. Stephen Tien Wong	1988
Mr. John P. Wetherill, IV	1967	Ambassador John Wood	2003
Mr. Thomas J. Whalen	1976	Mr. Thomas A. Woodley	1982
Mr. Thomas Wade Wharton	2003	Ms. Jacqueline E. Woods	2001
Mr. Thomas J. Whatley, III	1975	Mr. William B. Woods	2000
Mr. Leonard P. Wheat	1988	Mr. Hugh M. Woodward	1955
Dr. Belle S. Wheelan	1999	Mr. William H. Woodwell	1995
Mr. Douglas H. Wheeler	2002	Mr. Ramsey L. Woodworth	1995
Dr. Porter K. Wheeler	1990	Mr. Peter Bushfield Work	1968
Ms. Elizabeth Clarke Whitaker	2002	Mr. Willard A. Workman	1995
Mr. Michael D. White	1995	Mr. John Hamilton Works, Jr.	2001
Mr. Brian J. Whitehead	1996	Ms. Betty B. Wu	2001
Mr. Jeffrey Whitney	2001	Mrs. Deborah A.G. Wulff	2002
Mr. John Adair Whitney	1966	Captain Jerome Berton Wyble	1951
Ms. Margaret H. Whittaker	1997	Mr. Josh T. Wymard	2001
Mr. John F. Whittemore, III	1976	Mr. John J. Wynn	1998
The Hon. Faith R. Whittlesey	1993	Mrs. John Wyser-Pratte	1995
Mr. James K. Wholey	1992	Ambassador Jiechi Yang	2003
Mrs. Joseph L. Whyte	1951	Mr. David Y. Yao	1995
Mr. Grover T. Wickersham	1977	Mr. George M. Yates	1997
Mrs. Robert B. Wickes	1961	Mr. Stephen T. Yelverton	1986
Dr. Walter J. Wiechetek	1997	Mr. Stephen George Yeonas	1954
The Hon. Jane S. Wiegand	2002	Dr. Clayton K. Yeutter	1989
Mr. Gregory H. Wierzynski	1980	Mr. Paul A. Yhouse	1998
Mr. John H. D. Wigger	1948	Judge Robert J. Yock	1992
Mr. Paul Michael Wihbey	2002	Mr. Yasuo Yoshioka	1998
Mr. Michael Wilbon	2001	Mrs. Elizabeth W. Young	1976
Mr. Robert Charles Wilburn	2000	Mr. Robert Joseph Young	1975
Rev. Robert A. Wild, S.J.	1997	Mr. Thomas J. Young	1991
Mr. Alan J. Wilensky	1992	Mr. Alaa-Eldin Youssef	2002
Mr. William D. Wiley	1997	Dr. George W. Yu	1992
Mr. William B. Wilhelm, Jr.	1994	Mr. Tristan A. Zaia	1997
The Hon. William W. Wilkins, Jr.	1991	Mr. Paul R. Zalucky	2002
Mr. Richard B. Willett	1972	Mr. Robert M. Zatkowski	2000
Mayor Anthony Williams	2000	Mr. Robert Charles Zimmer	1974
The Rev. Dr. David Williams	1979	Mr. Joseph Robert Zimmerman	2003
Mr. Dennis R. Williams	1972	Mr. W. Robert Zinkham	2001
Coach Gary B. Williams	2000	President Elisabeth A. Zinser	1989
Mr. George P. Williams	1996	Mr. Criton M. Zoakos1998	2003
Mr. James V. Williams	1994	Ms. Carolyn C. Zollar	2000
Mr. John Brinton Williams	2003		

INDEX